THE GREAT TRANSITION

Bridges to the Afterlife

Ann Frazier West

BALBOA.
PRESS

A DIVISION OF HAY HOUSE

Subtle Bodies Courtesy of Martin Brofman, Ph.D. www.healer.ch The Healing Chapel at the Rosicrucian Fellowship Headquarters, Mt. Ecclesia in Oceanside, CA Courtesy www.rosicrucian.com

Balboa Press books may be ordered through booksellers or by contacting:

Balboa Press
A Division of Hay House
1663 Liberty Drive
Bloomington, IN 47403
www.balboapress.com
1 (877) 407-4847

Because of the dynamic nature of the Internet, any web addresses or links contained in this book may have changed since publication and may no longer be valid. The views expressed in this work are solely those of the author and do not necessarily reflect the views of the publisher, and the publisher hereby disclaims any responsibility for them.

The author of this book does not dispense medical advice or prescribe the use of any technique as a form of treatment for physical, emotional, or medical problems without the advice of a physician, either directly or indirectly. The intent of the author is only to offer information of a general nature to help you in your quest for emotional and spiritual well-being. In the event you use any of the information in this book for yourself, which is your constitutional right, the author and the publisher assume no responsibility for your actions.

Any people depicted in stock imagery provided by Thinkstock are models, and such images are being used for illustrative purposes only.
Certain stock imagery © Thinkstock.

Printed in the United States of America.

ISBN: 978-1-4525-8480-5 (sc)
ISBN: 978-1-4525-8481-2 (e)

Library of Congress Control Number: 2013918244

Balboa Press rev. date: 1/30/2014

For my three remarkable women: my mother, Kathryn, my friend, Patricia, my teacher and friend, Ann, and for all of my other family and friends who pave the way for me in Heaven, it is with my boundless love and gratitude that I dedicate this book to you.

The afterlife is a realm of transformation—of body, mind, and spirit—a place lovingly reflecting the consciousness of each individual and his or her place in the great cosmic dance of eternity.

—Lee Lawson, Artist, Author

TABLE OF CONTENTS

PART 3 GUIDE TO AFTERLIFE CONTACT

FOREWORD

I N OUR HUMAN WORLD OF form and function, the penetrating discussions of death and the possibility of life beyond death are increasingly familiar. All persuasions of people including research scientists, medical and non-medical alike, scholars, writers, philosophers and, of course, religious and spiritually minded persons openly seek to answer the ancient query, "If a man die, shall he live again?"

The unending quest for meaningful, thoughtful and insightful understanding regarding this question is now regularly presented in major Hollywood movies, television series and a growing host of books, academic and scientific bodies whose focus is on studying the physical as well as the spiritual nature of death, including the survival of our unique individuality beyond death.

Grieving men, women, their family and/or friends and loved ones can find DVDs, books, support groups and many available sources for comfort in stories of surviving loved ones and their often extremely personal experiences around loss, death and the afterlife.

In *The Great Transition,* Dr. Ann West shares with us her very specific life events, truly extraordinary experiences involving her own beloved mother, a teacher and a close life-long friend whose deaths were integral to her own deepening spiritual journey. Her wit, candor and clarity weave a tapestry of the basic world view teachings surrounding death. She invites us into discovery that reveals what many others, both professional and non-professional have learned, as well as her own discoveries about life beyond death—profound, powerful and eminently useful—and I dare say practical knowledge.

Dr. West describes in vivid detail life in the next world as revealed in her own dreams and intriguing visions. Her research includes some of the truly great classical literature including Anthony Borgia: *Life in the World Unseen*; Dresser and Rafferty: *Life Here and Hereafter;* Raymond A. Moody, Jr, M.D.: *Reflections on Life After Life;* W.T. Stead: *The Blue Island*; and Rudolf Steiner: *Life Between Death and Rebirth.*

The new student, the grieving spouse, partner, beloved or friends, as well as the spiritually minded seeker, experienced or not with the existence of a realm of life beyond death, will find here answers, deep insight and information not ordinarily available in one place or body of research. Dr. West shares some deeply personal discoveries about her own journey, her own brush with death, her exposure to reincarnation, other religious philosophies including metaphysics. This very personal journey is informative and most revealing indeed.

Anyone seeking to gain a synthesis of the after death experience will find value, insight and I dare say inspiration in this deeply researched and intriguingly written text.

This work could easily become a seminar, class or course on the development of our contact with Higher Realms or on the requirements as they pertain to the highly refined training and sensitivity of the medium whose human body vehicle is the "doorway" for other worldly contact.

Dr. West offers a glimpse, perhaps even an intimate view of her most sensitive life events as they relate to her family, her mother, her friendships. We are invited to "listen in" on conversations she had with those she loved—beyond so-called death.

This book will take you on a very unusual journey with warmth, wit and wonder. As one thinks and reflects deeply about what is called the afterlife, as presented by the author, one is reminded that we are always connected to those who have gone before us. Our work, as Dr. West suggests, is to refine our inner awareness sufficiently to be more aware that those we love deeply and profoundly, spiritually weave in and out of our lifetimes to be a major part of the eternal fabric of our lives.

Leroy E. Zemke, Spiritual Teacher, Minister, Intuitive Counselor, Author,
St. Petersburg, Florida, 2013.

PREFACE

Creating Bridges to the Afterlife

"WE'LL BE FRIENDS FOREVER, WON'T we, Pooh?" asked Piglet. "Even longer," Pooh answered.

This was the message on the front of the last Christmas card I received from my "forever friend," Pat Larson. In January 2001, Pat made her transition from this life to her new life in another dimension.

Pat and I met through our very special spiritual teacher, Ann Manser, and we became close friends as a result of our love for *the work* and for Ann Manser. Ann was a spiritual teacher, the founder of a wisdom school, *Pages of Shustah, Inc.,* and author of the study materials by the same name, the designer of cards for divination and the author of other ancient wisdom studies. In one of Ann's classes that I attended in her home, she mentioned Pat Larson's name. I immediately knew that I somehow knew Pat. I also knew that I had no reason, on the material level, to know her. I had not met Pat nor had I ever heard her name before that evening. Then how did I know her? To me, it was obviously a soul recognition. I knew her energetically through the sound of her name. I could not explain it in any other way. Because we lived in different states, Pat and I didn't actually meet each other until we attended a Spiritual Frontiers Fellowship Conference about two years later. We immediately became friends and treasured our spiritual kinship and devoted friendship over the next twenty-five years. We called ourselves *twin souls* because we felt that we were indeed twin souls, compatible in so many areas of our thinking, feeling—in our lives overall.

The dreaded day came when Pat made her transition and I could no longer pick up the phone and know what my beloved friend was up to at any given time. We had plans to travel to the British Isles in that summer of 2001. But now there would be no more adventures together—not in this dimension. My work schedule kept me busy during the day and some evenings, but I chose Thursday evenings to devote to Pat. I bought a journal to use specifically for my communication with her, writing notes to her and writing down any impressions I felt that I received from her in meditation, and for recording my dream visits with her. My first entry was nineteen days after Pat's transition, and the following is the beginning of that entry:

> Precious Pat, my Forever Friend,
>
> It has been nineteen days since you departed the earth plane. Sometimes it feels like an eternity and at times I can almost feel you by my side. Just knowing we can no longer share a companionship in Earth events is extremely difficult for me. We both thought we had so much more time. I've had such a need to just pick up the phone and hear your precious voice at the other end of the line. There are so many things I want to share with you. I'll still share them. I just don't feel prepared to receive your responses in a conscious way. Perhaps you can help me with that. I find myself wondering—a lot—about what your life is like in your dimension.

Later, in May of the same year, I wrote to Pat that I knew she was trying to respond to my notes to her but our communication seemed very one-sided because of my lack of ability to bring through her messages. I wrote to her, "I'm going to ask Steve Engel (our psychic friend in Oregon) if he will make contact with you for me." I planned to do that on the weekend, but the very next morning I had an email from Steve saying, "Pat Larson is hanging around me. I didn't know Pat all that well and I don't know why she's here." My email reply to him was, "I sent her to you, Steve. Please find out what she has to say."

Steve sent me an email a couple of days later with a short transmission from Pat. I was ecstatic! I had many questions for her, so Steve agreed to make another contact with her for me. The second transmission was much longer, with descriptions of her dwelling, her work and her workplace, her service and leisure activities. She transmitted a feeling of love and peace and personal fulfillment in her new home. At the end of her message she offered to help me learn to prepare myself to receive her transmissions. She told me she had much to share and would like to be able to do that at some future time. She made it clear that my development of accuracy may take a rather long period of time but that I would eventually be able to have conscious contact with her and with others in the higher dimensions. This was an exciting possibility, and so we scheduled a starting date for the next week.

The benefits of this work with Pat over the past twelve years, now, have been invaluable, not only in the knowledge I've gained about the afterlife that awaits us all and in the communication with my loved ones, but I feel that it has expanded my consciousness, and my spiritual growth has taken on an accelerated development that I could not have imagined. Before my mother made her transition she said to me, "Please keep up your work with Pat.

It will be important to us someday, too." Little did I know that it would happen so soon. She made her transition in 2003. The work *has* been important to us. Contact with Mother has been very real and often.

The communication is still very possible with Pat, with Mother (Kathryn) and with Ann Manser. Our contacts are not as frequent as they were at first. In fact, our visits take place more in my dream state than in the waking visions and conversations in meditation in the earlier times. There are reasons for this: they are all progressing in their dimensions and moving farther away from the Earth frequency so that their efforts to make the contact with me seem a bit more complicated. My own life becomes more demanding at times, and it is easier for them to communicate with me in the dream state when my mind is less cluttered and I'm more open and less ego-directed.

I have friends who are very fine and well-developed psychics; some who are professional and use their gifts in counseling others. I am not a professional psychic and I've never thought of myself as being psychic. However, I believe I'm intuitive and sensitive to the energies of others in this dimension and in others beyond the Earth dimension. My psychic experiences have been primarily spontaneous ones throughout my lifetime, and I assumed experiences like this were normal for most people. I do believe that for those who desire it, psychic ability can be developed. Eventually, we will all regain the psychic sensitivity that is natural to the human race and that has been lost to so many over eons of time as we have traded our sensitivity to the spirit worlds for our exploration in material living.

One morning, several years after I began my work with Pat and had learned to a certain extent how to communicate with her and with my mother and Ann, I woke up with a strong impression to write this book. I was involved in working on a manuscript for a book about *color*, and this particular morning I felt that I was being *told* that I must put that work aside for now and write about my experiences with spirit communication. It was an exciting thought—sharing my wonderful *other world* communications with others—many others, perhaps.

What began as a story about the three remarkable women in my life evolved into sharing my own spiritual journey. This was where it became a little difficult for me. I was a professional psychological counselor at an earlier time in my life and so it was always about someone else's journey. Now, the focus would be on my own personal journey. My editor and Author Advocate, Patrika Vaughn, liked the stories about the three women who had so much influence in my life, but she said, "This is your story; there needs to be more of your personal life in the story. What brought you to this point—the point where you became interested in communicating with the spirit world?" I didn't want my story to become an ego trip, so I had to sort out my feelings about it and realize that the reason this story must be told is to assure my readers that this kind of communication is possible for anyone who desires it.

Much of my knowledge and expertise in this study of death and transition to the worlds beyond our physical world comes from my early career in the medical field as a registered nurse and almost fifty years of metaphysical study which includes esoteric and mystery schools such as the Rosicrucian Fellowship; Builders of the Adytum (B.O.T.A); as a student and teacher of metaphysical subjects at the Temple of the Living God, St. Petersburg, Florida and the Sancta Sophia Seminary and Light of Christ Community Church in Sparrow Hawk Village, Tahlequah, Oklahoma, and also from selected studies in Theosophy and Anthroposophy; in workshops as a student and as a presenter through the years. During these years, I have also functioned as a spiritual counselor and healer and a spiritual and metaphysical teacher in many private classes and workshops.

How is communication with the spirit world possible? Are there energetic portals that connect us to other-worldly beings? Are there portals to other dimensions and even to other times? We just need to open our minds to either ancient metaphysical teachings or modern quantum physics to find some answers to these important questions.

Much has happened since I began writing this book. More loved ones have made their transition, and I'm learning new things about this process. I continue to learn more that I want to share with you, to make additions . . . and one day I realized that this could go on and on and it would never quite be ready to publish. So I am publishing my work in progress. It is not my intention to convince you of a belief in the afterlife but more that the sharing of my personal adventures with you might inspire you in your own search for the truth.

Spiritual communication is *spiritual science*. It is also *physics* taken to the quantum level and beyond, to *metaphysics*. It is an energetic exchange between conscious beings that does not require a physical body to communicate. All that is required of us to create the *bridges to the afterlife* is a loving heart, an open mind and a little discipline.

ACKNOWLEDGMENTS

I AM DEEPLY GRATEFUL TO so many people who have patiently supported and encouraged me in the preparation and writing of this book. To my editor and professional Author Advocate of A Cappela Publishing and my friend, Patrika "Pat" Vaughn, who understood my thesis for the book from its beginning stages and whose knowledge of metaphysics and its particular language supported my formal and informal research and gave me the confidence to carry out this project, I am grateful and indebted. At one point, Pat traveled and stayed in my home with me and kept me on-task making editorial changes during her seven-day visit, and importantly, she taught me that there was a balanced rhythm to follow, allowing a time for rest and relaxation and a nurturing of the spirit. My heart full of love and gratitude go to my daughter, Wendi Elizabeth West, who not only encouraged me with her loving spirit and support all along the way, but offered her superb copy-editing and formatting skills and artistic expertise as well as her well-developed literary competence. To my son, James "Jim" Frazier West, another heart full of gratitude for his professional technological skills and patience in time spent teaching me some basic technological skills on my computer and sometimes just doing it for me. He has been here daily for me at times when I couldn't remember how to "think like a computer."

To my favorite psychic counselors, Reverend LeRoy E. Zemke, Steve A. Engel and Robert "Bob" Murray, I extend unending gratitude for their depth of spirit and exemplary gifts of the ability to communicate with the Spirit World and for their support and encouragement of my psychic development. They have so willingly shared their wise counsel and insights from their experiences with worlds beyond our Earth plane. LeRoy is my close friend and spiritual teacher and has kept in touch by phone and periodic visits to check my progress as well as to inspire me and to validate this work.

To my sister, Mary Elizabeth Wilson, who has so willingly come to my aid with her skills in computer technology and formatting, and my uncle, Dr. Ted M. George, I express my deep appreciation for their loving and ongoing support even at times when they weren't sure of what I was up to.

My Dream Group which met bi-weekly for a few years accepted the challenge of helping me interpret many of my dreams that urged me to stick with this project and to bring it into manifestation when I was dragging my feet and not always confident that I could bring it to fruition. They deserve much gratitude. Thank you, Janet Tuck, Karen Davis, Becky McCarty, Joyce Johnson and Cynthia Brown. Cynthia has since made her transition, and I've had some contact with her in her new dimension now.

My life is filled with friends and family who have remained interested in this book. Most have understood and all have been a constant inspiration for me. My deep and sincere gratitude is extended to all of them and especially to those who understand my thesis and continue to inspire and support me to the end. My warmest appreciation goes to Jane Corley, Alice Valiquette, Becky McCarty, Charles Pickering, Davene Davis, Marie Neuberger, Patricia Gailey, Caroline Kiev, Martha Littles, Dianna Kay Marsden, Susan Humphrey, Diane Birnbaum, Inna Shapiro, Dr. Luby Chambul, Trina Madonia, Chris Larson, Mary Ann Watjen, Colleen Harwood, Louise Scott, Ashley Hamilton, Deborah Saad, James Murray, Sam Lewis and my daughter Julia Kathryn West.

To Katharine "Kate" Armstrong for her pressured last-minute editing expertise and to Stephanie Cornthwaite, my check-in-coordinator and all the involved staff at Balboa Press, I offer much gratitude for their kind words, expert guidance and tremendous efficiency.

This book would not have been written without my *three remarkable women,* all on the other side of life: my mother, Kathryn Parrotte, my closest friend, Patricia "Pat" Larson and my spiritual teacher and friend, Ann C. Manser. They cared for me, encouraged and inspired me and loved me while they were on the Earth plane and they continue to do so from their homes in other dimensions. They inspired this book which started out with the title, *Three Remarkable Women,* and it expanded, with their encouragement through meditation and dream visits to encompass more about the whole transition process. They have all three been my collaborators in this work from our hearts. I am forevermore grateful for these beautiful souls who have touched my life and the lives of others so deeply.

I feel blessed that I had the loving support of two other close friends who made their transition before the book was completed. Dr. J. Thomas "Tom" West, my former husband and friend and father of our four children, asked to read some of the manuscript for this book as he was being treated for cancer. He lived long enough to read the first ten chapters and expressed how helpful the information was to him at that difficult time near the end of his life. I am grateful for his valuable feedback on each chapter as he read it and for his critical analysis and testimony to its meaning for him. He has been in close touch and has cheered me on to completion from his side of life. Joan C. Pinkston made her transition within weeks of receiving her diagnosis of cancer. Joan and I were friends for most of our adult lives and together we were students of Ann Manser and LeRoy Zemke. Joan read chapters of this book and gave me helpful comments, and for that I am grateful, but it is for her loyal, loving friendship and continuing contact that I am most grateful. Thank you, Joan and Tom.

INTRODUCTION

The greatest illusion is that mankind has limitations.
~ Robert A. Monroe

SEVEN YEAR OLD EDOUARD WAS dying of leukemia when he asked his mother to remove his life support. He said, "Mother, turn off the oxygen, I don't need it anymore." His mother honored his wish and turned the machine off. Edouard held his mother's hand and smiled a big smile, saying, "It is time." Then he left.

The story behind Edouard's philosophy began when he was three and a half years old and became associated with a local group that followed the precepts of Vedanta, a system of Hindu philosophy. By the time Edouard died, the Vedanta swami believed his tiny friend was the reincarnation of a holy man. The group's head nun commented, "He was not a normal little boy. He was so full of understanding of his suffering, full of understanding of God." It was Edouard's fascination with the Vedanta philosophy that gave him the belief that death was "like a passageway, a walk into another galaxy." He also shared, "If you don't hang onto your body and let yourself ease away, it is not so painful."

We all die to this Earth plane, physically. But do we really die? Or do we just take off our physical bodies and go somewhere else to live? Some say that dying is just a part of life and that we continue living in other dimensions. If people were asked if they would want to live somewhere besides on Earth, I wonder how many would actually say yes. In fact, it is difficult to carry on any meaningful conversation about dying without revealing an underlying or even blatant fear of the subject. Why do we not have more curiosity about the thing that is inevitable to all life forms? When loved ones die, many of us wonder where they are going and if we will see them again. It does not seem fair that we spend a part or even all of a lifetime being close to someone, and then they are gone. We cannot see them, hear them, touch them, or communicate with them in any way—or can we?

In *Life After Death*, Deepak Chopra, world renowned medical doctor, author, and spiritual teacher states, "the standard assumption is that no one really knows what happens after we die. But the Rishis (Sages of Vedic India) asked the question, *why don't we expect to know?* Instead of being unknowable, perhaps the afterlife is something we haven't looked at hard enough. And if so, why not?"[1]

In his book, *The Kingdom of the Gods*, a treatise on orders of angelic hosts, Geoffrey Hodson says that "Man can know the facts. Faith need not be blind. Man is endowed with all the faculties necessary for complete knowledge both of himself and the visible and invisible universe. Extended vision is one of the required faculties. By its development and use, the boundaries of human knowledge may be gradually advanced until *noumenon* and *phenomenon* are fully investigated and ultimately known as one."[2]

I believe that it is possible to learn to communicate with our loved ones who have slipped into perhaps another dimension. I believe that they want that communication with us as much as we want it with them. I believe that, in most cases, we are missed by them much as we miss them. Perhaps they have a distinct advantage over us and can actually peer into our world much more easily than we can be aware of theirs. Anthony Borgia, author and medium, in the transcripts of his communication with a 'dead priest,' Monsignor Robert Hugh Benson, has written, "It was never intended that the two worlds, yours and ours, should be treated as two worlds apart, never having at any time communication with each other. Why should not our two worlds hold regular and natural converse with each other? That intercommunication does exist, has always existed, and, moreover, will always exist. It may have been—and is—carried on by the comparative few, that is true, but that is the loss to the majority."[3]

Because enough people have wondered about this phenomenon, there is a growing trend of research available on the subject. Research to date includes different types of contact ranging from development of our own telepathic abilities and those of gifted mediums, to a more formal approach using sophisticated electronic equipment sensitive enough to register and identify subtle vibratory frequencies from the other side of life. Some of the better known names in the area of afterlife research include Dr. Elisabeth Kubler-Ross, a writer and psychiatrist who has produced a monumental work in this field; gifted medium, Muriel Williams, and her friend, Professor Ian Currie, with their telepathic contact between dimensions; Robert Moss with his instructions on how to contact our loved ones in spirit via dream visits and inter-dimensional travel; George Meek and his development of electronic communication with highly sensitive instrumentation; and Dr. Gary Schwartz with his extensive research in the Human Energy Systems Laboratory at the University of Arizona. This and other important research will be discussed in more detail later.

Many people have had the experience of communicating with those in other dimensions and dismiss it as imagination, not believing they have had a real contact. I have had such experiences for most of my life, but it was not until recent years that I became aware of the possibilities for increasing my awareness of those subtle contacts. As have many of you, I grew up with some vague idea of "going to heaven someday." But what is heaven like? Why do I want to go there? Why do I have to leave this life? These are some of the questions that came to me as a young child.

I enjoyed spending time alone in the top of the maple tree in our front yard, or sometimes on our steps far enough down the bank below my house that I couldn't be seen and have my cloud-gazing interrupted. On a particular summer day, I sat wondering about how we got here and why we spend time growing up and learning so many things and then someday we just die. In that moment, I felt a presence of such love and comfort; I felt I had been enfolded in the most gentle and magnificent arms. I heard a soft and kind voice speak to me, "Someday, you will know the answers to your questions." I was elated, and for some reason I told no one about my wonderful and extraordinary experience. The reassurance of that loving angel was with me through many future trials. It was only a short time later that I would have to say goodbye to my beloved father who died from a brain tumor one week before my eleventh birthday.

About a year before Daddy's death, I sat in his lap in the rocking chair while he read a book to me called, *Seven Simple Sermons on the Second Coming of Christ*. He finished the book, and I begged him to start over and read it again to me. He did, and we discussed it in great detail, in a child's language, of course. I was particularly fascinated with the elaborate descriptions of heaven. I could picture the streets paved in gold, and the jeweled gates, and the kind people I would meet. This vision of such beauty and love did indeed make me want to be there someday. It helped me to establish in my mind a real abode for my father after his transition from this world, although there was something changeable about that setting, too. What was changeable was my own consciousness as I grew and matured.

We are told that our lost loved ones live on in our hearts. That is true. They do live on in our hearts, and we have our memories of them, and memories of our personal relationships with them. We are also told that we will see them again someday, and for many that is a vague promise that requires a lot of faith in the unknown. The truth is many of us really don't know what to do or think about our loved ones who have moved on. Can we in some way continue our relationships with them? Are they still involved in our lives here? Can they help us through our earthly trials? Can we be helpful to them in some way?

It is my intention, by sharing my own experiences, that I might help you to discover new ways to approach the loss of loved ones in your life, and new possibilities for making contact on some level with those who now reside in other dimensions. Perhaps you will have a clearer understanding of what separates our dimensions and what you might do to remove these perceived obstacles to the communication you desire with those you love. Grief is a natural response to loss of any kind, especially to the loss of those who are so dear to us. When there is a better awareness of what is taking place on both sides of life during this time of grief, the sting is sometimes less severe. It helps to know that our goodbyes do not have to be so permanent. It is comforting to know that the connection is still there and that there are ways in which this connection may be enhanced, allowing for a somewhat less painful journey for both you and your departed loved ones. It has been helpful for me to visualize my parents as very much alive—living in a beautiful new environment, brimming with youth, energy, and enthusiasm in their return to their real home. In a way, I have been able to develop a whole new relationship with them, honoring them for their dedication as my parents, but also anticipating a reunion celebration with them someday.

We can hold certain beliefs through an intellectual knowledge of them, but until we have experienced them in action they do not become a real truth for us. In this book I shall share my own truths with you, truths formed from actual personal experience. I have three stories to tell you about three remarkable women who, through their presence in my life, have taught me some of the most significant lessons I will ever know. My contacts with them took place during their lives on Earth and now from where they are living their new lives in other dimensions.

Ann C. Manser is a spiritual teacher who revealed much to me about who I am and why I am here. Pat Larson, my closest friend during our twenty-five year friendship, taught me the meaning of friendship at its highest level where souls connect and love and support each other. My mother showed me deep love and compassion, the courage to meet life and its challenges and how to keep moving forward through all and any circumstances of life. When one finds souls like these on her path, she doesn't give them up easily . . . and so I didn't!

Some people stay in our hearts forever.

PART I

Foundations

CHAPTER 1

A Journey beyond Time and Space

Beauty is not in the face;
beauty is a light in the heart.

~ Kahlil Gibran

NEVER, IN MANKIND'S HISTORY, HAS there been a time when the desire to explore has not existed. In fact, the desire to explore our environment appears to be inherent in our very nature of being. The boundaries of the human environment continue to expand, even to intergalactic proportions during our present lifetime. We know this to be outer space exploration; but what do we know about inner space exploration? This route to discovery has been active since life began, but relatively few have committed to the minimal amount of time required for such extraordinary inner knowing.

Let us suppose that you have been offered an opportunity to explore a new world, and that you will be accompanied by the most compassionate and knowledgeable guides imaginable. You will be required to leave your loved ones behind for a while with a promise that you will be reunited at a time in the future more convenient or appropriate for them. Your mode of travel will be comfortable and quick, much like stepping from one room into another or entering a lovely garden through a special gate aided by assistants whose task it is to ensure your comfort and minister to your every need along the way. Before you begin your exploration of this new world you might want to rest a bit to feel refreshed. So a safe and comfortable place will be provided for you for that purpose. Now, take a deep breath, open your mind and heart and let us be on our way for an intriguing hypothetical journey.

You might find yourself in a lovely garden, in a quiet woodland setting, near a lake or waterfall, or in the quiet private home of a friend or relative. Your imagination will take you where you in your own heart most wish to be. The climate will be mild and comfortable at all times. Should you take a notion to enjoy a dip in the lake, your skin and clothes will dry instantly when you get out of the water, so you will not need to be bothered with extra baggage on this journey. Colors will be more vibrant than those you are accustomed to seeing. In fact, there will be additional colors that will be entirely new to you. Flowers seem to greet you with pretty little smiles and songs. Songbirds and fluttering butterflies accompany you along your pathway of blooming bushes and trees. Do you recall the Walt Disney movies such as Mary Poppins with the gorgeous wonderland of flowering trees, apple blossoms, cherry blossoms? There might even be a golden glow of light illuminating your surroundings, much like the light found in many of the paintings of Maxfield Parrish, or like the magical glow of the sun sometimes seen after a rain.

As you travel along your pathway, making new discoveries with every step, you will come to the realization that not only do you feel lighter and more energetic, without any of the aches and pains or handicaps of the past, but you even look more youthful. You seem to glow with an inner light. You are used to communicating with your voice, using your vocal cords, and suddenly you realize that you are reading the minds of your guides before they have a chance to express their thoughts vocally. They seem happy with your discovery and they agree that mental telepathy is a much more efficient form of communication. Right away you become quite adept at this new way to converse. You never tire from walking, and your wonderful new guides realize from all your many questions that there are already myriad places on your list that you wish to explore. They then explain that any place you might want to visit is only seconds away and that to wish to be there is to be there instantly. You decide to take in the local sights first before embarking upon any lengthy travel and enjoy the lovely homes and the happy-looking people you see working in their gardens along the way. Farther along the path you speak to people sitting on park benches under flowering trees, some by a pond or a lake, simply enjoying each other and the sounds and scenes of infinite peace and beauty.

In a short time you have reached the edge of a small village bustling with people, but not crowded. People are casually walking in and out of art galleries, music halls, libraries, science laboratories and other establishments of interest. There is no commerce. In this world if there is something you wish to own you simply concentrate on the object, make your intention known, and it will manifest for you.

You may partake of a concert, a theater performance, a ballet, or a film. Some of these performances will be given outdoors on a picturesque hillside, others in great halls or open-air theaters. The movies are shown publicly, or you may choose to view them in your own home, alone or with friends. There are libraries where they are kept for your convenience. No money is used in this world beyond Earth time and space, so you will be charged nothing for your entertainment or enjoyment of the arts.

There are social activities for every personality. You discover that there are dances, concerts, science exhibits, and sports events of all kinds. Meandering along the pathway you can see to your right a baseball diamond with players actively enjoying the game and spectators cheering them on. On down the path you are delighted to find a lively tennis game in progress, particularly if this was your sport of choice throughout your lifetime. As you travel a bit farther into the countryside you arrive at a lovely blue lake with sailboats, canoes, houseboats, row boats and any other kind of boat or raft you can imagine. People are having a splendid time swimming near the beach. You become interested in a game of volleyball being played in the sand and stop to watch for a while. So much fun! Happy relaxed people are laughing and joking with each other, just enjoying pleasant company.

In the distance you spot a group of mountain climbers scaling a particularly challenging peak. As you move closer you observe that the climbers are very adept with their climbing skills; they seem to move smoothly and effortlessly. Beyond the mountain lies the ocean. The waves are ideal for surfing and you eventually see a few surfers perfectly balanced on their boards. The seaside, it turns out, is a popular place to meet and walk and picnic. The children are especially carefree and happy—so busy putting their artistic talents to work on the unique architecture of their sandcastles. Some are actually large enough for the children to play inside.

What a lovely day! What an enlightening tour! Tomorrow you will have decided to schedule a museum visit to a very special and unusual museum. You will be shown a living record of the evolution of life as it has unfolded over millions of years of Earth time on our planet. After this intriguing excursion you have been promised a relaxing evening at a large outdoor symphony concert where you will listen to some of your favorite music, or a concert where you can enjoy the music representing your own culture and watch the delightful show of color the musical notes produce.

Your kind and thoughtful guides tell you that tonight there will be a celebration of an important life lived on Earth—your life! This celebration has nothing to do with a life of fame or your academic accomplishment, nor even with whatever material wealth that you have been able to acquire. It has to do with the fact that you lived the unique life that was yours to live with respect for others with whom you shared the planet with patience and perseverance, with courage and fortitude for the trials, tribulations, and tasks set before you, and gratitude for the blessings bestowed upon you.

The setting for this celebration is by the ocean, and the party will begin on a large patio situated on a grassy slope above the ocean below, lined and dotted with lush green trees and flowering plants of many colors. It is never dark in this dimension, however there will be lighted lanterns strung on tree limbs above the patio to add to the festive ambience. Following the initial social interaction with your guests outdoors you will be escorted into a grand banquet hall decorated with the most exquisite works of art, statuary and more magnificent flowers and greenery. The ceiling gives the illusion of being domed, but it is actually open to the heavens. You will know this when you see an occasional bird enter the building through the opening.

You will be able to hear the voices of angels as they serenade you softly in the background throughout the evening. The tables will be covered with elegant white cloths and set with the finest china, crystal, and silver. In this new dimension you will be with all of those you love, and you may be surprised at the attention you will receive.

Your homecoming has long been anticipated by those who love you and had to leave you behind. You will see people you haven't seen for many years; friends and people to whom you are related, some who passed on before your birth or early in your life. Your parents might have both been gone for several years, your grandparents for many years. There could be aunts and uncles and friends whom you have missed for a long time; a sister, a brother, a child. They will all be there to greet you and to congratulate you on your "homecoming." You will indeed be the honored guest, for you have now joined them all—all of your loved ones who arrived before you in this other dimension which some call "heaven."

The journey you have just taken is based on a composite of experiences, including descriptions of the afterlife as revealed to me in visions and dream visits, as well as those shared by others in their writings. In the Holy Bible it is expressed that "In my Father's house are many mansions . . ." or levels and spheres of afterlife experience which surely include all cultures and many ways of life. Sylvia Browne speaks of the possibility of meeting beings from other planets who may appear in our "Earth heavens." Robert Murray writes about a planet similar to Earth, and its inhabitants. While the imagery above may indeed be true for some, it could be quite a different experience for others. The point is that those "many mansions" exist beyond those we are aware of through our five senses. And that is because we have at least six senses, and once we have developed the other senses—senses beyond the physical realm, we can move among other 'mansions' and have contact with those who no longer exist in physical form on the earth plane.

CHAPTER 2

Is Afterlife Contact Possible?

For those who believe, no proof is necessary.
For those who don't believe, no proof is possible.

~ Stuart Chase

MOST OF US ON PLANET Earth would agree that our lives here are journeys in time and space. We take for granted that we occupy space in some location or in varying locations on the planet. Our individual time lines, as far as we know, begin with our birth and end with our death. During this lifetime we experience many events, some of which are significant enough to be celebrated in some way. Let us suppose for a moment that we could extend that time line like a continuum into another dimension. If we could do that, then what we call "death" might be just another event on that same time line—one that might even call for a celebration of an Earth life lived and loved for many years or for just a few.

Stay with me for a moment as we imagine a little farther. In many cases we are granted the privilege of time to say: "So long for a while" and "We'll meet again" as the curtain goes down on our part of life's drama. There are others whose lives come to an abrupt halt because of war, accidents or other unpredictable occurrences. It is sometimes difficult to feel closure with those loved ones whose lives have ended so abruptly. Those of us left behind often remain in a state of shock for a long time. Try to imagine, then, that we can have an ongoing relationship with those we have "lost." How would that happen? Where are they? What are their lives like now? What do they do? When I tell you about my three remarkable women, I shall tell you about Ann Manser first. When Ann passed on many years ago I was not aware that an ongoing relationship in my conscious waking state was a possibility except perhaps through stories I had read about mediums who "contacted the dead." I began having spontaneous experiences that told me—in no uncertain terms—that Ann was very much alive. She reported in from time to time in my dreams or meditations, but it didn't occur to me that I could make some of our contacts happen when I desired them.

Many years later when my friend, Pat Larson, passed on I was more aware of the possibilities of this kind of contact, but I still thought I would need the services of a psychic medium. Pat was my closest friend and I had to know where she had gone and what she was doing and how she was feeling about her new circumstances. I did engage the services of a psychic, eventually two of them, both of them men whose ability and integrity I trusted. I received a lot of wonderful and credible information which only made me want more. It was through the first psychic that I became aware that Pat wanted me to learn to make the contact on my own. She explained that it would take a while, but with discipline and perseverance it would indeed be possible. Pat taught me from the "other side" how to make contact with her, step by step. It is a wonderful feeling to know that my beloved friend is just a whisper—actually a thought away.

By the time my mother, Kathryn, took her turn to pass on to the next dimension I was somewhat familiar with the possibilities, and so was Mother. While she was still in the physical dimension we had conversations about the possible conditions of her future home, and we knew we wanted to maintain contact with each other. She knew Pat, and she knew of the work we were doing together to make our contact possible. She urged me to continue that work so that she and I could keep in touch as well.

What if you could have some assurance that you would be able to see those you love someday again? Many of us have grown up without any of that assurance with the exception of perhaps a strong faith. As children most of us accepted the beliefs of our parents and grandparents as our own—beliefs that originated in whatever religious orientations our families espoused. Do these beliefs still satisfy you? As you may see they didn't continue to satisfy me. I had very strong feelings that there was much more to the story than what I had been taught in my Sunday school. However, Sunday school and the church of my childhood did provide a necessary foundation for my evolving perspective.

There are numerous theories and philosophies about life after death, and many question whether there really is a Heaven. Is there any proof of an afterlife? Scientists within the past two centuries have investigated and published their results in professional journals and nonfiction books for the public to read and evaluate. Their findings have been conclusive for a life after death in some other place or level of existence and also for the possibility that we on Earth can have ongoing contact with our loved ones in those other levels or dimensions. For many of you this may already be a reality. You have had strong feelings of a spirit's presence. You have been guided to just the right book on your shelf for an answer to a question or a problem. Perhaps you have had dream visits with a loved one—it felt real and you just knew you were actually with that spirit for that time.

I was busy putting books on the shelves in my library one day after the move to my present home, not long after Mother's "death." I was lamenting over my absence when she needed consoling and reassurance after a traumatic event in her life. At the time that she needed me my husband, Tom, was taking his sabbatical from the college where he was teaching psychology. We had moved our family from Florida to Carmel, California for several months. The children were in school there and Tom was involved in research projects along the coast of California. I couldn't leave them at that time to go and be with Mother at her home in Tennessee, and now, many years later while shelving books in my library, I was conjuring up what I perceived as neglect of my beloved mother when she must have needed me most. I was, for the moment, deeply engrossed in feelings of regret and guilt, being hard on myself for not being available to comfort her during her time of need. I was a little puzzled when I found myself walking across the room and automatically lifting a small book off the shelf. I had no particular book in mind so I was unaware of the reason for that momentary impulsive action. The book I found in my hand was *Gift from the Sea* by Anne Morrow Lindbergh. Inside the front cover I read an inscription—from me. I had sent Mother the book in September of the year we were away, right at the time of her difficulty. Also inside the book she had tucked the note that I had sent with it. It was a note full of my words of love and compassion for her. I also found in the back of the book a letter I had written to her a couple of weeks later, another expression of my deep love and caring. I then recalled that there were telephone conversations, as well. Although I couldn't actually see Mother standing there in the library summoning me to walk over to the shelf and pull out that very book, I was absolutely sure of her presence. She knew I cared and she wanted me to remember that I had expressed my caring to her when it counted. Needless to say, I was able to forgive myself for 'being so neglectful.' There are many ways and many signs of the ongoing presence of our loved ones in our lives. We just need to pay attention.

You might ask, "Why do I want to make contact with those in the afterlife?" Some of you might not feel the need to make contact at all. Others might like to know that their family members or friends are all right. There could be times when you feel a need for some help from their dimension or you might want to know how you can help someone there. Suppose a parent or a spouse leaves this life unexpectedly and there are unresolved matters that you would give anything to resolve in some way. There are still things you can do to reach some feeling of completion and put your heart and mind at rest. You can visit a well-recommended medium to make the contact. You can write your loved one a letter or find a quiet place and speak with him or her. You can say a prayer giving thanks for peace and love in the relationship or you can mentally affirm forgiveness on the parts of both of you as you go through your busy day. You can also request a dream visit in which you might be able to discuss and resolve your issues. Robert Moss reminds us that "The guides who come to us in dreams put on masks or costumes adapted to our level of understanding. There is an old

Greek saying that 'the gods love to travel in disguise." You have the idea. Now create some tools of your own.

Prayers and gifts of love are much appreciated by those on the other side. An example of such a gift might be a visualization of the loved one's spirit being wrapped in white light or in a rose light of unconditional love or even a stream of roses or hearts going forth from your heart and surrounding them. Their progress to the higher levels of their current dimension is supported by this action. Your prayers and loving thoughts have an actual beneficial effect on the recipient, spiritually and emotionally, helping them progress to more rarified dimensions. Making a gift in their name to a charity or someone in need, to your favorite cause or their favorite cause, will honor them and call forth much gratitude for all involved.

Those in the spirit world are very aware of and involved in our earthly activities. Once a bond is made with another soul it is there for always. It is especially felt by those in the spirit world and honored by their attention to our needs. Renee Bridges says that "they eagerly watch for opportunities to assist."[1] There are laws in their dimension which do not allow them to interfere with our free will. So only if we ask for their assistance will they do whatever is necessary on their side to help us on this side.

Kathryn (Mother) has used objects around the house to dramatically get my attention. I was in an auto accident several years ago while I was living in Oklahoma. While in the hospital in Tulsa Mother came from Tennessee to see me, and she gave me a little clown doll (pictured) with a music box inside. Sometime in the year before her transition I mentioned the clown, and she responded with, "You still have that silly old clown?" I told her, "Yes, I'll keep the little clown," and jokingly I continued, "it will always remind me of you."

About six weeks after Mother had made her transition I rolled out of bed one morning thinking about how long she had not felt well during the last couple of years of her life and noting how she still got so much done. She took such good care of her house and was always available to do things for other people—especially her family. On this particular morning I took Mother's camera out of a drawer, sat down on my bed and attempted to determine if there was any film in it that needed to be developed. I picked up the manual and was reading in it when the little clown music box, high on a top shelf of the bookcase, began playing. It played a few notes and stopped. Then it played a few more, and in a few minutes it played again. Poppy, my Himalayan cat, came over and sat by me and appeared to be watching "something" or "someone," so I began talking to Mother. I thanked her for being there. I closed my eyes and tried to "hear" or get some thoughts from her. I guess I was still a bit too emotional, so I wasn't able to pick up any information at that time. But a little later, as I sat working at my computer, I had a very strong urge to call my daughter Wendi in Vermont.

Wendi couldn't be reached by phone, but later in the day I was able to reach one of her friends who told me that Wendi had been pretty ill over the weekend. She promised to check on her after work and leave her a cell phone if she needed one. I was finally able to reach her and learned that her own cell phone wasn't charged and she had been too sick to get word to me in any other way. Before we hung up I told her how I had been led to call her. There was a long pause followed by, "Mom, that's incredible! I've been talking to Grandma and asking her for her help." I responded with, "Well, Granny sure came through for you, didn't she?" I flew to Vermont the next day to take care of my daughter. Wendi had asked for help and she had received it. Mother had discovered a way to get my attention and her plan worked. I've heard from her through the funny little clown many times since that first experience.

Another time, Wendi was visiting me and we were both in my library working at our computers. I was sitting at my desk and Wendi had her computer on the library table. We took a short break and began talking to each other. She suddenly stopped in mid-sentence and asked, "Mom, what is happening up there?" She was pointing to a top library shelf and we both watched as a round wicker basket, which had been standing on end against the wall, was now rolling across the shelf without any visible assistance. I immediately thought it must be Mother. I spoke to her and told her I was delighted that she had dropped in to see us. Since Mother and Wendi were close, I felt that she would be comfortable paying us a visit like that.

During my research for this book I read about what was involved for the spirit to make contacts like those mentioned. Apparently, it takes a tremendous amount of energy and skill on the part of the spirit in another dimension to propel the force it takes to penetrate the density of our reality. Many times, early in their experience in a new dimension with all new laws, they must have assistance from spirits who have had more experience making contacts with the Earth dimension. You might want to ask a loved one on the other side to choose a way to make contact with you—a way to let you know when they're around. You might make a suggestion such as playing a music box, moving or knocking over a small object near you, or turning over a photograph on your desk or table. He or she might impress your mind with a favorite song you shared, and you will begin humming or singing the song. Your loved one might not take any of your suggestions but have his or her own way to get your attention. So ask for the method of contact and then pay attention!

Clown Music Box gifted to me by my mother (Kathryn)

CHAPTER 3

Afterlife Beliefs of Major Religions

Do not believe in anything
simply because you have heard of it.
Do not believe in anything simply
because it is spoken and rumored by many.
Do not believe in anything simply because
it is found written in your religious books.
Do not believe in anything merely on the
authority of your teachers and elders.
Do not believe in traditions because they
have been handed down for many generations.
But after observation and analysis, when
you find that anything agrees with reason and is
conducive to the good and benefit of one and all,
then accept it and live up to it.

~ Hindu Prince Gautama Siddharta,
Founder of Buddhism—563-483 B. C.

RELIGIONS THROUGH THE AGES HAVE viewed death or the crossing over into a new dimension in somewhat ambiguous terms. For some, there is anticipation of glorious transformation into a state of bliss or heavenly paradise. For others there is a fear of punishment and torture in a hell of fire and brimstone. Metaphysically, there is some foundation for such notions, although "heaven and hell as understood by the masses and unenlightened clergymen are a distortion of the reality underlying those states."[1]

To the metaphysician, so-called death is just another phase of the human journey. There is no birth and there is no death. The journey goes on where there are just different levels of awareness. When the dying move out of the physical realm into the spirit realm they move beyond physical sensory perception and learn a whole new set of laws which correspond to their new environment. Contact between the physical and the spirit worlds is possible under certain conditions and circumstances. This will be discussed in greater detail in Chapter 20.

Some religions allude to a heavenly existence of eternal rest. "A heaven of ease and idleness is a static state. Inertia does not exist in the universe. All is in motion and in a continuous flux. Everything is in a dynamic state moving toward a higher expression and manifestation. It is a place of continued education for the evolving soul, where the mysteries of the universe and Cosmic laws are studied. One also spends one's time in heaven serving the whole of creation in various capacities, according to one's innate abilities and talents. In heaven, angelic beings are adorned with their purity, love, and other positive virtues."[2] What are supposed to be wings, as represented by painters in their artwork, are simply magnetic radiations streaming from their light bodies, according to metaphysical teacher, Leonard Lee. [3]

Whether you believe firmly in a religious theory of your own about what happens after death, or you believe that death is the end of life in any dimension—or if, as with many of us, you have had first-hand experience either through personal contact or a near-death-experience (NDE)—you might be surprised to find that many more people are aware of an afterlife than you thought. Stay with me while we explore some personal experiences and pertinent research on this intriguing topic of life after death.

Heath and Klimo state in *Handbook to the Afterlife* that "the reigning Western scientific paradigm today is, for the most part, a physical reductionist one." They explain that reality "can only be understood scientifically in terms of our currently known physical reality, with its three dimensions of space and its fourth dimension of time, and with its accepted realms of matter and energy." Many scientists now call themselves dualists, adding to the physical aspect a nonphysical aspect of reality which allows for the possibility of survival of the spirit at death and an afterlife of some kind.

For those who subscribe to a belief endorsed by a particular religion or denomination, your personal afterlife beliefs might be based on the doctrines and rituals of that religion. For some, a composite of beliefs from more than one religion or a combination of religion and science or of spiritual science might be more comfortable. You might want to be open to growth or expansion in your own consciousness and allow your beliefs about the afterlife to grow and change accordingly.[3]

This chapter is continued in Appendix A

CHAPTER 4

What Happens When We Die?

All changes, even the most longed for,
have their melancholy; for what we leave
behind us is a part of ourselves; we must die
to one life before we can enter another.

Anatole France

IN MY SEARCH OF LITERATURE on the topic, "What happens when we die?" authors have stated that being born into this physical, material world is traumatic for the soul being born, a much more difficult experience than leaving the body at death. I do not recall any personal death or near-death experience but I have had a definite recall of my own birth into this life through a *rebirthing* experience.

It has been suggested by several authors that being born into the physical world is a death experience in itself. One dies to the dimension from which he or she comes and is born into another dimension, the Earth dimension in our case. And as we die to the Earth dimension we are being born into another dimension to pick up life where we left off on Earth as we are able to adapt it to our new abode. The way of the new life in the next dimension will be discussed in a later chapter. As a point of comparison between the experience of being born and that of dying, I shall relate my own *rebirthing* experience and its attending effects.

If you have had rebirthing sessions, privately or in a group with a trained rebirthing facilitator, you will be able to relate in some way to my experience. If you haven't, let me first give you a couple of definitions, a brief explanation of the process and some reasons for it.

Sondra Ray, rebirthing facilitator and author, states that "Rebirthing originally started, it was thought, to heal the birth trauma. This is a major part of it. However, we have learned that it is really a spiritual purification process, and letting go of birth trauma is only one part of that much greater, all-encompassing process of going for God."[1]

Leonard Orr is the founder of rebirthing, and he was my first rebirthing facilitator. He defines rebirthing: "As a new yoga, rebirthing is not a discipline. It is an inspiration. It is not teaching a person how to breathe, it is the intuitive and gentle act of learning how to breathe from the Breath itself. Intuitive Energy Breath or Conscious Energy Breathing is the ability to breathe Energy as well as air. Conscious Energy Breathing is the most natural healing ability of all." He also states that "Rebirthing also means to unravel the birth-death cycle and to incorporate the body and mind into the conscious Life of the Eternal Spirit—to become a conscious expression of the Eternal Spirit."

In his early rebirthing sessions Orr's participants were submerged in warm water with a snorkel for breathing. My former husband, Tom, and I and a few friends were early participants, and our hot tub was used for Orr's St. Petersburg, Florida sessions. The warm water was of course a simulation for the amniotic fluid that nourishes and protects the fetus in the womb, and for me the rebirthing experience was very comforting.

Several years after this first one, I had another rebirthing opportunity. I was living in Nashville, Tennessee then and became a member of a group who worked together in a political, social, and metaphysical effort revolving around Barbara Marx Hubbard's "Campaign for a Positive Future." We invited an internationally known yoga teacher and rebirthing facilitator, Janabai Harrison, to conduct a workshop and private sessions for rebirthing.

About sixteen participants arrived one evening at the home of two of our group members, each bringing a sleeping bag as instructed. Water was seldom used for rebirthing sessions by this time, so we laid out our sleeping bags on the floor across the spacious living area and took our places stretched out on top of them. Janabai gave us a brief introduction then she turned on some quiet meditation music. Before she began her guided meditation I became very aware of my resistance to being there. *There are too many people here—some I have never even met. Why did I agree to this rebirthing session? Why didn't I wait and make another private appointment? I won't be able to relax and go within and do my inner work with all of these different energies here.*

My negative inner monologue continued until Janabai began to guide us to our own inner sanctuaries. Her voice was soothing, rhythmic and melodic. I was almost immediately transported back in time to my own birth. I had used self-hypnosis in the past, and this feeling was very similar. At once I was the infant being born and also the adult observer interpreting the process. I found my consciousness in the infant body being propelled toward the birth canal inside my mother's body by the rhythm of her contractions. I had no fear, but I was aware that things were rapidly changing for me. I suddenly felt myself being lifted out of my infant body supported by two breathtakingly magnificent cherubs, one on each side. I felt completely loved and protected in their hands. It was not long before my tiny body had been delivered and "I" was then placed back in that little body with the attendant senses of a physical being. I do not know what others experience as birth trauma because I felt none during that part of my birth process. The trauma, the disturbing and somewhat painful part of the birth, was the harshness of my new environment. It was overwhelmingly noisy—the clanging of instruments and containers and the adult human voices all *shouting* as the doctor and the nurses rushed about. The overhead lights were brilliant and blinding. The separation from the warmth and insulated quiet of my mother's body was the most difficult time in the whole process. This rebirthing experience far exceeded my expectations once I gave in to the process. The trauma of landing in a new environment of lower vibrations might be something useful for young parents-to-be to keep in their awareness when their future children are being born.

Consider that, in comparison with the birth process, many have told of leaving their body during the process we call a near-death-experience (NDE) and leaving all pain behind them, thereby suggesting that birth might be more traumatic than death. In both instances, those of birth and death, the spirit is leaving one dimension and entering another one where the laws of life are quite unlike those learned in the dimension being left behind. There is quite an adjustment to be made to the new dimension, but reportedly there are guides who help us to adjust and adapt in any dimension where we might find ourselves.

Most of us still living on Earth spend more time planning a two-week summer vacation than we spend trying to find out what is in store for us at the end of this lifetime and how we can best prepare for it. Perhaps we have grown up in homes with a busy lifestyle, or we have become complacent in the belief that there is no obvious way to explore possibilities of a life beyond our life on Earth. Or worse, we may have been brought up to believe that we are all sinners and we don't want to think about the consequences of our so-called sinful lives on Earth. This last reason appears to be pretty much the same viewpoint held over from beliefs of orthodoxy hundreds of years ago. In earlier centuries the Christian church fathers taught their followers about the dire consequences that awaited those who sinned and didn't follow the man-made traditions of the church. This apparently was done in order to exert their control over the church members at that time and is unfortunately still being used by some churches today as a method of control. There are many reasons that we have neglected to put much thought into a life beyond the physical life, but fear still seems to be a prevailing obstacle to this knowledge.

Have you ever heard someone say, "Well, there is no way to know if we survive death, or if there is even a life after death, because no one has ever returned to Earth to tell us about it?" I believe that people who make a statement like that simply have not been interested enough or are perhaps too fearful to research the topic and find the abundance of material and research that is available. The Dalai Lama states that "death is a part of all our lives. Whether we like it or not, it is bound to happen. Instead of avoiding thinking about it, it is better to understand its meaning."[2]

According to some orthodox religious views, death is the big separation of loved ones and their reunion is not possible until after the Day of Judgment. Esoteric Philosophy differs in this viewpoint teaching that death cannot affect the higher consciousness but only separates the lower (physical) vehicles of those who love each other. Could it be that we only feel separated from each other because those of us left in the material world have not developed our higher psychic faculties to a degree required to be aware of our loved ones in other dimensions? Helena P. Blavatsky, a founder of the Theosophical Society, insists that there is no such thing as death at all. The natural moving from one dimension to the next is often very aptly expressed as *the great transition*. This term *transition* is defined by Webster's New World Dictionary simply as "a passing from one condition or place to another." This might be a concept similar to a pupa leaving its cocoon and emerging as a butterfly.

For some people, especially those who have spent time in regular sessions of prayer and meditation, the great transition is another exciting adventure. It isn't unusual for one experienced in the practice of meditation to visit the afterlife worlds and bring back information on life there—to gain knowledge from someone who already resides there. Information can be in the form of visions, clairvoyance or clear-seeing; clairaudience or clear hearing; clairsentience or clear knowing; and/or trusting the voice within. We are all capable of any of these gifts for communication, and we use some of them without realizing it. When we become aware of them they can be further developed and used more consciously. Most of us have used them all, however there is usually one dominant channel for each person that seems to work better than others.

My mother told me about a clairvoyant experience she had when she was going through an emotionally traumatic time in her adult life. She was kneeling beside her bed in prayer and suddenly became aware of being watched. She opened her eyes and saw a masculine figure robed in white standing nearby. She described him as a "wise and compassionate being who was probably there to comfort me." It frightened her because it was so unexpected. She said she was sorry later that she had scared him away, because he disappeared just after she had acknowledged him. I suggested that he probably didn't leave at all but that she had been in such a state of heightened awareness she was able to look into his dimension. When she felt fear she changed her own state of awareness and was no longer able to see him. In other words, she removed herself from the frequency of the vision by lowering her vibratory frequency.

To many people the great transition doesn't exist. For some it is a matter of not believing or seeing how it can be so. Or, the recognition has not yet occurred that it is possible to be a soul wearing a body—a soul having a physical experience. These people often identify so strongly with the physical body that they see themselves as a body with a soul, and when that body dies the soul dies with it. Modern research proves this to be a false assumption and has been able to prove the survival of the soul and the spirit that animates the physical body. The next chapter will explain this in more detail.

Because of the vastness of the subject that we call death and the afterlife there is apparently no definitive source on our Earth plane that can accurately describe the experiences of the process of death or the soul's destination following that process. In order to give you a glimpse of this journey through the transition we call death and the life that follows I have drawn on many resources that I hope will, in some way, put some pieces of the puzzle in place for you. These resources include published articles and books by people who have had direct experience of contact with those in the afterlife or who know someone who has had direct experience; published research by scientists and others with strong credibility in the field of survival of the soul and afterlife contact; first-hand experiences of friends and colleagues, some of whom are well-known for their exceptional work as psychics and mediums; reports of near-death experiences (NDEs); and my own personal experiences in contact with loved ones, acquaintances, and pets on the other side of life through meditation, dreams, out-of-body-experiences (OBEs), and spontaneous phenomena.

My very first experience with death was with the death of my own father, so close to my heart, when I was almost eleven. He began having severe headaches and dizziness and other characteristic symptoms of a brain tumor only a couple of weeks before the tumor claimed his life. His last words to me were words I shall remember forever. He called me to his bedside and said, "Shirley Ann, if I were to put you in a box full of diamonds you would outshine them all." I knew at that moment that it was the last time I would see my daddy—and it was. The ambulance came and took him away to the hospital, and within a few days I learned that my precious father was "with the angels in heaven."

Several years after my father's death it was necessary for me to meet "Death" face-to-face again. As a student nurse, losing an occasional patient to death became an unwelcomed but accepted part of my training. It was always difficult to see another human have to give up a life, often prematurely.

While I was a student I fainted in the operating room the first time I observed surgery for a brain tumor. I was especially attentive and emotionally involved the first time I was assigned to care for a patient with a brain tumor, a seventeen-month-old boy whom I discovered was a distant cousin of mine. The child lived, but I was not able to follow his progress because he lived in another city.

What was it like to die? Did it hurt? Was it hard? Did anyone help you? Do you get to see God? These are a few of the questions I wanted to ask my dad.

There are numerous accounts written about near-death experiences (NDEs) that seem to follow similar patterns, yet there are unique features for each person having the experience. These stories told through the years by people who have died on the operating table, during childbirth, during an accident and in myriad other situations, and have then been resuscitated, have served as clues for us about the death process and as well have given us some idea of possible destinations in an afterlife.

When the time of transition or death of the physical body comes it is thought that it is the High Self that chooses the exact moment of that release and initiates the process. The High Self can be defined as the spiritual part of one's consciousness, the divinity or spark of God within each of us.

"The purpose of human life is spiritual, intellectual, cultural and physical evolution," states Geoffrey Hodson, "the gradual unfolding from a latent state to the full power of spiritual maturity. The development of the four lower or material vehicles (physical, etheric, astral, mental) accompany the development of the powers of the human spirit. In the divine sparks of humans the potential for spiritual powers is present from the very beginning. A lost spiritual Soul is an impossibility in nature, for the true Self is immortal, eternal and indestructible."[3]

"Be ye therefore perfect, even as your Father which is in heaven is perfect"[4] will be literally obeyed by the spiritual Self of all human beings. This is an impossible goal for one lifetime, is it not? Try to conceptualize the Self as an Oversoul, the Monad, or the Divine spark in each of us originating from the Divine Source. From this Oversoul, the highest spiritual part of each of us is like a seed containing the potentiality of the parent plant which is God or the Supreme Source of all that is. The "seed is sown or born on Earth, puts forth shoots, stems and leaves, and eventually it flowers. The resultant human individuality in its four vehicles is strengthened by the winds of adversity, purified and refined by the rain of sorrow, beautified and expanded by the sunshine of happiness and love, and ultimately reaches the fully flowered state."[5]

Elisabeth Haich, in *Initiation*, tells of meditating on the meaning of life and death. *"Death,"* I thought, *"death again and again!"* She suddenly heard a voice from within speak to her saying: "Death? Why do you persist in seeing but one side of truth? What do trees and nature reveal in spring? Life!—again and again! Life and death alternate in an everlasting circle. Death is but the other side of life." "In this moment I saw quite clearly, that as life recedes from the tree and its leaves in autumn, the leaves become lifeless, empty husks, fall off and die. But only empty husks! The essence of life which has lived in the leaves now rests in the tree and bursts forth again in spring, clothes itself anew with a material form and becomes leaves again, repeating its eternal cycle. The tree inhales and exhales life, and only the leaves change, only the outer shell! Life remains eternal, for life is the eternal *being*. And I saw even further: The fountain of eternal existence—human beings call it '*God*'—breathes life into man, just as the Bible says that God breathed life into Adam's nostrils. Then God inhales again, withdrawing his breath, so that the empty husk falls: The body of man dies. Yet life does not cease at this moment, it clothes itself with a new body, in an eternal cycle and moves on, as everything in this world lives and moves in rhythm, from the orbit of the planets to the breath and pulse of every living creature."[6]

The evolutionary process is everlasting without any conceivable beginning or end. When human perfection is finally attained, advancing with each life lived, there is still higher attainment to be reached. Perfection suggests finality, and Hodson suggests that perfection can only be attained in a relative sense. Each incarnation brings with it the challenges with enough friction to polish another facet of one's greater being, each polished facet another step in the direction of relative perfection. "The spiritual Self of every individual is a God-in-the-becoming, whose future splendor, wisdom and power are entirely without limit."[7]

In order to better understand the process of transition in greater detail, it will be helpful at this point to know something about the *seed-atom* and the *silver cord*. Atoms of the dense or physical body are renewed from time to time, but one atom remains as a permanent one. This permanent atom is called a seed-atom and remains stable throughout the life being lived in the physical body. It is withdrawn at death and will become the nucleus for another physical body for the same soul in a future life. The results of the experiences of the life just lived are impressed upon the seed-atom which is situated in the left ventricle of the heart, near the apex. When a person dies the seed-atom is released traveling to the brain along the pathway of the pneumogastric nerve, leaving with the higher vehicles, the astral, mental, and spiritual bodies, between the parietal and occipital bones. These higher vehicles are still connected to the physical body by a slender, silvery cord. The rupture of the seed-atom causes the heart to stop, but the cord remains intact until a panorama of the life just finished is reviewed.[8]

The vital body, the vehicle next in density to the physical body, is sometimes called the etheric double. This body is the exact blueprint for the physical body and it carries vitality to the physical body by way of the nervous system. If we would develop our psychic vision to a level where we could view the etheric double we would be able to diagnose and treat illnesses before they manifest in the physical body. There are some who are able to do this but they are not often taken seriously by the mainstream population. If a person loses a part of the physical body, a leg or an arm for example, it continues to exist in the etheric double. This is what some people are able to feel, which they call their phantom limbs. At death it is the vital or etheric body that contains the panoramic images of the life just ending.

Max Heindel cautions against cremation or embalming the body during the first three days after death. The vital body is still with the higher vehicles, and these subtle bodies are connected by the silver cord to the physical body. Heindel says that during this time any post mortem examination or other injury to the physical body may in some measure be felt by the soul going through the releasing process. When cremation takes place before the end of three days it tends to disintegrate the vital body which should remain intact until the life panorama has been etched into the astral body. The astral body becomes the vehicle of conscious expression in the next dimension. It is around the end of the third day that the silver cord snaps releasing the higher bodies to the higher realms. At this point the physical body is completely dead. [9]

Of extreme importance is the peaceful atmosphere that must be created for the person experiencing the dying process. Loud grief and other intrusive distractions can interfere with the attention a soul must give to the values of the life being left behind. The departing soul is able to read the pictures from the seat of the subconscious memory through the vital body. Everything in one's life is remembered and at this time it is seen in reverse order, from the moments before death back to the time of birth. These pictures are being impressed upon the higher vehicles or bodies, but there is no feeling attached to them at this time. They will be reviewed again at a later time in the astral world—a world of feeling and emotion where one remains for a time. Usually a peaceful surrender to the process of release is achieved if the conditions are kept quiet and serene.

Alice Bailey tells a story about the experience of a surgical nurse who had been an atheist and who began to question her unbelief after having witnessed a "curious phenomenon" frequently at the time of death of some of her patients. She stated that, "at the moment of death, in several cases, a flash of light had been seen by her issuing from the top of the head, and that in one particular case (that of a girl of apparently very advanced spiritual development and great purity and holiness of life) the room had appeared to be lit up momentarily by electricity."[10]

In another incidence, "several of the leading members of the medical profession in a large Middle West city were approached by an interested investigator, by letter, and asked if they would be willing to state if they had noted any peculiar phenomena at the moment of death. Several replied by saying that they had observed a bluish light issuing from the top of the head, and one or two added that they had heard a snap in the region of the head."[11]

The transfer of the life forces of the physical seed-atom to the astral body is the beginning of clinical death. These life forces will be used as a nucleus for the vital body of a future embodiment. Seed atoms from the other levels, the astral and mental atoms, are transferred to the appropriate subtle bodies to be used in the astral dimension. The astral body is the visual equivalent of the physical body. Heindel advocates cremation over burial of the physical body because "it restores the elements to their primordial condition without the objectionable feature incident to the process of slow decay."[12] This of course is an individual choice.

In cases of suicide a person who is attempting to evade the difficulties of his life might find himself more alive than ever in his new dimension and with a feeling of emptiness until such time as when his normal death would have come. According to Annie Besant, ". . . you may destroy the body, but not the appointed period of sentient existence." She says that the higher vehicles do not separate until that predetermined time of the end of life that has been cut short by suicide. Until that time the spirit is as mentally alive as before and is subject to the desires and cravings of his Earth life without the means to satisfy them. At the time when the natural death would have occurred, his four higher levels of consciousness reunite, and then the final separation occurs, and he may pass on to higher realms and begin his further development there."[13]

There is a whole new life awaiting us as we leave this physical level of existence, our school of life here on Earth. It is not a place where we can be idle, and there is no awful Judgment Day according to my research on this topic. We judge ourselves, not in a moral way of *shoulds* and *oughts,* but to process and determine more appropriate ways we could have employed to handle certain situations.

Now, let us go back to the transition process itself. I want to relate to you the story of one person's transition from Earth to the spirit world as told in the mid-twentieth century by a priest in the spirit world through a medium named Anthony Borgia, in his book, *More About Life In the World Unseen.*

Borgia met his spirit communicator while he was still in the physical body. A well-known priest, he was reportedly the Monsignor Robert Hugh Benson (1871-1914), a son of Edward White Benson, former Archbishop of Canterbury. In Borgia's book, Monsignor Benson gives an account of his own death. He first reveals the fact of his gift of psychic vision as a priest on Earth and shares with us his ability to witness the passing of souls into the spiritual dimension while he was still living a physical existence. At his own passing, at the age of forty-three, the Monsignor recounts his experience as being labored due to his physical illness, but not painful. He recalls that in the days prior to his transition, at times he floated away from his body in the bed and gently returned. At times when he might not have seemed conscious to those who attended him he could see and hear all that was going on around him. He knew the time had come for him to leave, and he was eager to be gone. He suddenly felt a great urge to rise, there was no physical feeling, much like in a dream. He realized as he began rising above his body that no one in the room was able to see what was happening. He could see his body lying on the bed, but the real part of him was alive and well. He noticed that he was wearing his usual clothing, clothes he would wear around his house. He knew he had *died* and that he was very much alive and feeling better than ever before. Death was painless. He was met by a former colleague in this new world, "and the new sensation of comfort and freedom from bodily ills was one so glorious that the realization of it took a little while to comprehend fully. I was waiting with excitement for all manner of pleasant revelations of this new world, and I knew that there could be none better than my old friend to give them to me. He told me to prepare myself for immeasurable number of the pleasantest of surprises, and that he had been sent to meet me on my arrival."[14]

The Monsignor and his friend spoke, using their vocal cords. This method of communication later shifted to the use of mental telepathy which is the usual mode of communication on those levels. The mind, belonging to the spirit, expands and has access to much more knowledge than it holds when it has to filter through the limiting physical brain. The two men walked for a short time and then the friend suggested a more efficient method of travel. The Monsignor was told to take the arm of his friend and to close his eyes if he wished. He immediately experienced a sensation of floating which became more rapid as they went on. When they stopped, and he opened his eyes, he could feel a solid surface under his feet. They had arrived in a lovely big home—his own home. It had been improved in a way he had not been able to accomplish with its earthly counterpart. He discovered that there is a continuity of life and most decidedly a continuity of memory—and where there is memory, there is a past.[15]

"Sleep and death are brothers, the ancient Greeks used to say. The process of going to sleep is indeed similar to what happens at death."[16] In life on Earth, during our waking hours, the spirit body and the physical body are inseparable. They are attached to each other by a magnetic cord, called by some a silver cord. This magnetic cord was mentioned earlier, and it is an elastic life line which enables our spirit body to travel throughout the earth, the universe, or the spirit world while the physical body is asleep. As long as this cord is joined to the physical body a person's consciousness is in the physical world upon waking. When the magnetic or silver cord has been severed at the time of death the spirit is then free to live in its own element, and the physical body, no longer having the indwelling spirit to animate it, will begin to disintegrate like an old garment no longer useful to us. So the only difference between sleeping and death is whether or not the silver cord is still attached. It isn't physical, so it cannot be broken like an ordinary material cord.

In my research, both in literature and in my personal experiences, I've learned that there is always someone to meet us on the other side. It might be a family member or a friend. It might be someone we have called upon. In cases where there are no friends or relatives available, a worker in that dimension is appointed to greet new arrivals. One explanation of this circumstance is that those spirits who have volunteered to greet new arrivals in the *heaven world* are alerted, by someone in charge of a central office, of an imminent arrival. It is apparently all done mentally. A flash of light is sent toward the person making the transition. The appointed invisible helpers are aware of the light and are attracted into the *thought beam*, finding themselves in the exact spot where their services are needed. For example, the Monsignor and his friend, Ruth, another invisible helper, were sent to the bedside of an eighteen-year-old young man who was dying. They found him in his own bedroom at home. Ruth positioned herself at the head of the bed with the Monsignor at the patient's feet. They soon realized that the patient could see them but others in the room could not. They reassured him that everything would be all right and that they were there to help him. When the time of departure came, his spirit body began to rise above his physical body. "To the relatives in the bed-chamber, the boy was dead and gone. To Ruth and me he was alive and present," reported the Monsignor. He further stated, "I held him in my arms, as one would a child, while Ruth again placed her hands upon his head. A gentle movement of her hands for a minute or two to ensure that the boy would be peacefully comfortable, and we were ready to start upon our rapid journey to our home." The journey was soon over, and they placed the young man on a comfortable couch and awaited his awakening. When he opened his eyes he could see a lovely view out the window and was amazed at the beauty of his new surroundings. Ruth and the Monsignor were there beside him to explain what was happening to him, his transition into a new world, and to keep him from becoming frightened by the changes that had taken place a short time ago. They also explained to him that he would need a short rest to regain his strength and energy before exploring his surroundings. They gave him some fruit to eat which seemed to help restore his energy.

In the afterlife dimension food is not physical, but some new arrivals still feel the need to eat and so there is a counterpart to the foods in the earth dimension available. It is the essence of the food that the spirit is able to ingest. The period of rest is different for everyone upon arrival in this new world. Some need a very short rest and others might need days or weeks or longer depending on the vitality lost during an illness or shock received from a sudden death. Sometimes people who have crossed over, not believing there is an afterlife, have trouble seeing and hearing at first. They are so blinded by their long-held beliefs that death is the end for them that they are not open to the help they could readily receive on their arrival in a new dimension. Some are so difficult to convince that they have died and are in a new dimension that they wander for years in a dim mist, not knowing that all they have to do is to ask for the help that is available for them. Helpers try to get their attention, but they have shut themselves off from sound and sight and have not yet opened themselves to learning how to effectively use their spirit hearing or seeing mechanisms.[17]

"The average earth-dweller has no notion what kind of place *the next world* can possibly be, usually because he has not given much thought to the matter. How those very same people regret their indifference when they eventually arrive here in the spirit world! *Why*, they cry, *were we not told about this before we came here?*" The Monsignor tells us that "The passing from earth to the spirit world is not a religious affair, whatever. It is a purely natural process, and one that cannot be avoided. Living a good life on earth is not a religious matter. What really counts in our earthly lives is the motive behind our deeds."[18] It is loving, respecting and serving mankind that is important, according to many resources for this work. Service to humanity is service to the Creator.

CHAPTER 5

Other Dimensions

*Just when the caterpillar thought the world
was over, it became a butterfly.*

~ English Proverb

WHAT WILL LIFE BE LIKE for us in the next dimension? You can pick up five books or more that describe what it is like in other dimensions and you will get five or more very different perceptions because there are so many different dimensional levels to contact and visit. Ultimately, where we end up has everything to do with our level of vibratory frequency— our consciousness. The law of attraction is very much at work here.

"After birth, death is the greatest privilege that comes to mankind. If death did not occur, there would be old age, feebleness, poverty, pain and suffering forever; with it (death), splendid life on through the ages, progress, perpetual youth and vigor. Such is the heritage of all who have lived or who shall live in the ages to come as inhabitants of this plane; such are the benefits coming through dissolution."[1]

Ann Manser states that "death on the physical plane is a reward for work completed. The end of a physical life only comes when the personality has finished the work of that particular period. Understanding this, death can be met with trust and with love . . . and with unselfishness."[2]

In Alice Bailey's *Esoteric Healing,* Master Djwhal Khul states that "Death itself is a part of the Great Illusion and only exists because of the veils we have gathered around ourselves."[3] Death is essentially a matter of consciousness. We are conscious one moment on the physical plane, and a moment later we have withdrawn onto another plane and are actively conscious there. He further explains that death differs from sleep in that two streams of energy, one from the heart and one from the head are withdrawn and the body disintegrates. In sleep, only the stream of energy anchored in the brain is withdrawn and our awareness is focused in another dimension. As we become more aware of this process and the memory of experiences in other dimensions becomes intentional, we can program ourselves to remember more of those *other-world* experiences.

As a preface to this chapter about life in a new dimension I shall offer a brief rudimentary lesson in physics in an effort to explain the state of matter in the afterlife.

A law of physics states that matter is neither created nor destroyed; it simply changes form. Edward Randall in his book, *The Dead Have Never Died,* tells us that if we are to understand that "there is continuity of this life, and that spirit people have bodies, live in a material universe, and have homes similar to our own, it is necessary to explain the conditions which make such a state possible; we must know the law through which life holds continuity." He further explains that "there is a material universe beyond the physical; there is an etheric universe within and outside the physical; and the entire universe is composed of matter in different states of vibration or modes of motion. These truths must be understood before a single individual can comprehend the continuity of life—that the so-called dead have bodies, form, feature, and expression, and that they live on intelligently in a world as material as this, continuing their progression. Our dissolution will not end our individuality. Everything that possesses the property of *gravitation* or *attraction* is classed as matter. The mind, or its thought, is the force that creates everything on earth. A thing is conceived mentally before it is manifested.

Randall states that "if the universe is material, matter does not cease to be when it ceases to be tangible." He further points out that "matter slow in action is subject to the law of gravitation, and therefore physical; and matter so rapid in vibration as not to be subject to the law of gravitation is etheric. Matter is only changed in density when it ceases to be physical. Mind is matter raised to its highest degree of atomic activity when it holds within itself inherent power of intelligent direction. Certain forms of matter may be changed by chemical action and advanced to the spiritual state; then by the reduction of atomic motion the same matter may be restored again to its former condition, to hold once more physical expression."[4]

Randall also explains that "we must know the law through which life holds continuity" if we are to comprehend this transition from an earthly existence to a spirit existence. "Matter is either solid, liquid or gaseous. If solid, it is strongly cohesive. If liquid, less so. If gaseous, the atoms may be said to bump against each other and rebound. For example, ice would be at the lowest frequency or the densest form of water, and vapor the highest in frequency." Matter is tangible and visible to the physical eye as long as it is subject to the law of gravitation, or we can raise our vibration to another level to be aware of and perceive what is invisible. But if we are in the domain of spirit, as in meditation or thought, we are not subject to the laws of gravitation when the vibration is increased beyond that point. "The line of demarcation, therefore, between the spiritual and the physical is the point where the law of gravitation ceases to have influence."[5] In addition to the materialist worldview of physics, the more recent development of quantum physics has emerged based on the primacy of consciousness. "Consciousness is the ground of Being."[6]

The purpose of this discussion of rudimentary physics is an attempt to clarify the continuity of consciousness in the invisible regions of our universe. Just because our physical eyesight is unable to see beyond the vibratory frequency of material life it does not mean that life in the higher dimensions does not exist. For those who have developed a visual ability of higher frequency there is no question about its existence.

Paramahansa Yogananda reminds us that "different cultures and sects conceive of heaven according to their racial, social, and environmental habits of thought: a happy hunting ground; a glorious realm of endless pleasures; a kingdom with streets of gold and winged angels making celestial music on harps; a nirvana in which consciousness is extinguished in an everlasting peace."[7]

Jesus said, in John 14:2 in the New Testament of the Christian Bible, "In my Father's house are many mansions." Yogananda interprets this: "These many mansions include comprehensively the Infinitude of Spirit, the Christ Consciousness sphere, and the diverse higher and lower planes of the causal and astral realms. In general, however, the designation of heaven is relegated to the astral world, the immediate heaven relevant to beings on the physical plane."[8] These many mansions are the many subtle planes in the spiritual world, explains Barborka.[9] Death, and birth in the astral world are merely a change in consciousness. When the physical body dies, a being loses the consciousness of the physical and becomes aware of his subtle astral form in the astral world. This does not intend to imply, however, that all consciousness of the physical world is annihilated, but rather that one's attention will be primarily in the next dimension where our vehicles or bodies are compatible with the astral atmosphere.

We live in a solid, material, physical world and wear *solid* physical bodies. The physical or material world is where our consciousness resides. When we leave our bodies during sleep we are conscious on another level in another of our bodies—one of the more subtle bodies which we occupy.

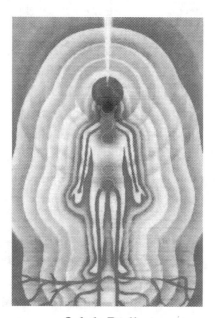

Subtle Bodies

There are three bodies or levels that I shall define and explain before we focus on characteristics of the astral world. At any given time we use the body which is supported by the vibratory frequency of the environment in which we find ourselves. On this physical earth our physical bodies are supported by a seemingly dense, material world. This three-dimensional world is perceived only through our five senses, for the most part. Everything existing in our natural world is energy in a more or less compact or congealed stage of vibration, exhibiting weight according to its mass or distinguishing gravitation. "The cohesive property of *maya's* creative vibration holds together every (particle) of matter present in the universe. Sand mixed with water and molded into a sand man looks enduringly solid; but when the water is evaporated out of it, that illusion falls apart. Likewise, the illusion of a seemingly solid human form is held together by the adhesive power of delusion working through the mind. The relationship between consciousness and the body is such that at death the body disintegrates because the mind and consciousness depart; but as long as consciousness remains in the body it works hard to hold together the atoms, cells, and organs—in spite of the effects of disease and aging."[10]

The subtle astral body or level of consciousness is the seat of the mental and emotional natures of a human being. It is a body of light and the second of three sheaths that encase the soul. Yogananda explains that "the powers of the astral body enliven the physical body, much as electricity illumines a bulb."[11] It is important to know something about the astral body because it is this body through which our consciousness will function in the astral dimension where we will reside after *death*, in the afterlife. Elements making up the astral vehicle are categorized as mental, emotional, and pranic. Prana can be defined as sparks of intelligent finer-than-atomic energy that constitute life.

The causal body resides in the realm of ideas where there are many categories of thought or idea elements. The causal body is an idea-matrix for the astral and physical bodies. When disease or other causes bring on the time of death, the heavy *overcoat* of the flesh is shed. The soul, however, remains encased in the astral and causal bodies.

Yogananda further teaches that the physical desires are rooted in egoism and sense pleasures. Astral desires are centered in enjoyment in terms of vibration. Astral beings, those who have passed into the astral dimension, hear the ethereal music of the spheres and are entranced by the sight of all creation as an expression of changing light. Astral persons also smell, taste, and touch light. Astral desires are thus connected with an astral being's power to precipitate all objects as forms of light and to undergo vivid experiences in thoughts or dreams. While still in the physical level of existence, a person uses and is more or less conscious of all three of these vehicles, the physical, the astral, and the causal bodies. When our senses are active, in tasting, smelling, touching, listening, and seeing, we are working principally through our physical bodies. When our powers of will and visualization are exercised we are working mainly through our astral bodies. Our causal medium finds expression when we are thinking or diving deep into introspection or meditation; the cosmic thoughts of genius come to the person who habitually contacts his causal body. This process of contact can be conscious or unconscious. In this sense, a person may be classified as chiefly *materially minded* (physical level) or *energetic* (astral level) or *intellectual* (causal level) depending on the level one is accessing at that time.

Now, where is this astral plane or dimension in which our loved ones reside and where we shall one day reside alongside them? There are many, many astral levels with innumerable astral beings. Astral inhabitants use their astral vehicles to travel from one planet to another—faster than electrical or radioactive energies. Just try and imagine that! The astral world is made up of subtle vibrations of light and color and is hundreds of times larger than the material cosmos. In fact, it is said that the entire physical creation "hangs like a little solid basket under the huge luminous balloon of the astral sphere."[12] It might be helpful to visualize a cone-shaped continuum with Earth at the nadir and each dimension expanding exponentially and becoming less dense or more rarified as the frequency increases. There are countless astral solar and stellar systems much like our material suns and stars that roam in space. Astral suns and moons are lovelier than our physical ones, and the astral day and night are much longer than on Earth. In fact, some authors have stated that there is no night in the astral world. I suppose that has something to do with the level contacted in the astral realm. The higher the levels and frequencies, the lighter and more refined and they become.

Those who have been privileged to view parts of the astral universe report that it is beautiful, clean, pure, and orderly. There are no blemishes. An even temperature like an eternal spring is maintained with an occasional luminous white snow and rain of multicolored light. There are many opal lakes, bright seas and rainbow rivers to be found throughout the astral dimension. This dimension is inhabited by millions of astral beings who have come more or less recently from the earth. This level is what some call Summerland. There are also myriads of fairies, mermaids, fish, animals, gnomes, and other spirits all residing on different astral planets according to their own karmic qualifications.

You might wonder if you will be sharing your region of the astral world with spirits of questionable character. Various spheric mansions or levels are provided for both good and evil spirits. The *law of attraction* is automatically at work when we reach this dimension, and astral beings of different grades are assigned to suitable vibratory quarters. We are attracted to spirit domains whose vibratory frequency is similar to our own. Good spirits are able to travel freely within compatible frequencies. Harmful ones are confined to limited zones and are not permitted to mix with those of higher vibrations. Killing, wars, or negativity of any kind will not be found in the afterlife regions. "There are no two places in the spirit world exactly alike. Each place—yea, even each sphere is the separate creation of the particular class of minds that have created it, and those whose minds are in affinity being drawn to each other in the spirit world, every place will bear more or less the peculiar stamp of its inhabitants. The souls which are now inhabiting the lower spheres are simply passing through the process of education needful to awaken into active life and growth the dormant moral faculties."[13]

Is there a place called Hell? Hell is the name that humans have given to a place or condition opposite to Heaven. In his book, *Wanderer in the Spirit Lands,* Farnese, a medium, takes us on a journey with the soul Franchezzo, whom he says lived and died in the 19th Century. His journey in the afterlife takes him through many levels or spheres of heaven where he describes the inhabitants of those spheres and the type of consciousness and frequency that determined each particular habitation. In the lower levels he speaks of the consequences of drug addiction, among other examples of broken laws of nature: "I passed a number of vast caverns called the Caverns of Slumber, wherein lay a great multitude of spirits in a state of complete stupor, unconscious of all around them. These, I learned, were the spirits of mortals who had killed themselves with opium eating and smoking, and whose spirits had thus been deprived of all chance of development, and so had retrograded instead of advancing and growing, and now they were feebler than an unborn infant, and as little able to possess conscious life. In many cases their sleep would last for centuries; in others, where the indulgence in the drug had been less, it might only last for twenty, fifty, or a hundred years." He goes on to explain that the growth of these addicts has been retarded for many years, many lifetimes, and may take "many generations of time to learn what one generation on earth could have taught them."[14] This is only one aspect of the *hell* that one can create for oneself.

Deepak Chopra states, "Hell is farthest from God because it represents the low ebb of consciousness. When we become disconnected from ourselves, a sense of deserving-to-suffer begins. Hell is the suffering you think you deserve. As consciousness evolves, *Satan* will become more unreal."[15] On a lesser scale, we humans are often guilty of self-punishment on our earth level of consciousness, and we tend to want to blame others or God for the things that happen to us. How many times have you heard someone say, "It was God's will that Uncle George was taken from us." Or, "I don't understand why God let little Lucy become so ill." This kind of thinking allows people to avoid responsibility for their own conditions. Along this same line of thinking, shouldn't we take more responsibility in our preparation for the future we will have in the afterlife and beyond that in another incarnation? Why would a loving God want to punish us? Perhaps our own soul is responsible for our education and for leading us to experiences that balance our behavior in a nonjudgmental and matter-of-fact way. Some Eastern religions call this karma.

Edward C. Randall[16] tells us there are seven spheres, each containing many planes of existence in the afterlife dimensions, and that we are able to move from lower to higher planes and spheres according to our growth in consciousness. These higher realms are purported to be reached through eventual mastery of the tasks required of us in the lower realms of experience. Randall was given names for each sphere to represent the focus of energy required while residing within that sphere of activity. They are as follows: the first sphere is one of restitution, where a spirit is able to release unwanted earth conditions; the second sphere is one of preparation, a period of study to gain knowledge of the self and natural law; the third sphere is one called instruction, where the spirit is able to teach those still living in the lower spheres; the fourth sphere is one of trial and temptation, testing the integration of one's acquired knowledge of the laws learned in earlier spheres; in the fifth sphere of truth, error and falsehood are unknown; in the sixth sphere all is harmony; and in the seventh sphere, the plane of exaltation, a spirit becomes united with the great spirit of the universe. It is said that the spirits of this sphere maintain their individuality, however. This one is far beyond our comprehension at this time. Randall reports that his spirit source tells him that the majority of normal people from the earth plane arrive on some level of the third sphere. According to my research there are several levels in each of the spheres and those in lower levels cannot travel to the higher levels but can communicate with them telepathically, as we can from our Earth plane. However, it is taught that those in higher levels can visit the lower levels when there is a reason to do so.

Will I have a body in the astral dimension? What is it made of, and what will it look like? Beauty in the astral world is known as a spiritual quality, and in most cases the astral form is an exact counterpart of the last physical body possessed by a person. Think for a moment about how we as inhabitants of the physical world become so obsessed with staying youthful in appearance. The physical dimension is the only dimension where the pull of gravity causes cellular disintegration and causes our physical bodies to age. When we leave our physical bodies behind and move into the astral dimension we have left behind the part of us that ages. So we emerge in the new dimension in our youthful images of the astral realm. We can choose an approximate age from our Earth life from which we would like to create our appearance for our new life. Occasionally, someone chooses to retain his old-age appearance. Perhaps one has achieved and identified with a level of respect at an advanced age, or in order to be recognized by certain individuals in the earth dimension or a higher dimension, one might manifest the appearance that would be familiar to the observer.

Through intuition, all astral beings see, hear, smell, taste and touch. It has been said that they have three eyes. Two are replicas of our physical eyes. The third and most important is the eye used for astral vision, the one that is related to the pineal gland and pituitary body and for the most part undeveloped during our physical sojourns. Those of you who practice meditation may readily relate to this information, because a by-product of regular meditation is the stimulation and opening of the third eye, the result of which is the psychic gift of clairvoyance. Dr. Douglas Baker reminds us, "We have powers latent within us. All of us manifest them when we are asleep. If we could retain consciousness while the physical body sleeps, our psychic powers could be recognized and used by us in waking consciousness. As a soul, man possesses all these powers. In the descent into our world of Illusion, we have lost memory of our souls. To restore that memory, as Self-Remembrance, constitutes the unfoldment of the third eye."[17] "You'll remember the third eye, which facilitates what is called Etheric Vision, as the enigmatical organ of mythological history. It is the eye of Horus of Egyptian mysticism; it is the poised snake of the Caduceus; it is the horn of the Unicorn; it is the biblical eye of *if thine eye be single thy whole body shall be full of light.*"[18]

The third eye area is called the brow chakra or the *ajna* center by those familiar with the chakras or energy vortices along the astral spine in Eastern teachings. The third eye is not an endocrine gland even though it is associated with both the pineal gland and the pituitary body. It is an organ that emerges with the spiritual growth of the integrated personality. Each chakra or center is a battery, Dr. Baker tells us, and all must be charged. The 'bulb' of the third eye may be *switched on*, and the inner vision is activated through meditation and concentration.

In my extraordinary experiences in the astral realms of the afterlife I have found spirit bodies to be as solid on that level as they are on the physical level. They were solid to me because I was present there in my own astral body during out-of-body experiences (OBEs) or lucid dream experiences. So what I deduced from those occasions was that if my body was composed of material of the same vibratory frequency as those of the spirits I was there to visit, then I could feel another's body of a similar vibratory frequency. In my first meeting with Ann Manser, in the afterlife dimension, she demonstrated this fact to me by pressing her shoulder against mine, allowing me to feel the solidity of her shoulder. There have been many times, in my OBEs or lucid dream visits with Mother and with Pat and with other loved ones, that I have felt and been aware of the solidity of their forms during a loving embrace or a touch of the hand. In one visit with my mother, I thought, *this is real—I can really feel her.* I later remarked to her "No one will believe this happened." I knew without a doubt that we were there together and that she had a definite message for me which I shall share in a later chapter about Kathryn.

During these visits with loved ones, I've been very aware of the appearance of their skin, their hair and their eyes. The skin looked unusually clear and healthy to me. It was flawlessly smooth and vibrant in color—translucent in a sense. I was particularly focused on my mother's complexion when I observed her in an afterlife restaurant setting during an OBE. She wasn't aware of my presence at first, and while I was waiting for her to notice me I was focused on how beautiful she looked—how perfect she seemed in appearance. She was dressed in a lovely light bluish-green silk street-length, short-sleeved and collarless dress with a blue and light green or aqua pattern of small flowers and was wearing a single string of pearls with single pearl earrings to match. But it was the unblemished and refined appearance of her skin and hair that captured my admiring attention.

In one of my visits with Pat she appeared on my right in an exquisite formal floor-length gown made of what seemed to me a winter white lightweight wool fabric with a mandarin collar that was trimmed in pale rose-colored piping. The dress was fitted at the waist and the skirt was flared from below her hip line. She looked absolutely gorgeous! Her smile was lovely and somewhat mysterious. She looked younger, her complexion was perfectly flawless like Mother's, and her hair was longer than I had ever remembered seeing it—perhaps shoulder-length and in a different style.

In Fred Rafferty's *Spirit World and Spirit Life*, in response to questions about how the spirit world dresses, his contacts tell him about their fashions:

"She wears delicate colors, as nearly all do: sometimes rose color, pink, or lavender, but in shades more delicate than any you know. We are never afraid of injuring our robes, for they are not subject to wear or soil."[19]

"We are clothed in garments that correspond to our mental and spiritual condition. You will appear in a simple white garment at first, and this will change as you change. Mental qualities express themselves outwardly, and different minds express different colors. Minds that are filled with doubt are sometimes clothed in incongruous colors. The destructive forces have coarse garments of the most discordant colors. They imagine themselves in gorgeous apparel. But they will sometime see themselves as they are, which will be when they reach out for something better."[20]

The clothes are made by thought processes, according to Rafferty. The spirit beings are clothed when they arrive in their new dimension, and a dominant color might be chosen by their own thought for use there, but this is changeable. Dress there "is more than external adornment, it becomes a sort of symbol of character." Our loved ones in spirit can appear to us in clothes which we are accustomed to seeing on them, but the clothes that are worn among those in their spirit realms are something like codes or symbols of their inner characteristics.

In speaking of spirit senses, Rafferty's spirit friend communicated, "We have been schooled by earthly teachers into the belief that once we have passed the gateway of death, the fair land of promise—the paradise, the heavenly home, would lie before us in all its perfection, and in one moment of rapture we would see and understand, and immediately all knowledge as well as vision would be ours. Instead of this instantaneous fairyland of delight, we have been told of the more normal one of growth, of steadily increasing knowledge, the continued unfolding of new fields of vision; and always beyond, the unending vistas of greater knowledge, greater marvels and greater joy."[21]

Apparently the spiritual vision is dim at first, and mistakes are made. Spiritual powers are not attained all at once, and spiritual vision may take a while to become dependable. This can cause an unnatural appearance of the surroundings. The hearing can also be blurred and indistinct. But it is suggested that everything still appears much clearer in the spiritual dimension than it does on the material plane.

When spiritual vision clears through learning how to use abilities of the spirit world instead of the optic nerves of our world, the vision is clearer than we can imagine. At some point inhabitants of that world must learn to discern material things and material events in the Earth dimension, as well. It is not a natural ability for them to see us easily or observe our activities. It can be done, but it is much easier for those who are "linked by a strong bond of attraction of love or sympathy."[22] We must provide the channel for the exchange of energy for it to work without a great deal of effort on their part. Spirit beings reportedly see our spirit selves, which are far finer than our earthly ones. The spiritual body as seen in our earth dimension is much like it will be when we leave this dimension, except that on Earth our powers are obscured by our five senses. Those five senses make havoc with spiritual logic and instruction. "Five senses! You have a hundred here, and all more perfect than any of the five. Then we have perceptions not dependent upon sight, hearing, touch, or taste. These belong to spirit intuitions."[23]

Authors seem to agree that at first there is little difficulty involved in spirit observation and communication with those of us still on Earth because our spirit friends are in dimensions whose vibrations are closest to the Earth vibration when they first depart this life. It is only after they have been in their new dimension for a while and have moved beyond their primary levels that they speak of having more difficulty making their presence known to us. My mother's frequent phenomenal demonstrations seemed to stop a few years after her transition. I still have the mental contact with her, but she does not often or perhaps is not always able to make her presence known to me through the dramatic means she used at first, such as moving objects around or playing the music box.

When asked about language, Rafferty and other sources have agreed that language is used in instances such as oratory, poetry, and lessons in their dimension, but that in ordinary conversation mental telepathy is more efficient and preferred. Mental telepathy, there, is a conservation of words when whole concepts are conveyed, and visual imagery seems to them to be more accurate than a string of words. When I have received information through meditation it has more often been presented in visions, in pictures or symbols representing a whole thought. This does not mean that it cannot be transmitted in words, however.

Spiritual hearing is developed through awareness and practice, just as spiritual sight is developed. It has been stated that we cannot imagine the beauty and perfection of sound in those higher dimensions. Our earthly ears cannot register the vibratory frequencies beyond the boundaries of our own five senses. Occasionally we mortals can have a glimpse of the higher worlds and a rare experience of the music of the spheres. I had one such occurrence when I attended a healing service at the Rosicrucian Fellowship International Headquarters in Oceanside, California. The atmosphere was heavenly and accentuated by the celestial music, like a choir of angels that seemed to be piped into the room. It sounded otherworldly, and my companion assured me that it was, indeed, because she did not hear it. I believe that in such a spiritual atmosphere I was able to raise my own vibratory frequency to a level that enabled me to attune to higher realms during a part of the healing service.

Sylvia Browne's spirit guide, Francine, tells us to "picture the most beautiful thing you've ever seen and then multiply it by 100—then you might be close to imagining the beauty and composition of the Other Side. Several human-made structures, if captivating, are duplicated on the Other Side. We have buildings representing every type of architecture, although most of these reflect the classic Greek and Roman periods. We have huge forums where we listen to lectures and view the arts, tremendous libraries and research centers where we gather knowledge, as well as individual homes and smaller buildings for either residing or general use. We have fountains and plazas, courtyards and parks as well as gardens and meditation areas. Even the descriptions of Utopia wouldn't be enough to portray the splendor and efficiency of my side. It is indeed a paradise!"[24]

In addition, there are reportedly opportunities to develop your talents in the arts, in teaching, in sports, in almost any area of expertise you wish to acquire. I asked Mother while she was still in the physical dimension if there was anything she wished she had done in her life. She replied, "I wish I'd learned to play the violin." I told her it was never too late to begin. I can imagine that Kathryn, a lover of music, is now learning to play the violin.

Francine says that our bodies do not require any sustenance, such as eating, drinking, or sleeping. But there are times when one wishes to relax, or to eat or drink at social events as one's traditions dictate.

According to several sources, soon after a new spirit's arrival, there will be orientation activities. I've been privileged to attend these on occasion. It was very clear to me that the purpose of these orientations was to familiarize the new spirits with certain laws of the dimension and to provide opportunities for them to become acquainted with others who have recently crossed over. The first time I recall being involved was when Pat's orientation was taking place, about three months after her transition, in a large hall where we were seated across from each other at a long table. Dinner was being served and people were passing dishes to us from right to left. I remarked to Pat that not everyone present could see each other. She said she had noticed that, too, and pointed out a few people whom she thought could see us. It made me wonder later that if there was such a mixture of new arrivals, there might be those who had not yet gained use of their spiritual sight. After dinner the table was cleared away, leaving a spacious *dance floor* in the hall. A small musical ensemble began to play familiar tunes, and soon we had a folk dance being organized, complete with a caller. We were told to choose partners. Pat and I only knew each other, so we were partners. During my teen years I belonged to groups that held folk dances and square dances, so this was not a new idea for me. I couldn't help but wonder if Pat had ever done much folk dancing, however. We giggled and had fun with our attempts to follow the directions, stepping all over each other. There was a short break, and I was asking her questions about her new home when suddenly I was withdrawn from the scene and felt as if I was being suctioned back through a tube or tunnel to my sleeping body in my own bed. I could still see Pat bathed in a brilliant light at the other end of the tube, and I was still asking her my last question, "Is it beautiful where you live?" As this scene faded away, I was waking up, and I immediately turned on my light and reached for my journal where I recorded everything I could remember. The experience was so vivid that I felt as if we had just spent that time together on the earth level.

About a month after my mother's transition, she was able to share with me some of her orientation activities. This particular occasion was an outdoor picnic. I recall a lot of trees and greenery, and most of those attending were attired in swimwear or were in some way very casually dressed. We mixed and mingled, eating from plates of picnic food we carried around with us. I recognized only one other guest, Jan, a friend who had made her transition over a decade before this time. We had a nice visit, and I learned that she had been an organizer of this outing. Mother seemed very much at ease and enjoyed meeting potential new friends. When it was time for me to leave, I crossed back over to my side of life by way of a hot air balloon connected to a cable.

Having to work for a living is only an earthly condition, so many of the occupations found on Earth are not needed in the afterlife. In the afterlife dimension, one works to help others, whether it is in direct service to others in their dimension or ours, or in some other occupation that will aid Earth inhabitants in making new scientific discoveries. It is said that the scientific knowledge is so far advanced in those realms that information transmitted to Earth can be only as sophisticated as the mentality on Earth is capable of conceiving and comprehending. In addition to science, medical or other areas, there are studies in almost every field of knowledge you can imagine, including business, the arts, education, agriculture, athletics and the animal kingdom, to name only a few. When I asked Pat about her work, she told me she was involved in working with those on Earth who were open to transmissions from her dimension to receive knowledge about specific areas of study. She was very involved in some research on animal communication, at the time, and wanted to get the information through to those who could receive it. Her work will change, she said, and she will learn more about blending energies and using color in specific ways for healing. Sometime later she will learn how to work with the energy for healing animals. She will also be involved in teaching, continuing her work from her life on Earth in the ancient wisdom teachings, but on a higher level. Pat said that she is able to see the earth plane very clearly, however at times it takes a special energy or an apparatus called a reflection screen, like a flat television screen, which she uses to tune in to our dimension.

Through Bob Murray, a very fine psychic and author, Mother (Kathryn) told me about some of her work and her daily schedule a few years after her transition. At that time, she was working with children and animals and the communication between them. She was teaching children respect for other kingdoms through their care of the animals and through their work with flower gardens. When I was a young child of three or four, she planted a very small flower garden for me to care for. I remember the feeling of responsibility it gave me, and it has certainly provided a lifelong appreciation for the beauty of flowers.

Mother has a full schedule doing things she likes to do. She is doing some research into genetics, teaching, working with infants who have crossed over to her dimension, and enjoying her flower gardens. I shall share more about her life and Pat's in the chapters written specifically about them.

Life is continuous; there is no death, but a shift in consciousness to a level that is already a part of our make-up, but one that we have not been conscious of using. If we use our color spectrum as an example of a continuum of vibratory frequency, there are colors below and above our visible spectrum that we are unable to see with our physical eyes. As we develop our inner vision, our ability to see dimensions beyond the earth dimension is possible. Moving into a new dimension of the afterlife does not appear to offer a completely different experience for those of us moving from the earth plane. However, there are adjustments that we must make that will involve the laws of those regions—laws which enable us to navigate easily—and to speak, see and hear more efficiently and more easily. Our earthly law of gravity is not in force there, so we will no longer have the resistance to it that depletes our bodies of energy and stamina.

The descriptions in this chapter of possible lifestyles and activities are found on the astral level, usually the first stop on transition from earth life. This level is the closest in vibratory frequency to our world and one that does not seem drastically different, at least where human patterns and activities are concerned. Spirit beings manifested there remain there for varying lengths of time, however they can choose to move upward to other levels when they are willing to progress through various studies and service to others. A move in any direction depends on one's soul growth and personal level of consciousness.

PART II

Personal Journey

CHAPTER 6

Beginning My Journey

To exist is to change, to change is to mature,
To mature is to go on creating oneself endlessly.

~ Henri-Louis Bergson

THE FACULTY WIVES' BOOK CLUB meeting ended, and I was eager to go to Haslam's Bookseller to see if I could find our reading choice for next month's meeting. Although I had been involved with the Florida Presbyterian College (FPC, now Eckerd College) campus functions for a couple of years longer than other faculty wives there, I was the youngest in the group. Husbands of other members had been on the faculty of other colleges and universities and had answered the call to fill teaching positions at an innovative new college in St. Petersburg, Florida. These more seasoned faculty wives took me under their wings. Tom and I had been affiliated with the college a year before other faculty families began to arrive. He was on the original staff as Director of Admissions and recruited the first few classes for the college. I was all eyes and ears as I learned the ropes of being a good and supportive faculty wife.

Haslam's did have the book. It was a new book by Nikos Kazantzakis, *The Last Temptation of Christ*. Masterfully written, I struggled to comprehend it, but in my youth I did not fully grasp the universality of the author's message. I found my own religious foundations being shaken as the author portrayed the Master Jesus as earthy and human like other men of Earth. It was too much. My young psyche could bear no more. I became so obsessed with a new way to view the story of Jesus that I no longer knew what to believe. It had always been so simple—so easy to believe the biblical interpretations of my church's elders. A new variable had been introduced through the story Kazantzakis was telling, and my whole belief system was challenged—was crumbling inside me. Now, I no longer felt secure. I didn't know what to believe. I found myself turning away from anything that reminded me of the church. I wouldn't listen to church music on the radio—no Bible reading, no church attendance. I continued to take our children to church, but I didn't participate. Where was the truth? It was a difficult year. All that I had believed and relied upon and identified with—even my faith was stripped away. I felt naked, defenseless. Who spoke the truth? I began to see the limitations of the Church Fathers. After all, they were human, too. I fell into a deep depression. This went on for at least a year.

Enough! I no longer wanted to go through this alone, and for the first time at the end of that year I fell to my knees and begged for help. "Show me the way," I cried. Help came immediately. Within two hours of my cry for help I received a phone call from a friend inviting me to attend a healing service at a local metaphysical church that evening. I was open, ready to explore new pathways—pathways free of the dogma and judgment I had experienced in the houses of worship I had loved and been a part of for so many years.

It is a universal pattern that old structures have to be destroyed to make room for new ones. In keeping with that pattern I went through a period of time when old religious constructs were being eliminated, and in my case pretty quickly. Not everyone has to give up outgrown beliefs in such a dramatic way. Some are able to replace them one-at-a-time with a gradual allowance for new viewpoints. In my case, I suppose I was immersed enough in denominational dogma that it took this drama to blast off the first layer and create an opening for new thought on spiritual ideologies.

My friend and I attended the healing service. The small congregation filed down to the front of the sanctuary dividing into shorter lines in front of four men and women who served as healing channels. As the senior minister placed his hands on my shoulders, he said, "You have been asking *show me the way.* Be assured that you are being shown the way and you are opening to your new life in very significant ways."

How did he know my very words? I've never even seen this man before. I began having dreams that indeed indicated to me that I had chosen the right path for myself at that time. Elders dressed in white robes standing in brilliant light began to appear in my dreams giving me guidance and encouragement.

My life was changing rapidly. I felt like a magnet pulling toward me experiences I needed for learning about higher aspects of myself. Books seemed to jump right off the book store shelves. There was so much to learn. I was in Haslam's again when I discovered a section of intriguing metaphysical books. The book that jumped off the shelf for me on this day was *The Rosicrucian Cosmo-Conception* by Max Heindel. I bought it and took it home with a plan to read and study it every day.

Each morning I sang as I cooked breakfast for my young family and made school lunches. Highly motivated, the household chores were done in record time. Now it was time to read the book. Every morning, for three weeks, I feverishly read and pondered the words of Max Heindel. Some days I spread a sheet or blanket in the backyard under the pine trees and, while listening to the sounds of nature, I read his beautiful words about God's creation, the heavens, the angels and many other concepts I could not even begin to comprehend at that time. I was filling up to overflowing with knowledge about the Cosmos until I couldn't read another word. I put the book under my bed and decided it was time to integrate some of what I had read. Later, I would pick it up again and read some more. In the Introduction to this book you are now reading, I told of the angelic presence who enfolded me in her arms and said, "Someday you will know the answers to your questions." When I looked through the table of contents in Heindel's book, I felt it surely had answers to many of my questions. I felt that this was the beginning of that *someday*.

Three weeks went by, and I fished the book out from under my bed and began reading again. In the book, I discovered some information on a course of study called Rosicrucian Philosophy from the Rosicrucian Fellowship in Oceanside, California. I subscribed to the course, studied the lessons, answered the questions and mailed them back to an assigned teacher at the Fellowship. I was so hungry for this information and its application. I learned more about concentration, prayer and meditation. As I began to use that knowledge, I opened to new insights into many areas of my life.

In the summer of 1969, Tom and I bought a Starcraft tent-top camper, hitched it to our station wagon, packed enough clothes for a family of five for several months and headed for California. He was taking his sabbatical from the college that year and chose to do some work along the coast of California: in Big Sur at Esalen Institute; in Haight-Ashbury with Abraham Maslow; and in other locations important to him for his research into the counter-culture of the 1960s. Since he would be traveling along the coast for much of his work, he asked me to choose a place for us to live and for the children to attend school. It didn't take long for me to decide on Carmel-by-the-Sea on the Monterey Peninsula. I contacted the Chamber of Commerce to find schools and in the process I learned more about Carmel as a well-known art colony. By the time school started for the children, we were in a lovely rented home nestled in the woods overlooking Carmel Bay, only blocks from Carmel Woods School. The houses weren't numbered but were named like those in English villages. Ours was "Cheerio Tipp." Since mail came to residents at a central downtown post office, there were no mail boxes. Most front yards had wooden fences and gates with bells to alert residents to approaching visitors, and lovely flower gardens to greet them.

The children were happy in school, and I enrolled in Carmel Art Institute to study oil painting with John Cunningham. At that time there were sixty-six art galleries in downtown Carmel and a Community Art Center. I was in John's art class five hours a day on week days and I then wandered from gallery to gallery after class until the children were home from school. This was a bit of heaven. I found a guitar teacher in Carmel Valley and took classical guitar lessons as well. Tom and I took advantage of the famous massages, hot tubs and workshops at Esalen Institute, and a weekend at the Tassajara Zen Retreat in Carmel Valley. In later years, I revisited these favorite retreats a few times. We all went to Disneyland in Anaheim and made periodic treks to San Francisco. It was a joyous time in our lives.

The children easily made friends and enjoyed entertaining them, in return being invited to parties and sleepovers at their homes. Pizza parties with board games and action games were favorite activities for them. Our boys, ages eight and ten, wanted to earn a little pocket money and found "gainful employment" selling the weekly edition of the *Carmel Pine Cone* newspaper on street corners for fifteen cents an issue, keeping most of the profit. Carmel was like a small English village, and we loved living there in such a safe and storybook-like setting.

Our rented house had a long railed wooden porch with a front door and a Dutch door into the kitchen-dining room area. It was a luxury to be able to keep the top part of the Dutch door open to the outside world—no bugs! And no need for air-conditioning. The children had the lower level of the house with a bedroom shared by the boys and a room for Julie. The living area and our bedroom were located on the street level, and there was a family room on a split level above the living room. From this room we had a breathtaking view of Carmel Bay near the entrance to 17-Mile Drive toward the famous Pebble Beach Golf Course.

With Tom away for days at a time, and after the children were in bed, I had many evenings alone to read and communicate with family and friends on the eastern side of the country by phone, letter and cassette tapes. The taping was fun. My friend, Ginny, and I sent weekly messages back and forth between St. Petersburg and Carmel, which kept me from being homesick.

One evening, as I sat in the living room quietly reading, I heard a *knock-knock* in another part of the house. I froze—and it happened again—every few minutes! The timing seemed too rhythmic to be a random sound from outside. I slowly crept down the hallway in the direction of the knocking and stood there for a couple of minutes. Nothing happened. As soon as I went back to the sofa and sat down, it started again. I listened carefully and pinpointed it as coming from the hall closet door this time. I walked toward the door and the knocking stopped. Each time I sat down it started again. This became a routine occurrence during my so-called quiet evenings alone. One morning, Mark asked me why I had continually walked up and down the stairs the night before. "You never did come in our room, but I heard you going up and down, up and down the stairs." I knew I hadn't gone downstairs, so to avoid frightening the children I must have evaded Mark's question in some way.

It was not until our last day in Cheerio Tipp, when we were packing for the long drive back from California to Florida, that we were all convinced we had not been alone there. Added to the personal belongings we had brought with us we had accumulated quite a bit more in seven months. Our Christmas had been celebrated there, and I had many canvases from art school. I gave each of the children a large grocery bag and instructed them to put in the bag only things, like toys, they definitely wanted to keep. About ten minutes into that task six-year-old Julie bounded up the stairs, pale and excited: "Mom, I had my bag next to the closet with my toys in it and I went to the bathroom, and when I came back the bag of toys was all the way across the room!" My first thought was that one of the boys had moved it. I went downstairs to investigate. Both boys were sitting in their room, on the floor, busily sorting through their own toys. When asked if they had been in Julie's room they looked puzzled, which convinced me they were not guilty. Then Julie added, "Mom, I saw it moving itself!" Julie understandably refused to go back to her room and finish the job, so I took over from there. We never got to meet our ghost *face-to-face* but it was certainly not shy about benignly revealing its presence to us.

In October, Tom and I had attended a weekend seminar together at Esalen Institute and had left the children with friends. When we returned home, the children had decorated the porch with streamers, balloons, Halloween cut-outs and a big *welcome home* sign. Prominently displayed on the front door was a picture of our family drawn by eight-year-old Mark. He had each person named, so there was no mistaking the identity of the side-view pregnant figure—it was me! I complimented Mark on his family portrait, meticulously drawn and colored, and asked, "Mark, do I really look that big?" In actuality, I was quite petite. His response was "No, you're not big now, but you will be before our baby is born!" I didn't think I was pregnant, so I told him there wouldn't be a baby anytime soon.

A few weeks later, Tom and I were gone overnight again. On our return this time we were presented with another picture drawn by Mark. In this one, I was holding a baby in my arms. Mark was convinced there was a baby on the way, and I was now really beginning to wonder. By Christmas I realized that I was in fact pregnant, but we decided not to tell the children about it until we were on our way home a couple of months later. On about the third day of our trip, driving through a long strip of desert, I suggested that we play "Twenty Questions." Before I could finish going over the rules of the game, Mark piped up with, "I know the answer—we're going to have a baby!" He got it! He hadn't let it go. We then had a lot of fun planning for our new little family member. How did Mark know before his parents knew? I still don't know the answer to that question. Perhaps it came to him in a dream. He couldn't explain it either, he just knew.

At the end of seven months, the first week in February, we left our new friends and acquaintances behind—and yes, our hearts, too. We said goodbye to Cheerio Tipp and started the long drive across the country back to St. Petersburg with a full camper. There was extra weight now, with many canvases from art school and other meaningful souvenirs from our West Coast sojourn.

My correspondence course with the Rosicrucian Fellowship had continued, and I was eager to visit the International Headquarters at Mt. Ecclesia in Oceanside, California while we were in that part of the country. We pulled into a campground in Ventura, California to spend the night. The next morning I was up early to fix breakfast for the family, then off to Oceanside and Mt. Ecclesia. I left Tom and the children at the seaside campground and told them I would be back sometime around noon or early afternoon.

A sign on the arch above the road which read "The Rosicrucian Fellowship" assured me I had arrived at my destination. Not far into the grounds I saw another familiar symbol—the five-pointed star emblem with the rosy cross superimposed on it. I found a place to park and walked to the nearest building to ask about the schedule of events or services offered that day. Already, I felt as if I had landed in a different dimension. It was so quiet, so peaceful. The birds' songs were the only audible sounds except for a gentle breeze in the trees. I opened a screen door that led me into a large room which was apparently a dining area. There, I found a few people eating breakfast. A woman sitting alone at the table nearest the door saw me come in and graciously stood up and welcomed me.

"Good morning . . . and welcome. You look a little lost. Is this your first time to visit us?"

"Thank you, and yes, I drove in for a short visit this morning, and this was the first building I found open."

We introduced ourselves and then Margaret continued, "We're having breakfast now. Let me get you something to eat."

She insisted on getting a tray with poached eggs, toast, and a glass of orange juice for me and invited me to sit with her. Since I had grabbed only a banana for a breakfast-on-the-run, I accepted her kind offer.

"We're all vegetarians here. I hope you don't mind the absence of meat with your eggs." I assured her that I didn't.

"Would you like to follow our morning schedule with us or would you prefer to wander around the grounds?"

I replied, "I'd much prefer to participate in your program and get a feeling for what it might be like on a daily basis." Margaret became my wonderful guide for a tour of the retreat and morning services.

"Our first stop, then, will be at the chapel for a vesper service," she explained. No one spoke after entering the room. It was completely quiet—a feeling of great reverence. There were more people present than I had expected on a Saturday morning. Some were in prayer and meditation before the brief service. We were led in singing a couple of songs from the song books, and we listened to a short scripture lesson. When we were back outside on the path again we could whisper to each other. I was reminded of my weekend at the Tassajara Zen Retreat where no one spoke above a whisper within the grounds of the center itself. Both places had a strong atmosphere for healing—with such beauty and the uplifting sounds of nature.

"Where do we go next?" I inquired.

Margaret pointed to a building on our left. "This is the Healing Chapel," she said. "It's my favorite of all! You'll see!"

Inside the building, all conversation stopped again. There were seats where about twenty-five people sat in prayer and meditation. I followed suit. Finally a woman arose, performed a short candle-lighting ritual, then offered a healing prayer and read names from letters of prayer requests. I recalled that I had sent names to them for prayers in the past, and now I knew their procedure for working with the prayer requests. The interior of this building was breathtaking. The ceiling was dome-shaped and painted a sky blue with all the signs of the zodiac represented by symbols in a circle around the base of the dome. Throughout the service I could hear the most exquisite soft and uplifting music playing. It sounded like a choir of angels humming in melodious unison. The phrase, "on wings of song" took on a whole new meaning as I listened and meditated to the celestial melodies I was hearing.

When Margaret and I were on the outside pathway again, I whispered to her that I thought the healing chapel was the most sacred place I had ever been and that I especially enjoyed the music. I asked her if the music had been piped in somehow or if there was some kind of equipment hidden in the chapel sanctuary. She looked at me in complete puzzlement and said, "Why, there was no music in the chapel. No, we have no way to pipe in music." We were both silent for a few moments. Then she looked at me again and confirmed what I was thinking when she added, "I believe you heard music of the angels. I didn't hear anything at all." And this was only the beginning of a day of extraordinary experiences.

We finally came upon the book store, and I wanted to browse a bit there. I was surprised that the store was open on Saturday. I bade my lovely guide a grateful goodbye and a good life, and so we parted. I found a few books I couldn't live without, made my purchase and started toward the car. I wished that I could stay longer. I wasn't ready to leave this spiritual place inhabited by angels—some of them mighty Beings. I wanted to sit and meditate a while longer and just soak up the positive vibrations all around me. I knew I needed to go back to the campground, though. The family would be packed and ready to go as soon as I got there. I got into the car and tried to start it. It wouldn't start. It was a new station wagon, but it wouldn't start. I tried several times, unsuccessfully. What could I do now? This was a time before cell phones. I had no way to get in touch with Tom. I decided to get out and sit on a nearby retaining wall under a big tree and meditate. That's what I'd wanted to do all along. Well, now I was being given the opportunity. After about fifteen minutes, I tried again. The car started, and reluctantly I left. This had definitely been one of those indelible experiences that would live on and on. As I had suspected, when I returned to the campground Tom and the kids were ready and waiting to get on the road again.

While Tom drove, I was busy looking over my new Max Heindel books, reading parts of them while the children read or played games in the back seat. Occasionally I would find a particularly profound passage and read it aloud to Tom. I soon realized that I wasn't seeing things the way I usually saw them. I was seeing them with a *mountain-top* viewpoint. It seemed that I was on top of the mountain looking down and seeing the whole picture—a new picture of creation and my part in it all! It was exciting! I could suddenly comprehend things in a way that I never had before. A whole new perception was being born. I couldn't get enough! We drove until suppertime then found a campground and set up our camper for the night. *They* set up the camper. We each had our assigned chores when it was time to crank up the pop-top camper. But this time I wasn't able to do my part. I was not even able to feel the earth beneath my feet, literally. What in the world was happening? I *floated* around almost in a daze. I tried to explain it to Tom, and he tried to understand. He volunteered to fix supper, because I couldn't focus enough to do much of anything on a mundane level. I was giddy and unsteady, and when it was time to go to bed I was ready. I wasn't functioning well at all. It wasn't scary, just inconvenient. The next morning I was more grounded, and we put in a full day of driving. I felt almost normal again with the exception of my new perception, and I liked that.

The next couple of years were full and happy. The children had to readjust to their Florida school, and our little Wendi was born in July after we returned home. I continued my art classes in Cortez, Florida with a well-known artist and teacher, Marilyn Bendell. For two years in succession I won Statewide Juried Exhibitions for my oil paintings and received commissions for my work. I began to attend services at the Temple of the Living God and joined this interfaith metaphysical church and educational center in St. Petersburg. Reverend LeRoy Zemke was the minister and dean of the educational program. I was a student, faculty member and board member at the *Temple* over the next several years, the most formative and one of the most fulfilling times in my spiritual development.

Early in that decade I had an unusual experience which shed some light on the suicidal ideation I had experienced a few years before. One afternoon as I lay across my bed for a short rest, instead of going to sleep I had a feeling that I was sinking into the bed. I was unable to move my body but was fully conscious and aware of everything in the room, as well as sounds outside the room. It was later suggested that I was probably having a trance experience.

Everything went white. In front of my eyes and inside my head there was a white *screen*. I could see images, and at the same time my consciousness was projected into the image of a young man—a man not quite thirty years old. I was that man as he climbed out of the second or third story window of a building and cautiously took a few steps along a ledge to a piece that jutted out perpendicular to the building. I, as the young man, was aware that a very important love affair had just ended for me, and I was so distraught that I didn't want to live. At once, I became aware of the crowd that had gathered in the street below and slightly to my left—the expressions on the people's faces, and the yelling. Some yelled, "Don't do it!" Others yelled, "Oh, go on and get it over with!" Still others stood there with looks of shock and dismay. Somehow, I was able to come to my senses and halt the act. I was already a few steps out on the projection from the building when I decided not to end my life. I began to very carefully back up. There was no room to turn around and go forward. My right foot slipped, and I fell to my death. As I was falling, the conscious this-life-observer part of me said, "Please don't put me through this again." Instantly, I was transported to an earlier happy scene in which I was the same young man on a baseball diamond wearing an old-fashioned uniform and playing baseball. The colors appeared faded in both of these scenes, indicating to me that they took place in some remote past.

In my current lifetime, I experienced a deep depression in my thirtieth year. There was more than one contributing factor of course, but on the darkest day of that depression I was trembling in fear and feeling an overwhelming compulsion to take drastic action. I believe that the above vision showed me in an earlier life as a young man of thirty who intended to take his own life, and when he changed his mind he accidentally fell to his death. It makes me wonder if what I was feeling in this life was an experience of a *bleeding through* of that former life and the dramatic way it ended. It is easy for me to believe that I was shown this vision to explain in part the suicidal tendencies I had at that same age in this life. Another possible support for having lived that life, which seemed to be sometime near the end of the nineteenth century or perhaps the early twentieth century, was the baseball scene. As a child, in this life, I loved to play softball. I played intramural softball at school but also regularly rounded up my neighborhood playmates for games, beginning in about the third grade and extending through junior high school. Sometimes the neighborhood boys even let me play baseball with them. On one occasion, I had to hit a home-run to earn membership in the boys' tree house club. I was excited to be the only female member of the boys' club until I attended their first meeting. Even though I liked the boys as friends, I found the meeting boring and never went to another one.

When I was thirteen, my mother, my sister and I were walking up the hill on our way home from church one Easter Sunday when I saw my seventh-grade sweetheart, Jack, coming toward us carrying a box of candy under his arm. He asked if I could walk with him, and with Mother's permission we fell behind them a little and walked together. As we approached the end of the street at the top of the hill, we saw some of the neighborhood kids playing softball in a backyard. They spotted us and yelled, "The bases are loaded and we need you to hit us home!"

Jack and I looked at each other. I was dressed in my Easter dress with a hat and white gloves, and for the first time, grown-up stockings and shoes with a little taller heel than usual. Stockings in those days came in two pieces and were held up by elastic garters—though not easily on my skinny legs! Jack and I both liked to play ball, and this challenge was too good to turn down. After all, they had said they needed someone to hit them all home. What a vote of confidence! We gave in, and Jack insisted that I go to bat first. I removed my gloves and hat and took the bat. The first pitch was too low, but the second one was just right and I hit a home run! I ran the bases as fast as I could run with my new shoes and stockings. "Oops!" I felt the stockings crawling down my legs. By the time I reached third base they were all the way over my shoes and flying like windsocks behind me. This was no time to worry about stockings. I made it to the home plate, very embarrassed but at the same time feeling happy that I had scored well for the team. I simply reached down, pulled off my shoes and stockings, and then put the shoes back on. I stuffed the stockings into my small purse and cheered Jack on as he made the next home run.

Yes, I was a dedicated ball player, and now I believe it didn't begin in this lifetime. One by one my childhood questions were being answered, and I was now on a roller coaster for the many enlightening experiences ahead for me!

**The Healing Chapel at the Rosicrucian Fellowship Headquarters
Mt. Ecclesia in Oceanside, CA**

CHAPTER 7

When the Student Is Ready

*In the silence of the heart, there is a meeting between
the master and the disciple. Both know something has moved,
some energy has been transferred, transmitted. The flame that
was asleep in the disciple is asleep no more; it has jumped
to aliveness and consciousness. This is the transmission of
the lamp. A strange situation is needed: the master has to
have it and the disciple has to be ready to receive it.*

~ Osho-Zen: The Solitary Bird, Cuckoo of the Forest

*You would not have called to me unless
I had been calling to you.*

~ Aslan to Jill in C. S. Lewis,
The Silver Chair

DREAMS HAVE BEEN A SIGNIFICANT vehicle for messages from the unknown and from aspects of my own soul for most of my life. I've recorded them in journals from early adulthood, and as I grew in knowledge and wisdom concerning such things I began to interpret or attempt to comprehend their cryptic meanings.

In October 1973, I had an unusually vivid dream which forecast my meeting with Ann Manser approximately three months later. In this dream I found myself in the home of a friend, a home elegantly set among pines and palms on a hillside reminiscent of those of the "rich and famous" on the coast of Southern California. Overlooking the ocean, in a balmy tropical atmosphere, the house was large and sprawling and decorated in creamy neutral colors with startling splashes of more vivid colors perfectly accessorized in pillows, in massive paintings and other works of art. The furniture was classic in design, neutral in tone, and fairly inconspicuous, contributing to the overall tasteful simplicity of a peaceful ambience. A more dramatic theme was produced by an overlaid pattern of light throughout the modern structure, brilliant in some areas with figures in light and shadow in other areas. Potted plants, trees and flowers breathed a natural life into the vastness of space in this exquisite dwelling.

People, people, people—everywhere there were people, but without a feeling of chaos except for the relative confusion invading my own mind. I seemed to be aware of inner changes vying for my undivided attention; changes taking place in mental-emotional regions, or were they perhaps in the deeper more spiritual regions? As I wandered throughout the mansion, preoccupied with a bulging sense of urgency and unable to identify its source, I discovered a luxurious spa. Perhaps a long relaxing soak in the tub would help to clear my senses. I disrobed, drew a warm bath and sprinkled in a bit of lavender to help soothe my swirling thoughts and feelings. As I sank into the deliciousness of the setting and the moment, I gazed out over the magnificence of the ocean, its passionate surging and its rhythmic tranquility. I felt at one with nature as I was experiencing it. And even though some of my inner conflict seemed to melt away, I still felt a nagging unrest.

As I reached inward, searching for some enlightenment, I was aware of a disturbance in the water behind me. Someone had apparently slipped in to share my bath. I couldn't bring myself to look and see who was there, so I quietly slipped out of the tub, donned a swimsuit and lay in the sun on the deck for a while. I soon discovered that my friend, Marilyn, was also there. We visited, napped, and sunned on the expansive deck with several other guests.

Later, indoors, amid the activity of milling guests, I found myself sitting and playing a beautiful grand piano. Its tone was heavenly. As I played the piece of music before me, my delight gave way to mounting frustration. Bill, a family acquaintance, and his wife, Barbara, were standing to my right. Bill began moving the sheet music so he could better see the words as he sang along. Eventually the music had shifted so far that I could barely see it. I had to stop playing.

Still affected by the din of the gathering, and longing for understanding and direction, I left the party, alone. I soon found myself in a Navy shipyard speaking with a young sailor. I made an inquiry about how I might contact Madam Hoffmeister, a woman whom I thought might assist me in my quest. I was informed that she had recently moved to an eastern region of the country. After a long, uneventful journey, my bus delivered me to a mountaintop retreat. It was lovely—very hilly, green, and quiet. I noticed a building nearby. It was a regal structure with high walls of glass. I entered the building and found myself in a cafeteria surrounded by rooms marked for the teaching and practice of various music disciplines. As I walked down the hallway, I met two women. The elder seemed to be scolding the younger who was dressed for dance in her leotard. As the two parted, I stopped the older woman to ask if she knew how I could make an appointment to see Madam Hoffmeister. She told me that Madam Hoffmeister was very busy and it was useless to try to make an appointment with her. I thanked the woman and sat on a nearby bench wondering how I could see this important person. The younger woman bounced back toward me after the other one had left. She was a pretty blond, bubbly and friendly. She asked if she could help me. I told her I was there to see Madam Hoffmeister, and that I would be willing to wait for an appointment. She promised to see what she could do and to return as soon as she had something to report. A few minutes seemed to pass and the young dancer reappeared to tell me that I could have Madam Hoffmeister's first appointment at eight-thirty the next morning. I thanked her and assured her that I would return at the appointed time. I was ecstatic! As I made my exit from the building I looked toward the sky. In the air just above me there was an explosion—a beautiful profusion of color. The dream ended.

This dream was such a lucid experience that I felt I had in actuality been in those places and with those people. It was so much a part of my consciousness that it was comparable to an actual holiday in the physical realm, except that it touched me on a much deeper level within myself. Sometime in the next several weeks I met a Jungian dream analyst named Patricia "Pat" Granger, and I engaged her counsel to help me interpret the dream. When I had finished telling her the dream, in all its detail, she asked questions regarding my feelings and thoughts about it. Then she asked me if I knew the meaning of the German name, Hoffmeister. I told her I didn't. "It means *high master*," she said. I countered with, "but this is a woman." She looked amused and reminded me that "women can be masters, too." She told me, with a twinkle in her eye, that the dream would eventually make more sense to me and that I would recognize Madam Hoffmeister when the time was right for us to meet. Finally, she told me to pay particular attention to the burst of color in the sky at the end of the dream. "Color will be significant for you," she said.

Later, I learned that Ann Manser had been a draftswoman at the Puget Sound Naval Shipyard, and I'm sure that my brief stop at the naval shipyard in my dream was a clear tip for Mrs. Granger, who I also learned was Ann Manser's sister-in-law. Keep in mind I had not yet heard of Ann Manser at the time of the dream analysis with Pat Granger. Another sign was the time of my morning appointment with Madam Hoffmeister—eight-thirty. The numbers added together equal eleven, which was a number of great significance to Ann.

The congregation of the metaphysical church and educational center I attended, The Temple of the Living God, was like a family to me. I thought I knew most of its members and regular visitors. One chilly evening in January, 1974, I sat with friends on the back row in the sanctuary. I was thoroughly involved in the service when the back of the head of an older woman sitting on the third row of the middle section of the sanctuary begged for my attention. There was nothing at all unusual about her appearance. But I was transfixed; I lost track of time and of what was happening in the service. When I regained control of my conscious mind, I was puzzled and fascinated by the experience. At an appropriate time, I turned to my friend, Marilyn, on my right and asked her if she knew the woman. She whispered, "That's Ann Manser, the author of the Shustah work." I had heard the name, Shustah, but did not yet know what it meant. I am sure Ann Manser and I had been a part of the same congregation many times before. The student had not been ready.

After the service, Marilyn asked if I would like to meet Mrs. Manser and offered to introduce us. I was hesitant. My earlier experience had been a very powerful and extraordinary one. I could finally see her face, and I watched as she made her way through the crowd, speaking briefly to those who stopped to greet her. Who was this woman? She was obviously important to a lot of people. They greeted her with such respect; warmly, but in a somewhat formal manner. While others were embracing each other, no one embraced Mrs. Manser. I did not take advantage of the opportunity to meet her that evening.

Intrigued with the event of the evening, I drove home thinking of nothing else. I was energized and spent a long time in my evening meditation which was focused on Mrs. Manser and questions about my being so strongly drawn to her. My meditation was rich with such images as I had never seen before. They were colorful and other-worldly and appeared to me in rapid succession. There were symbols such as a snow-capped, misty violet-colored mountain, a white marble temple trimmed heavily in gold, high on a hill, a woven hemp peacock chair and a majestic vision of a Hindu-appearing teacher dressed in white with a white turban and a jewel hidden in the center of the turban. He sat at a banquet table draped with a white cloth—the whitest white I had ever seen. He faced slightly to his right with his left arm and hand on the table. On his ring finger there was another large and brilliant jewel—perhaps a diamond. At a later time, I asked Ann Manser about the Hindu teacher. I had painted the visions immediately after closing my meditation that evening. The first three symbols were rendered using pastels or colored chalk. The Hindu teacher was done in oil. Ann later told me this man was an inner plane teacher who had been with me for several years. She told me his name was a very long one and that he had given it to me the night I painted his portrait. She wanted me to recall the name. It took me several weeks to get a name that I thought belonged to him. Ann had written the name down to save and compare with the one that would come to me. I was driving home to St. Petersburg from an art lesson in Bradenton, Florida, along the approach to the Sunshine Skyway Bridge on Boca Ciega Bay, somewhat mesmerized by the sun glistening on the water when the name came to me in an instant! The name was Amahlamedananda. I then remembered thinking about two names as I had painted his portrait—Amahl and Amed. The *ananda* part of the name was not revealed until that moment. I called Ann to tell her, and she asked me not to tell her the name but to write it down and compare it, on our next visit, with the name she had written down. She wanted me to learn to trust my intuition. When we met again, we compared the names and they were a match!

Back to the Temple event when I first became aware of Mrs. Manser—I felt bold enough to talk with her about my experience a few days later. I phoned her. She listened attentively, and when I had finished my story she simply said, "I've been waiting for you to call." I was so startled by her statement that I was momentarily speechless. She went on, "There are three of you, all women, whose calls I have been expecting. You are the first to call." I somehow knew who the others were and named them for her. She said, "Yes, but please don't mention this to the other two women; they'll call when it is time for them to make contact." A second person called her shortly after this conversation. The third woman never called.

Over the next few years I was privileged to be one of Ann's students of the ancient wisdom teachings and Universal Law as interpreted and written by her in *The Pages of Shustah, The Holy Kabalah* and *The Evolution of Consciousness in the Fourth Kingdom;* the latter a collaborative work with LeRoy Zemke. I was already a student of Max Heindel's Rosicrucian teachings, and when I became a member of the Temple of the Living God I became a student of Theosophical teachings and other wisdom teachings through my participation in the educational program offered there. So a foundation was in the process of being built for my understanding of these esoteric concepts.

A new study group was formed. An earlier one was already in progress, made up of peer students of the wisdom teachings. We met once a week in Ann Manser's apartment to discuss a focus chosen by Ann, or sometimes one chosen by the students. This meeting inspired us to delve more deeply into the teachings on our own and contribute our investigative findings for discussion at future meetings.

In Ann's written work, the esoteric definitions of color and light represent vibratory frequencies on a continuum corresponding to levels of consciousness or our other dimensions of consciousness. Some reach far beyond our conscious experience in the Earth frequency. Certain principles are assigned to each color continuum following our Earth spectrum and continuing on into the Higher Worlds where colors unheard of here are expressions of higher principles. For example, the principle represented in an aura by the color green is that of the desire nature on the astral level from which it flows. On the physical or material end of a continuum it would have to do with physical or material desire. In the mental realm on the continuum the shade of green there might represent desires toward mental pursuits or certain educational goals. The higher up the continuum, the more refined the principle becomes in its manifestation. The desire nature emanating from the balanced green found on the higher end of the continuum might propel one toward the divine impulses of creative desire and a desire for perfection on those higher levels.

With my background in oil painting with pigment, I became enthralled with acquiring more knowledge of color as it related to light rather than pigment. From this introduction to color as a principle, the investigation of the uses of color has become a special area of my study through the years. I was invited by Ann to study privately with her for a time. We began the Kabalistic study using color in our meditations. The student was ready, her teacher had appeared, and she was beginning a journey of intense spiritual investigation into the realms of higher consciousness.

Ann Manser, 1926

Amahlamedananda

CHAPTER 8

A Remarkable Woman Named Annabelle

Annabelle: English combine of the
Hebrew Hannah and Latin Belle,
meaning "of grace and beauty."

~ Evelyn Wells

B ORN ANNABELLE HAUSAUER IN MILES City, Montana on June 11, 1896, Ann was one of six children; there were two sisters and three brothers, all of whom were musicians. Ann was the visual artist in her family. Her father was born in Alsace-Lorraine in France, and her mother was from Scotland. The family spoke English, German, French and Gaelic as common languages in the home. Ann attended the University of Washington in Seattle, studied painting and became an electrical draftswoman employed for fourteen years in the Puget Sound Navy Shipyard. She became a talented visual artist with watercolor her preferred medium.

Ann told of being carried on her father's shoulders as he walked through their town, Miles City, Montana, in a parade celebrating the turn of the century in 1899-1900. She was almost four years old and recalled that her father said to her, "Remember this day, Annabelle—you will not see another turn of the century in your lifetime." It was during this year, when Ann was four, that she had a terrifying recall of a former incarnation. From that experience her perception began to expand with an increasing ability to communicate with all forms of life.

During her young adulthood, while on an outing at Mount Olympus with a friend, Dr. Dean, Ann saw the magnificent force-field, the aura around Mount Ranier. "It was a beautiful healing apple-green," she recalled. This dramatic experience awakened her to her life's work in color and aura investigation. Her personal studies evolved from myths and symbolism into the deeper archives of color, auras and evolutions of the kingdoms. Her studies eventually concentrated on the revelations of the Holy Kabalah from which her Shustah and Kabalistic written lectures would emerge many years later. She developed the *Aurascope* in which she described the permanent aura of an individual in color and its corresponding principles and which she termed the "precise signature of the personality which it surrounds."

Ann had a special relationship with all of the kingdoms. She had delightful stories to tell about her work with the plant kingdom and direct conversations with the devas of that kingdom. Deva is a Sanskrit word which means *shining ones*. The devas are in the category of angels, nature spirits, all winged beings similar to the fairies we heard about as children. She told of an experience she had with a deva or nature spirit when walking through her dining area and hearing a tiny voice from somewhere saying, "I'm awake now." She looked all around her and she couldn't find the source of the voice. It happened again, "I'm awake now." It then seemed to be coming from under the buffet in the dining room. She got down on her hands and knees and looked under the buffet. Back in the corner against the wall was a forgotten Christmas cactus she had placed there for the period of darkness the plant requires before its blooming cycle. Its little deva was giving her a reminder. She immediately pulled the plant out into the light and watered it and reported that it was blooming profusely by Christmas.

There were awe-inspiring accounts of her experiences with the great storm devas, and her frequent contact with those exalted masters and beings beyond the human kingdom. But it was her little brothers and sisters in the animal kingdom who captured her love and devotion. She provided a home for many animals during her lifetime, and she never appeared too busy to offer a healing prayer or ritual for one of her little *friends* about whose suffering she was made aware. She canceled a class she was teaching one evening in order to perform a private vigil for a little cat that had died—our little cat named Puff.

Ann had many devoted friends and students who would have joyfully cared for her during her illness with cancer, but I was the only one of her students living nearby who was not expected to report for a nine-to-five job each day. I was a stay-at-home mom with four children, and they were wonderfully generous with me when I offered to take care of my friend and teacher, Ann Manser. Wendi, our youngest, was six and Jim, our eldest, was seventeen. Mark and Julie were fifteen and thirteen. I left each evening when Wendi was in bed and the older children were ready for bed and arrived at Ann's apartment before her bedtime and stayed with her all night. This routine began a little over a month before Ann's death in January, so most of it took place during the Christmas holidays. Each evening I unrolled my sleeping bag onto an exercise mat on her kitchen floor and slept there all night with one ear open to listen for her call in case she needed me. Then I stayed with Ann each morning until I cooked her oatmeal for breakfast and prepared her main meal to be heated at the noon hour for lunch.

The daytime hours belonged to my family, and the children were wonderful about helping with daily chores so we could do our Christmas shopping and enjoy a few holiday treats together. In the late evenings, I stole away to see about Ann. She always greeted me with a new story about her preparation for her transition from this life into the next. I listened attentively as she imparted her knowledge of dimensions beyond the physical dimension, knowledge to which I had never been exposed. She pointed out boundaries of the next dimension as they related to her living area, as many extended beyond the boundaries of the physical rooms. I had to stretch my imagination in order to comprehend some of the jewels she shared during these visits. I, along with other students, had studied many metaphysical concepts with her but these were experiences occurring on her pathway as she was gradually giving up her life on this plane. There were evenings when she wanted to talk about her early life in the Badlands of Montana and later in the Puget Sound area of Bremerton, Washington. I was intrigued by her stories about her family's journeys by covered wagon from their farm into town every three months to buy supplies of kitchen staples, fabrics, and other necessities. "Our kitchen was always stacked high with goods for days after our trip, until things were packed away properly and the fresh foods canned. I loved the way we felt so rich after one of our buying trips!"

There were fascinating stories about her life as a young adult. It didn't take much to get Ann started on one when she was feeling up to it. Some of them took place in a period of time when my own parents were still children. Ann's sister-in-law, Pat Granger, spoke of Ann's beauty as a young woman. She said that Ann turned heads everywhere she went. Ann was twenty-two and still living at home with her family on the ranch in Bremerton, but working in town at the Naval Shipyard. She had to walk about two miles each way, to and from work every day, in all kinds of weather. Her mother suggested that she find an apartment in town near her work and mentioned her idea to a friend, Dr. Dean, a lady physician in town. Dr. Dean had a vacant apartment for rent across the hall from her own, so Ann moved into it.

One evening I took some Christmas gifts to work on while I listened to the latest development in Ann's journey. She began chuckling as I took my usual place at her feet and made myself comfortable on the floor with the gifts spread around me. When I asked Ann what was so funny, she said, "You're sitting right up against Clare. She gets a kick out of that." I quickly got up to move, and Ann said, "No, she likes you there."

Ann explained to me that Clare was a Sandalphon Angel—"The Mighty Archangel Sandalphon, whose host of angelic beings are the Cherubim, and among many important tasks they work with the animal kingdom. The Cherubim or Sandalphon Angels also work at the gates of birth and death, opening and closing the avenues of consciousness when transition occurs in the animal and human kingdoms."[1] I asked Ann that if she had a choice would she prefer to know of these preparations beyond our dimension for her death or would she rather be unaware of them? She assured me that she wanted to know everything she could know about the whole process. I had moments of great anxiety, and many others of feeling blessed that Ann was able to share her dying with me. It was difficult at times and also necessary for me to be as open as possible. If I was going to be truly aware of what was happening, there was no room for a fearful attitude.

One night, Ann had a story to tell me of her retreat to the desert in her earlier years where she lived in a trailer for forty weeks with only her German shepherd for company. During this time, she was being prepared for a spiritual assignment of research, channeling and writing some valuable teachings. Her goal for this desert retreat was to spend time in meditation, contemplation and contacting higher realities and those higher beings who would assist her with the monumental task ahead of her. She was in touch with the Ascended Masters who would instruct her, lead her to research sources and help her to organize her written work in a graded or developmental form. The work would then be offered to those who would someday study it for their own spiritual knowledge and development. She spoke of times while she was writing this material when she would be awakened in the night and shown, psychically, specific pages and lines where she had made an error. She would immediately get up and make the correction. Over the years, Ann was more and more able to easily contact those spiritual Teachers in high places. Lord Hilo and Lord Dianthus were two of the Teachers, and during Ann's illness Lord Hilo reportedly became a frequent visitor.

Wendi, my younger daughter, and I went Christmas shopping just a few days before Christmas. When I awoke on that morning in Ann's apartment, I felt as if I were walking at least three feet above the floor. I had difficulty with my balance and was bumping into things. This experience was similar to the one I had at Mt. Ecclesia (Chapter 6). Later, as Wendi and I walked through the mall, this feeling began to subside, but only gradually. I was feeling high and giddy and was probably more fun for Wendi than if I had been more grounded. I discussed this feeling with Ann that evening. She thought that I might not be getting enough to eat or enough rest. A few days later when she spoke of Lord Hilo and his visits to her in the night to offer her healing and make her more comfortable, I realized that it could be his energy that was causing my *high* and affecting my balance. Ann agreed. Lord Hilo's energy or vibratory frequency would have been extremely high in comparison with my lower Earth frequency, thereby causing a dizzying effect on me. Ann was accustomed to his presence and knew how to prepare herself and adjust to his frequency. Ann said that she checked in on Wendi and me, intuitively, during our shopping excursion that day. "As you and Wendi walked through the mall among the Christmas decorations and to the music of the season, you were both surrounded by butterflies. You looked so happy, and little Wendi could barely contain her exuberance!"

Many of Ann's friends and students called for suggestions for Christmas gifts for her. She told me to tell them she needed nothing. But knowing she liked things like Godiva Chocolates and beeswax candles, her friends made sure she received an abundance of both. As her gifts arrived, I discovered stacks of boxes of Godiva Chocolates in her freezer. I teased her with the idea of writing a book about her someday, and she playfully retorted, "No one would want to know that I like chocolates and wine for breakfast." I responded with, "But that is just what would sell the book!"

Ann's health began to rapidly deteriorate after Christmas. Her medical diagnosis was cancer of the adrenal glands. We discussed the fact that she was beginning to need more care, and my family needed me, too. My schedule would have to change somewhat in order to make sure she was cared for. She agreed to go home with me the next day and let me take care of them all in one location. My older children had many ways to entertain themselves and spent a lot of time with friends.

Ann made her preparations to leave her apartment behind. A few of her belongings were gradually packed in the car and she was at last ready to go. I was concerned about moving her from her home, and told her so. Her response was, "I don't care if I never see my apartment again. I could leave and never come back." I knew of course that she had nothing against the apartment; she just wanted to leave her poor miserable body. She asked me to call Douglas, her friend and landlord, and ask him to "exorcise the apartment of all the pain and sickness" that had permeated it. The short trip, only a few miles to my home, was not easy for her. She felt every bump in the road and was terribly weakened by the ride.

After we arrived, Ann slept off and on all afternoon. As the sun began to set, I built a beautiful roaring fire in the fireplace and prepared a light supper for myself. I spent some time reading, then writing and often checking on Ann. She was exhausted and slept for most of the evening. While she was sleeping, I had a visit from an old friend, another Ann. We sat and talked by the fire for a while and continued our conversation with a cup of tea by the Christmas tree. It was the most relaxing time I had experienced for several weeks, and I expressed my thanks for that welcomed intermission. Wendi had very generously offered her light blue little girl room for Ann's visit, and Ann slept in her canopy bed. She explained that she had been told by an invisible teacher that Wendi's room had been lined with an impermeable other-dimensional material that would protect her room from Ann's pain and any other negativity. The lining would be removed after Ann was gone, and it would be clear again for Wendi's occupancy.

The next morning I went in to check on Ann without taking time to dress for the day. Ann greeted me with a smile. "I watched the sun come up this morning, so this room is on the east side of your house. The seven colored rays came in that window then two of them disappeared. Soon the sun was up. I like this room. It's so pretty and it smells so fresh. There is a little place just outside that window where the nature spirits play all the time. They just love it out there. Is that the back yard?"

"No, it's actually a narrow strip next to the hedge between this house and the neighbor's house. There are flowering tropical shrubs planted along that side of our house. No one uses that area; it isn't often traveled."

"That's why they feel so at home then. Where is the sun now?"

I pointed to its approximate position. "By now, it's about nine-thirty in the morning."

Ann changed the subject. "This is your day. I want to spend a lot of time with you. I have things to say to you."

I told Ann that the children all spent the night with friends and that I would be able to be with her all day.

Ann then asked, "Do you remember when it was that Joan gave you the Shustah card[2] reading and told you she saw a man waiting at the end of the path for you?"

"Yes, it was just a few weeks ago. She couldn't see his face but she recognized him as being someone we both know," I recalled.

"Joan was right . . . there is a man. His name is Tom." Ann softly sobbed. "Not the Tom you know . . . but the same person. He'll be different . . . he will be so different that the people who know him now won't recognize him then." Her sobs came and went.

"Did your in-depth study tell you much about Tom? Was your work together mentioned in it?" In-depth studies are psychic readings, yet more than that, given by Reverend LeRoy Zemke. These readings delve into soul qualities and commitment on those spiritual levels, and one's life purpose.

"No, I learned that we were priests together in a life in Thebes and formed a close bond of friendship at that time," I answered.

"Well, you're halfway through a block of work you're involved in together. About the time of your decision to separate back in the summer, Tom was given a choice on a higher level to make—the choice between being a scorpion and becoming an eagle."

"Tom's Sun sign is Scorpio," I offered.

Ann began to weep again as she continued, "He made his choice . . . to become the eagle. You must give him a gift of an eagle in some form sometime." I later gave Tom a silver half-dollar coin with the eagle side facing outward on a chain to wear as a pendant. "He will be going through such changes in his consciousness in the years to come that his physical appearance will change . . . his face will be so different that people who don't see him often won't recognize him. Your whole family is involved in this work that you and Tom are doing on another level. Since you began this work, many incarnations ago, you have worked out many problems that have come up during this time. There are four problems which you have tried many times to work out on other levels. You have not yet been successful in solving those problems, so they had to be objectified in this incarnation."

"Oh my . . . our children! They represent the four problems?"

"Yes, all six of you went into a conclave before you came in this time. The children each agreed to do this for you. Each one represents a different problem. As soon as you are able to recognize the problem, and it's only one principle with each one, the problem for the child will disappear and the child will be free to be on his or her own."

Then I asked her, "Can you tell me something about the work that Tom and I have agreed to do?"

"No, I can't tell you that. It has to do with the wisdom teachings, however. You must live your life a day at a time. Do the work at hand. Look for signposts . . . you'll recognize them. Watch for the signs in your children. Take it a day at a time," she advised.

Ann changed the subject again, "I don't know where I am in relationship to the rest of the house. Maybe I'll feel like walking out and letting you point out where the other rooms are located. It's interesting that you're the one to work with me at this time and that you had the light blue room with the east window for me to use."

Ann kept asking about the position of the sun throughout the day. I told her I had given some thought to the light blue room before I brought her over to the house, but I didn't know about the east window.

"Do you know what the implications of my being here could be?" she asked.

"Yes," I said. "I want to share something with you. Several months ago I realized somehow that I would be with you at this time. I don't know how I knew it, but I did."

"I wonder how you knew that. Your inner teacher must have told you."

"You just reminded me of something, Ann. In November of last year when I was studying the first lecture of the Kabalah with you, you read the Shustah cards for me. One thing you told me was that my teacher and I were working together on something on the inner planes that would be completed in December, 1976. Well, this is December, 1976!"

She responded with, "I told you right, didn't I?"

"Yes, I believe that I have been through some deep inner process of preparation for this experience with you."

Ann Manser, 1976

CHAPTER 9

Closing a Chapter

A teacher is one who makes himself
(herself) progressively unnecessary.

~ Thomas Carruthers

IN THE BOOK, NOW OUT of print, *The Beginnings of the Sixth Root Race* by Theosophist C. W. Leadbeater, the author describes a time in the future when dying will be more a matter of moving out of our worn-out bodies at will. He says that we will know when that time comes and the body has lived beyond its usefulness and a person begins to find his powers failing him. He seems to be able to just move out of his body in his sleep. He will not drop the body as long as it is useful. He will not feel at all that he is giving up life, but only that he is changing a worn-out vehicle. Leadbeater claims in this work to have been given a clairvoyant view of many aspects of this future Sixth Root Race. "The fifth great period (fifth day of creation), during which we are now living, saw the coming of the fifth root-race.[1] What happened next with Ann Manser made me wonder, when I later read this book, if she had also read it.

The second night that Ann stayed with me was full of surprises and unusual events. The evening was a cold one, so I built another fire to help warm the house. The children were all staying with friends again. Ann kept asking me for more cover. I had the thermostat turned up as high as I dared above the usual temperature for our house. Her room felt warm to me, but I brought more blankets and laid them on top of her. When it was time for me to turn in for the night I let the fire go out and Ann heard me getting ready for bed in Mark's room. He was not there, and his room was close to the room she occupied, so I stayed there where I could hear her if she needed me. She called me into her room and said, "I would like for you to sit with me for a while." I of course complied and pulled a chair over next to her bed. I also began to feel cold, very cold, so I piled more blankets on top of both of us. That didn't help much. I finally realized that the cold was coming from inside our bodies somehow. I didn't understand it and asked if Ann could understand what was happening. She termed it a "psychic cold" and said there was a lot of activity from other dimensions in the room at that time. If she hadn't sounded so tired and weak I would have pressed for more explanation. The right side of my chair was against the right side of her bed so that I was facing her. She reached over with her right hand and took mine and held it for a long time. I prayed for her comfort. After a while she fell asleep and released my hand and I put my head down on the edge of the bed to try to get a little sleep, too.

Almost two hours passed and Ann awoke. In a disappointed, almost agitated tone, she woke me with, "What happened? I'm still here! Where have *you* been?"

"I've been asleep, sitting here with my head on the side of your bed," I told her.

"Where was your head?"

I showed her just where my head had been and she became more agitated as she chided, "I couldn't leave because your crown chakra was too close to my solar plexus. Your energy kept me here!"

It was at that point that I realized her plan was to just slip out of her body and end her suffering. She had not shared this part of her plan with me, and I had no specific instructions except that under no circumstances should I admit her to a hospital. She had been adamant about that while she was still at home in her apartment. Now she was changing her mind, and she ordered, "Call an ambulance and take me to the hospital!"

I reminded Ann of her earlier wish to not be admitted to the hospital under any circumstances. She was just as adamant now about being admitted. This created a real dilemma for me. I didn't think I could make the decision alone so I tried to wake myself up enough to phone our friend, Douglas. I was able to reach him and together we decided it was best to admit Ann to the hospital. I called for an ambulance and quickly got myself dressed and told Ann what was happening. I was so glad my children were away and being cared for that night so I had the freedom to take care of Ann and go with her to the hospital. She was admitted to a small private hospital near my home, and I stayed with her there the rest of the night. I was not able to relax enough to nap, so I pulled out a pen and small notebook and composed this little poem to pass the time.

The Time Is Not Yet

Away from the shell you traveled in *space*.
A start, abrupt halt,
then your winged journey began.
Your tracks were silvery, a web
made of lace.

Where is the illumined one,
Her work well done—
Who labored, kept vigil
through night and through day,
who left her High Master in the Hands
of her Holy One?

Oh Lord of Green Fire, soar.
Take her upward and
penetrate each veil as you climb.
Go onward, go forward to new levels sublime.
There, let her see her pattern
complete and entire.

A fragment of your consciousness
could not break away,
exalted Teacher—your life held in sway.
The cord, almost severed, coiled up as in waiting.
Oh what have I done to bring on such as this?
You agonized . . .
Then you returned to the shadow, the darkness,
the illusion you met.
Once more sheathed in pain,
the mystery regained.
The time is not yet.

For the next few days, Ann had a steady stream of young doctors and interns in her room. One in particular made frequent visits to check on her. I soon learned that she was teaching him, giving him esoteric information and he kept returning for more. On his first visit she drew him a picture of the configuration of her adrenal tumor and its exact position and location in her body. Having been a draftswoman at a naval base in her earlier years, the drawing was a pretty accurate rendition of what she could see, psychically. She had not yet had any X-rays or diagnostic tests done when she made the drawing. X-rays were ordered, and after they were developed the doctor brought them in and asked to see her drawing again. There was an almost perfect match. He was of course amazed, and he asked if she had seen other X-rays of her tumor before then. She told him no other X-rays had been made but that she was able to use her own "X-ray vision" and see what was happening inside her body. He was then so intrigued that he was by her side as often as he could manage to find the time, holding her hand, asking questions and listening to her discourses on various metaphysical concepts.

Ann was given a thorough picture of her condition and then asked to make a decision about her treatment. She chose to have the tumor surgically removed. She was eighty years old and I asked her if she would like another doctor's opinion. She said, "No, I've made my decision." On the morning of her surgery she asked me to go into meditation, while she was in the operating room, to see if I could locate her consciousness during her surgery and tell her later what I had found. I was allowed to walk beside her as she was being transported to the operating room. Not knowing if I would see Ann in her conscious state ever again, I walked absent-mindedly to the OR waiting room and tried to calm my mind and obediently go into a meditative state.

Fortunately, I was the only person in the waiting room for quite a long time and I had the privacy to take my time and make the preparation I needed for meditation. Sometimes I think these things are planned and set up on another level. When I felt prepared, I had no trouble achieving a deep level of meditation and went almost immediately to a place in a forest of giant redwoods on the West Coast of the United States, possibly in Washington State. There was no conversation, although I was keenly aware of Ann's consciousness in a spot on a redwood stump where the sun had found an open space to beam through the giant trees and rest there. The forest was restful and still with the exception of a slight breeze that softly whistled through the treetops. I was content to be there for what seemed like hours bathed in a Presence which seemed both awesome and serene. I found myself withdrawing from the experience just in time to hear others entering the waiting room, and I was eager to tell Ann where I had found her consciousness. That location made sense to me because of her early life in the Pacific Northwest.

After her surgery, Ann was in the Intensive Care Unit for the remaining twenty-four hours of her life. I was allowed to see her for fifteen minutes during every scheduled visiting time; in the morning, afternoon, and evening. She was sleeping when I saw her on the evening of her surgery. The next time I was allowed to see her was on her first post-operative day. I was there waiting when visiting hours began. Her eyes were closed, so I gently took her right hand in mine and just held it. I felt that she knew I was there because she was able to give my hand a slight squeeze now and then. I suggested that she just rest and not try to communicate with me that time, and I told her that I would be back to visit in mid-afternoon. I was there again when visiting hours resumed. Ann seemed a bit more able to communicate with me this time. She wasn't able to speak but she gently squeezed my hand again and tried to communicate with her eyes. I told her about my experience with her consciousness during her surgery. She squeezed my hand in response. I had the distinct feeling that she was still somewhat disengaged from her physical body and was trying ever so hard to connect enough to speak to me. She was making a valiant effort, and knowing my time with her was getting shorter I again suggested that she conserve her energy for healing and let me do the talking. I promised to be back for the next visiting hour, bent over and gave her a kiss on her cheek, and as I was leaving we had an unmistakable communication through a powerful eye contact.

In that last eye contact, I believe Ann was telling me goodbye although I was still so hopeful of her survival that I was not very open to her message. I ran an errand, picked up Wendi from our neighbor's house, and we went home. About a half hour after my arrival at home I received a phone call from a nurse at the hospital informing me of Ann's passing. A part of me knew the news the phone call would bear. Wendi was in the room and heard my conversation with the nurse. As soon as I hung up the phone, Wendi began crying and asked if Mrs. Manser had just died. I held her and told her she had. I didn't weep at that time; it seemed that Wendi was doing that for me. I held her and talked with her about how Ann had wanted to leave and go on to live with the angels and not suffer any longer. Wendi had met her only once. I had taken her by Ann's apartment because I wanted them to have some physical contact with each other in addition to the spiritual connection I knew was there. It had been a brief contact, with Ann at the top of her stairway and Wendi just inside the door at the foot of the stairs. Wendi knew Ann was important in my life—she was very attuned to people in that way.

Ann had given me some money before her surgery. She told me that in the event that she didn't make it through this surgery I should buy something nice for the doctors and the staff who had attended her. She was so appreciative of their care and wanted me to express that to them for her. Knowing how much Ann liked Godiva Chocolates, I bought a large box of them and wrote a note indicating her wish to thank them and then I presented it to them. Those who were there at the time gathered around and spoke kind and loving words about her. I felt she would indeed be pleased.

Ann's life was celebrated in a lovely memorial service held at the Temple of the Living God and officiated by her closest friend, spiritual consultant, and her student in earlier years, Reverend LeRoy Zemke. Many of her students, locally and from a distance, were present to honor their beloved friend and Teacher with a capital "T." Ann C. Manser's legacy lives powerfully on through her wisdom school called Pages of Shustah, Inc. and her written work studied by groups and individual students in the United States and throughout the world.

In some of our late night discussions, while Ann was still living in her apartment, we talked about death, about making our transition to a new abode in the afterlife, and in particular about her own transition which was imminent. She shared with me her mental task of "building a place in the inner planes," the subtle dimensions, "where I can go to have my review of this life." She described a location in the etheric realms of the Nevada desert, a *shack*, she called it, from which the Las Vegas skyline was visible. I asked her why she was building a shack when she could build anything she wanted, to which she replied, "A shack is all I'll need, and I have pleasant memories of my retreat in the desert in the early years." She also suggested that it might take her about three weeks to get to a completion stage of her afterlife review. Ann had completed this phase of her spiritual work, was not afraid of dying, and in fact was ready to move on and begin the next phase of her *life*. During one of our conversations we discussed the possibility of our communication across dimensions after her transition. I made a deal with her. I promised her I would do whatever was necessary to control my grief for her if she would help me make conscious contact with her three weeks after her transition. She knew I could easily receive information through my dreams, and often in meditation I would be aware of presences and contacts through visions and symbols. So she promised me she would appear to me in some way in three weeks after her passing.

Ann had performed *miracles* of this kind before. For example, when our cat, Puff, died, my daughter, Julie, was devastated. I called Ann to tell her about Puff and how his demise was affecting Julie. She told me to see if I could get Julie, age eleven then, to sit with me and meditate and say prayers for Puff. She said, "I will work with Julie and try to help her see Puff." She then asked me if Puff had a favorite place indoors. I told her he slept on Julie's bed a lot. Julie declined my invitation to meditate together but wanted to light a candle and pray for him in her room, alone. I helped her to get ready and then went to my own room to meditate. I hadn't been in meditation very long when I heard a gentle knock on my door. Julie asked if she could come in. She said she was sitting and praying for Puff when she suddenly looked up and he was curled up on her bed where he always slept. It was very comforting for her to see him and to know he was okay and had come to visit her in his favorite place. She was able to tune in at other times and see him briefly or sense his presence around her. I immediately called and reported Julie's experience to Ann. Recalling this experience, I knew Ann would be able to help me know when it was time for her to make contact with me.

CHAPTER 10

A Visit to Another World

*The Other Side is, indeed, beyond the normal
sensory perception of humankind. It's another
dimension at a higher frequency of matter.
In actuality, it is reality!*

~ Sylvia Browne

IN KEEPING WITH MY VOW I was able to control the emotional expression of my grief for Ann. However, I designed my own review of our many conversations together and her teachings as I had sat at her feet, an eager and obedient pupil. On the day before I expected a visit from her from the afterlife, I made sure I was doing things that would help to raise my vibratory frequency so I wouldn't miss her contact. I was careful to spend the day being positive and happy, listening to classical music, reading uplifting passages, and eating light meals—almost fasting. In the evening, just before bedtime, I said my prayers and went into meditation in order to create an *atmosphere* for my meeting with Ann. We had an appointment and I was confident and expectant. I knew I would hear from her, if not in meditation then certainly in a dream that night.

The next morning the sunlight streamed in my window and I suddenly sat up in bed not knowing if I had seen Ann in a dream! I couldn't remember a dream with or about her. I felt such disappointment. I didn't blame Ann; I took responsibility for not being properly prepared or not recalling her visit. I would try again that night. Perhaps something beyond my control prevented the contact. It was a school day for the children, so we had breakfast, made lunches, and the older children were off on their bikes to school. I drove Wendi to school, then I came back home and immersed myself in routine morning chores when I suddenly became so sleepy I could barely stand up. I managed to get to my bedroom and lie down across the bed. I didn't fall asleep, however, but everything went dark. I could still feel my body but couldn't move it. I later decided that I had gone into another trance state. I heard music on the radio three rooms away in the family room. My mind was suddenly awake and more acutely aware than usual, and then there was a light just in front of my face! Ann appeared before me, close enough for me to touch her if I could have moved my hands.

Ann was happy and smiling and began talking to me. We talked about recent events which had taken place before and after her transition. I automatically slipped out of my body and she took me to see places she wanted me to know about—a theater setting which I thought might be a teaching auditorium, for example. She spoke of recent incidences in the hospital and how she felt about them. As we talked, we projected ourselves to the locations that were the subjects of our conversation. She then seated herself somewhat above me on a natural rock throne-like structure. I saw sand around us, so I assumed we were in the desert. As she talked, I became aware of her auric emanations which formed a vast rainbow of colors around her. The pulsating colors were magnificent, shimmering and sparkling. There were colors that I had never seen on the earth plane. Each color seemed to slide or melt into the next one. This of course formed some of the colors which were not familiar to me. I do not know just how far her aura emanated from her more solid-looking body. I caught brief glimpses of colors which seemed to stretch a great distance away—perhaps measuring almost a mile, but I was unable to hold the frequency for more than an instant. So I couldn't even determine how close the colors might be to those with which I am familiar. I knew they were there and I wondered how much farther those emanations traveled that I was not able to see at all. I kind of gasped in the middle of something she was saying and then I burst out with, "Ann, I see your aura!" She looked amused and responded with, "Oh you do, do you? Describe it to me." I proceeded to describe what I was seeing and she assured me with, "Yes, you do," and smiled. She soon suggested that we change locations. She had more to show me.

After telling me to wait there for her, somehow Ann projected me to the new level or location. As I waited, I realized we were still in the desert and I could see that there was water in front of me—a couple of feet to my left and a little below me. These were clear pools tucked behind some very large boulders. I supposed this represented an oasis. Ann soon entered the scene from my right and walked over to me and pressed her left shoulder and arm to my right shoulder and arm. She felt so solid and so real that there was absolutely no doubt in my mind that she was actually there. Since we were in the same dimension at that time, our bodies on that level appeared to be solid to me. With my physical eyes I could not have seen her body and the surrounding environment—only with my inner vision, my third eye, could that have happened. She then walked into the pool, directly in front of me, and submerged herself to waist level. She explained that the pool was a "healing matrix" and that she would come daily for a while for the healing of her subtle bodies.

The experience ended and I regained my physical sight and my ability to move my body. I could see the digital clock in the room which indicated that the time was 11:11 A. M. Even the numbers were significant. The number eleven was a special number for Ann. Her birthday was on the eleventh of June. She died on January 4, 1977 which when added together is the number eleven, numerologically. If you'll recall the dream I related at the beginning of this story, my appointment with Madam Hoffmeister was at eight-thirty the next morning. The sum of the eight, three, and zero is equal to eleven. Ann produced her written *Pages of Shustah* and *Holy Kabalah* in sets with eleven lectures in a set. So the 11:11 on my clock was indeed a confirmation of my visit with Ann in her dimension! This out-of-body experience with her was much more convincing than a dream could have been for me. What a gift! Ann's gift of showing me that she was indeed alive and well was profound in itself, however another dimension to her gift was that it would change the way I perceived the passage called *death* forever. It helped me to understand, first hand, that when we leave this earth level, this densest material dimension, we make a transition to a dimension which is less dense but appears solid when we are conscious in its more subtle frequency. Scientists tell us, over and over, that everything is energy vibrating at different frequencies. The Earth frequency is just vibrating at much lower frequencies than those of the etheric, astral, and higher planes. We have to transcend the Earth frequency to be conscious in those higher planes.

Our consciousness, even while in our earthly material bodies, can exist on many different planes, each vibrating to a different frequency. These are not actual locations but different rates of vibration which can be accessed while our physical bodies remain in the same location. The consciousness can leave the physical body during meditation and visit different levels where it can gather information and access levels of wisdom. We all leave our bodies and travel in other levels of consciousness while we sleep. This gives our physical bodies a time to regenerate, and it gives our consciousness an opportunity to explore other realms of experience. For example, if you have a problem that you haven't been able to completely resolve on the physical level, you can present the situation to spirit or your Higher Self by writing it on paper and placing it next to your bed or under your pillow, or you can state it aloud and ask for insights for its resolution. Have you ever asked for help with a situation and had a dream that helped you to work it out? Perhaps you didn't recall a dream but you later had the insights you needed for working out the problem. The information is given on one or more levels of our consciousness and must filter through the lower levels of consciousness and the physical brain, the densest and most limited level. The essence of the solution will hopefully reach our conscious awareness, but we might not be able to identify the level of its source. Our dreams sometimes reach our conscious minds as extreme distortions of the reality from which they originate. If the dream content is not within the realm of our waking experience, our brain has to translate the message in a symbolic language which we may or may not comprehend. So you say, "I had the weirdest dream last night. It makes no sense at all." If you're not familiar with its symbolic language, it might surely be *weird* or *strange*. Most dreams are attempts of other levels of our consciousness to communicate with the conscious mind, the part of the mind that is more aware on this physical level.

"Our planes of consciousness can be broken down into four very broad categories: Physical, Emotional, Mental and Spiritual. Within each of these categories there are many sublevels of consciousness. In order for us to obtain knowledge and experience from each of these planes of existence, we have built interpenetrating subtle bodies corresponding to the vibratory frequency of the planes. The subtle bodies are just like a physical body inasmuch as they are perfected by exercise, and in this case mainly by meditation. So people who become interested in metaphysical, mental, and spiritual subjects stir these bodies into expansion. As a consequence, their consciousness can become aware and travel on all of the planes."[1] These subtle bodies have corresponding glands in the physical body that vibrate at a similar frequency, creating a link between the subtle bodies and the physical body. These links, or connectors, are called *chakras*, a Sanskrit word literally meaning, *wheels*. These major wheels of energy/prana/light are located in the subtle bodies in the brain and along the spine near their corresponding glands and can be seen by those with developed abilities on the subtle levels. One way we can relate to the subtle levels and chakras is to think of them in terms of colors, with the frequencies following the visible spectrum as most of us know it—from red to violet. Each color represents a continuum of principles for each level of consciousness as do the colors which can be seen in an aura around a person or other living things. This concept was mentioned earlier in chapter seven.

It can be simply stated that, for example, when our physical body grows old and less useful to us we can shed it like an overcoat and move into another dimension where we can wear more subtle bodies. Life never ends, it continues on other levels along with others who have made their transition to the same levels.

"There are different levels or *spheres* in the afterlife—from the lowest vibrations to the highest. On physical death we go to the sphere which can accommodate the vibrations we accumulated throughout our life on Earth. Simply stated, most ordinary people are likely to go to the third sphere—named *Summerland* by some. The higher the vibrations, the better the conditions—this will take us to the higher spheres."[2] We are informed that the higher spheres are too beautiful to even imagine. To Carl Jung, "what happens after death is so unspeakably glorious that our imagination and feelings do not suffice to form even an approximate conception of it."[3] For those with very, very low vibrations, very serious problems do exist." Franchessa related, "I was next sent to visit what will indeed seem a strange country to exist in the spirit world. The Land of Ice and Snow—the Frozen Land—in which lived all those who had been cold and selfishly calculating in their earthly lives. Love had been so crushed and killed by them that its sun could not shine where they were, and only the frost of life remained."[4] Does this remind you of C. S. Lewis's land beyond the wardrobe in *The Lion, the Witch, and the Wardrobe* of his *Chronicles of Narnia*?

In April 1912, at the sinking of the Titanic, the famous British ocean liner, a man named W. T. Stead lost his life along with hundreds of other passengers on the ship. Over the next several years he was in communication from the next dimension or spirit world with his daughter, Estelle Stead, who was still living on Earth. As recorded in their book, *The Blue Island*, everything seemed to him as physical and material as the world he had just left. He was welcomed by loved ones he had known on Earth, many who had been there for quite a long time. He described the great beauty of his new land with familiar appearances such as buildings: libraries, businesses, concert halls, halls of learning, apartments and houses. His first stop in the new world was on a level very close to the frequency of Earth and therefore only a gradual change from his usual habitat. In this, and in other readings, I've learned that there is a period of orientation experienced by all newcomers in order to familiarize themselves with new laws that differ from the laws of physics governing the material world.

Sylvia Browne states in *Conversations with the Other Side* that "Your true existence is in another dimension we call the Other Side. This dimension has a higher frequency of matter, which is beyond the realm of your five senses. It's a dimension where you reside for eternity, except for your sojourn to a plane of unreality (like Earth), where you temporarily dwell to experience and learn for the evolvement of your soul. The Other Side is your real Home."[4] Browne describes the beauty of the other side as glorious and "unbelievable." The lawns are lush and green, the flowers are larger and more colorful. There are wooded areas, mountains, lakes and oceans much like those found on the earth, however more beautiful than we can imagine. Not only will we be greeted by our loved ones, but our pets are waiting there for us too. She tells us that we will have bodies that look physical and that are more real to us than the bodies we have on Earth. We can choose our own features and colors and shapes. If we're a bit overweight in our physical body here, we'll be able to make adjustments there, and our appearance will be as we wish it to be. Most choose to look more youthful than when they left their Earth existence. Our social and educational lives continue on the Other Side with opportunities to be involved in any of the arts, sciences, philosophies, and athletics. There are infinite opportunities for service there, including healing, teaching and working directly with those left behind on the earth plane, and many, many more.

Through reading and studying the subject of the other side of life, I have learned that we will find ourselves residing on the level which corresponds to our own soul frequency and will therefore be with those of similar soul development. Farnese tells us that spheres in the spirit world are separate creations of "the particular class of minds that have created it, and those whose minds are in affinity, being drawn to each other in the spirit world, every place will bear more or less the peculiar stamp of its inhabitants."[5] We will be able to visit other levels if we wish. Again, "in my Father's House are many mansions." We can visit a higher level by invitation or arrangement and easily transport ourselves to a level below our own for a visit or for our own adventure or research.

During our life on Earth we can practice the following concept in preparation for our sleep time adventures each night. Watch your dreams . . . what are the paths taken in your night time dreams? What you read, see on television or think about just before falling asleep has for the most part a great deal to do with your dream life. You create a frequency which corresponds to the level of your dream travel. If your dreams become nightmarish or negative, check your thoughts and attitudes of the day or the fears that drive you in everyday living. However, sometimes nightmares are the only way the dreamtime is remembered or can communicate with us. In some cases it then brings important information we have not remembered any other way. Many inventions have come through nightmares; for example, Elias Howe and the sewing machine. The story is that Howe needed to figure out a better place to put the eye of the needle than in the middle of it. One night in a dream he was threatened with death by a group of cannibals carrying spears. The spears were shaped like needles but they had holes near the outer ends of the spear blades. On waking, he immediately made a model of this new version of the needle and created a sewing machine that worked well.

You might want to make a habit of reading and thinking about something inspirational or perhaps listening to soft classical or other soothing music just before falling asleep. A good way to clarify, and in many cases atone for your actions of the day, is to review your day backwards just before falling asleep. Backwards, because we see the effect of an action, and then the cause is revealed as we go back to an earlier time in the day. This exercise has a farther-reaching effect of helping us to be more responsible for our thoughts and actions in a preventive way, as well. Some teachers and writers have compared this concept to that of a sort of purgatory, a purging of negative attitudes or our life review soon after our arrival in the next dimension.

CHAPTER 11

More Contacts with Ann

*All realities and outcomes exist
simultaneously but do not interfere
with each other. Your perception
determines the shape of your reality.*

Penney Peirce

IN ADDITION TO THE STORY of Ann Manser and her mention of her life review in the *shack* in the desert, I had a dream visit with her not long after she came to take me on a tour of her immediate area of *heaven*. In the dream, which I interpreted as an actual visit to her dimension, I found myself knocking at the door of a small one-room cottage or *shack* in a desert setting. Ann opened the door and invited me to come in for a visit. She explained that she was still working on her afterlife review but could take a brief break. She was wearing a light blue batiste gown and housecoat that fell just below her knees. I felt very aware of her surroundings and so glad to have a few moments with her. There were windows above her writing table, not low enough to distract her from her work, but they gave her a view of the Las Vegas skyline when she stood up.

A few months later, I contacted a man to whom Ann had frequently referred as a fellow metaphysical teacher and writer. She had known him for many years. They taught many of the same concepts from different angles. I wanted to meet him and ask him more about my teacher in her earlier years of teaching and writing. He agreed to our meeting, and we scheduled a visit at his home in Sarasota. Don was a serious man, and he talked a lot about his early acquaintance with Ann and their mutual students in other parts of the country. He mentioned that he had met with her several times in her dimension after her transition. I could barely contain my excitement as he told me about looking for her and finding her in a shack in the desert with a view of the Las Vegas skyline. He added, "She is always wearing the same thing—a thin light blue gown and housecoat. She's very involved in her life review so I don't linger long when I'm there." When he was finished, I shared with him my own similar dream visit with her. His experience was certainly a confirmation for mine.

This was not the end of my contact with Ann. She has appeared to me many times in my dreams, although not as frequently as she did during the first ten years after her transition. I continued as her student on the inner planes (spiritual realms), in her dimension, and I recall many enlightening classes with her and her assistants. Some dealt with color as used for healing. When she had to be away for her own higher education and retreats or teaching assignments she provided substitute teachers for our classes. An interesting thing that happened in the classes was when she went around the table and asked her students personal questions, sometimes regarding signs of their spiritual development, the other students were unable to hear the individual answers. The information given was between Ann and the student. One question I recall being asked was, "And what do you do regularly to raise your frequency for your spiritual work?" My answer was, "One of the things I do is to listen to classical music." She smiled in approval.

In September 1979, I watched as Ann worked in a dream visit with a map of our world spread out on her desktop. She was very focused on cutting out our countries and trimming some of them, aligning them again in a slightly different configuration from what we see on our maps of the world today. As I thought about the dream, I couldn't help but wonder if she was showing me the way the world will look after some of the predicted Earth changes have taken place.

In the early 1980s, after I moved to Nashville to pursue graduate degrees at Vanderbilt University, I asked Ann in a dream if she would help me learn Universal Law on a deeper level. Just as there are immutable laws which govern physics or chemistry or biology in our material world, there are certain immutable laws which govern our levels of consciousness. For example, the Law of Action and Reaction or Cause and Effect, the Law of Cycles, Periodicity, the Law of Abundance and the Law of Attraction are but a few of them. She said to me, "But you know the Laws, just practice them." I then told her I wanted to know them in greater depth. She hesitated, looked away, then looked again at me through a half smile and responded with, "Yes, I will help you then." As my life became more and more complicated I finally realized that Ann was indeed helping me to learn Universal Law in depth!

Although my contact with Ann is much less often now, it does occur periodically, often as a nudge or a prod, and sometimes to show me a principle or a quality of which I need to be aware. Our contact is usually in my dream state and is always a special treat for me. I know that she is involved in very important work in her dimension and perhaps in other dimensions as well. Because of the strong connection we had on Earth, I feel that I can reach Ann when I need an answer to a worthy question or special assistance with something. If she cannot be available for me, she will send another spirit entity to assist me. I feel fortunate, indeed.

When Ann was still on Earth she occasionally phoned me with questions such as, "What am I cooking for my lunch?" . . . or "for my dinner? What am I wearing today?" She was trying to help me with my psychic development, and I would answer her sometimes with correct responses. She surprised me, when I was studying privately with her, by handing me her deck of Shustah cards and asking me to read the cards for her. Read for my Teacher? I almost had an anxiety attack right there! She helped me to calm down and impishly asked me again to read for her. I whispered a silent prayer and began my reading. My interpretations could have been all wrong, but she didn't correct me. She was very encouraging and thoughtfully expanded some of my interpretations so they made some sense in relationship to her life. I know now that she was attempting to inspire me to develop my sensitivity for this work now, as well as for use at that earlier time. Because I was very involved in my oil painting during this time period, she called me occasionally to check out the mixture of certain colors. She was a water colorist, but more important, she was reading auras and creating her *Aurascopes*.

Of course we were talking about different mediums, however I learned a lot from those explorations. Her work related more to light combinations while mine used pigment mixtures which are heavy and opaque. The combinations of colors and the results were very different, of course. What distinguishes the color studies of the Pages of Shustah from the mainstream teachings of other esoteric literature is the strong emphasis on deeper meanings and the delineation of color itself. With the Pages of Shustah color process, a way of translating vibratory frequencies into color, one can learn how to help others, how to better know oneself, and how to understand animals, among many other insightful experiences. For example, suppose you have an important job interview. A color you might use could be a golden-yellow, a color of creative expression and one-to-one communication. You might wear the color visibly or under your outer clothing or you might visualize it around you.

Color can be used as a tool for manifesting the vibratory frequency of anything in your life. Color can connect you with the thing you desire through the *law of attraction*. When you express a particular vibratory frequency, whether in thought, image, word, or action, it creates the environment in and around you that can attract to you anything else in the world that vibrates to the same frequency. The more specific and focused your expression, the better your chances are of receiving just what your heart desires. You must really *feel it*. This is the basic law of attraction. We can be attracted to people because of the colors in their auras, in particular their permanent auras, perhaps because of the compatibility of our auras. If you find your life full of conditions and obstacles that seem to deter you from realizing your goals, take a good look at the kinds of thoughts you're entertaining and the quality of energy you are expressing. Sometimes you can be aware of the energy you are putting out consciously, but often it is on a subconscious level and you must dig a little deeper to identify it.

The subconscious mind perceives things in a very literal way. For example, I made a discovery about myself when I went through the process of Rolfing (structural integration) many years ago. Before the Rolfing sessions, I had a habit of walking slightly on the outside of my feet without making much contact between my whole foot and the ground. I later became aware of my frequent use of the phrase, "I just don't understand." After the ligaments and tendons in my feet were lengthened by the Rolfing techniques, my feet were able to make full contact with the ground and for the first time in many years I was able "to stand on my own two feet!" As a result, my life went through some major changes. My subconscious mind interpreted my body language and thought patterns, before Rolfing, as my attempt to avoid standing on my own two feet.

My mother had surgery for the removal of cataracts on both of her eyes around the time I was becoming aware of specific connections between our subconscious minds and our health. I often heard her say, "I just can't *see* why that happened," or "I don't *see* why I have to do that." You get the idea. She was in fact programming her subconscious mind not to see. It appeared that her subconscious mind interpreted her comments literally to mean she couldn't see or didn't want to see. In both of these examples my mother and I were using negative affirmations even though we weren't aware of doing so. Louise Hay tells us that "Whatever we believe becomes true for us," and we become caught up in what Hay calls a "limiting belief" without realizing it. One of my favorite handbooks for learning about and working with mental patterns behind "dis-ease" is Hay's book, *You Can Heal Your Life*.[1] In this book she offers explanations of the patterns in our lives that cause *dis-ease*, and teaches us how to overcome them through development of new thought patterns and through affirmations designed for healing specific conditions.

If you study the meanings of colors you can use color to help create the vibratory frequency for the object or condition you desire. Pay attention to the colors that surround you in your home, your workplace and the clothes that you wear. Color has universal meaning, and we make it personal by the way we use it in our everyday lives. I have a favorite quote from Manser's *Pages of Shustah*, "From a half-hidden violet nestling under a leaf, to the gaudiest of sunflowers blazing over a board fence, is suggested the whole meaning of Cosmic Creation."[2]

The color red when used in a clear, vibrant shade can aid you in physical activity, courage and enthusiasm. You can use blue to expand the mind, and for reasoning ability in mental tasks. Pink is a magnetic color and the color of attraction and could be beneficial in any situation where you want to attract attention of many or of one person, as in the job interview. A clear, soothing green can be healing, and a vibrant emerald green can promote something you desire. I have several shades of blue in my own aura and I am attracted to blue in clothing. But at a particular time in my life I became attracted to shades of emerald green. I was wearing that color one day when Ann asked me what I was trying to promote. I must have looked puzzled when she began to explain that she had seen me in the color so often that she wondered if I was working on a project. I told her I had been working on a college admission application and was planning to go back to school. She said, "That's it, you're promoting your plan to go back to college." Rose is the color of Universal love, a kind and powerful compassionate color. Indigo apparently helped me prevent pain from a tooth extraction one time. I was able to avoid taking medication for the pain that I was told I should anticipate. Violet is a powerful color for transmuting a negative situation. For example, if you find yourself in a place around people where there is a feeling of negativity, you can visualize a brilliant violet light filling the room or the space around you and the crowd of people.

You are the magician, and it takes focus and intention to achieve what you want, but a successful outcome is certainly within the realm of possibility. I sometimes use a vision of cool violet flames consuming the negative energy of the space around me, especially if I find myself in a questionable public place that I cannot leave immediately. This benefits everyone in that place. White light is often used for personal protection and for raising the vibratory frequency of the space around you. The *Shustah* teaching goes beyond the physical spectrum of seven color bands and uses an expanded twelve-color spectrum which includes silver, light, cream, rose and russet. Color is a valuable tool you can use anytime, anywhere, because it can be used as a mental tool.

CHAPTER 12

A Remarkable Woman Named Patricia

"We'll be friends forever, won't we, Pooh?" asked Piglet.
"Even longer," Pooh answered.

~ A. A. Milne

EARLIER, I MENTIONED THAT ANN Manser had students all over the United States and in other parts of the world. She had a group of students in Omaha, Nebraska with whom she spent some actual class time on occasion. The coordinator for that particular class was a woman named Patricia "Pat" Larson. Pat was also secretary for Pages of Shustah, Incorporated, so Ann and Pat were in close communication regarding the work. Our class with Ann, in St. Petersburg, numbered six to eight students who met weekly around Ann's dining room table in her apartment. We studied and discussed specific material such as *The Evolution of Consciousness*[1] lectures, principles of color, dreams and other specific and general metaphysical topics. There was a time designated for open discussions on any topic we wished to explore. Ann was a teacher who knew how to draw answers from within our inner beings. She didn't supply all of our answers but demonstrated to us that we had many of them ourselves and showed us how we could access them when we needed them, through meditation and contemplation.

During one of our evening classes, Ann was discussing a topic with us when she referred to something being studied in Pat Larson's group in Omaha. This was early in our class association and I had not heard of Pat Larson. When she spoke Pat's name, however, I experienced what might be called an instant soul recognition. I think I interrupted Ann when I impulsively blurted out, "I know Pat!" Ann looked at me and said, "Have you been to Omaha?" Of course I knew I hadn't. I was embarrassed, and apologized for my impulsivity. I was also puzzled. Why was Pat's name so familiar to me, and why did I instantly feel that I knew her? Of course I didn't know her . . . or did I? I could almost visualize her physical being.

Earlier, I mentioned Ann's special talent for seeing and reading auras, the energy field in glowing colors around people and animals. Ann's ability went farther than that of most aura readers. She could attune to what she termed the invariant aura or the more permanent part of

85

the auric field, not to be confused with the changing or mood auras or the health auras seen by most clairvoyants. The invariant aura gives us a deeper understanding of where we have been, why we are here and where we are going. Ann read over a thousand auras in her lifetime and presented her interpretations in a written form which she called an *Aurascope*.

After my soul recognition experience with Pat Larson, Ann asked me to meditate and see if I could identify some of the colors in Pat's aura. She had already given Pat her own *Aurascope*, so Pat's colors were known to her. I carried out Ann's request and verbally discussed my impressions of Pat with her. Ann had suggested that I do a painting depicting an interpretation of the colors I saw with Pat. I didn't get that far, however I felt that Pat had some autumn colors—gold, light yellow, green, and perhaps a pleasant shade of red. These colors, according to Ann, were in Pat's aura along with several others, including some shades of blue. I eventually made a phone call to Pat, in Omaha, and told her about my experience. She was delighted, and we corresponded and communicated by phone and by letter until we met, almost two years later, at a Spiritual Frontiers Fellowship (SFF) Conference on the University of North Carolina campus in Charlotte. I saw her walking across the front of the auditorium the morning after my arrival on the campus and immediately knew who she was. We later visited and planned our schedules so we could attend some of the same workshops. We discovered that among our mutual interests was the exploration of the world of color and we attended an evening lecture on the Dinshah *Spectrochrome* methods of healing with color.[2] I later became the recipient of three original Dinshah *Spectrochrome* machines which I have used in healing for many years. The original *Spectrochrome* system uses five glass colored slides, or filters, mixed to produce twelve colors. An apparatus with a high wattage bulb, 500-1000 watts, is used to project the prescribed color onto an area of the body for the healing of that body part or organ. After the conference, Pat and I stayed in close touch by phone and mail, and especially during the span of Ann Manser's illness.

Several years after Ann's transition, Pat and the Omaha class hosted a Shustah conference in Omaha to which all of Ann's students were invited. Many of her students from around the country were in attendance. The conference was held at a local hotel in Omaha with Reverend LeRoy Zemke as our keynote speaker. LeRoy was one of Ann's first students in the Tampa Bay area of Florida and her close friend for many years. He was, and is, senior minister of the Temple of the Living God, a nondenominational church and education center in St. Petersburg. He is also a popular world traveler and teacher of spiritual law and spiritual development and their practical application in everyday living. In Omaha, we convened to discuss and make plans for the future of Pages of Shustah, Incorporated and to establish contacts with other students and coordinators of the work. A highlight of our social agenda was a party which was called a "Come as You Were" party. It was such fun to see people in costumes that depicted a former lifetime they wished to dramatize. The social director for this party had planned for each person present to give a five-minute synopsis of the life they attempted to portray. What fun it was to hear all of the different lives and periods of time represented! Many of the participants claimed to have had actual memories of those incarnations and others had received information about their past in past-life regressions from psychic readers or healers or therapists. A very popular and effective therapy now is "Past Life Regression" used primarily for identifying the origins of past life trauma patterns and healing those patterns that are causing some dysfunction in this lifetime.

Pat chose to dress for the party as a pioneer woman from the Wild West with her long gingham dress and pioneer bonnet. The life I chose to portray was one of a medieval maiden inspired by a visit to the Metropolitan Museum of Art in New York City. While visiting the museum I was drawn repeatedly to the medieval room of art and artifacts with very positive memories or feelings that I might have experienced a life during that era. Most of you have surely had feelings of familiarity with a place, a person or a situation, and I'll bet you've said something like, "I feel like I've been here before" or "I feel like I've known you all of my life." Many countries of our world were represented at this "Come as You Were" gathering with some of the guests dressed as beings or aliens from other planets. This exercise served as a learning experience of the possibilities of past incarnations as well as a great ice-breaker for becoming acquainted with fellow Shustah students.

We were fortunate to have a few students who were gifted with the ability to channel information from the spirit world. On our program for the conference was a woman named Virginia who graciously accepted the challenge of channeling for our contact with Ann Manser in her dimension. A list of questions for Ann had been formulated by students before our sitting was scheduled so there would be no interruption during the transmission. In that transmission, Ann gave us several directives for presenting her life's work to students, but her main advice at that time was to revise the work, not to change it but to update its form. This has now been accomplished, complete with charts and illustrations.

Pat and I developed a close friendship over a twenty-five year period of time, investigating past incarnations we felt we had shared, gathering information from various psychic readers on our relationships in those lives, and asking how we could best work together in this lifetime. We were separated only by miles and made good use of the United States Postal Service, our telephone service and airline service often to visit and do our work together. Pat often said, because we didn't live near each other, "What a waste of compatibility!" I agreed wholeheartedly. We established that we were and are indeed "forever friends!" We were *sure* we were twin souls and at times we knew just what the other was thinking about on any given subject. It delighted us that we were so "in sync." We had some extraordinarily deep discussions about our metaphysical studies and work, with our levels of comprehension and about it all being completely compatible. When we traveled together by automobile we liked to take a particularly challenging book or other piece of reading material and read to each other with detailed and in-depth discussions of our reading topics.

Pat and her husband, Bill, with another couple owned a lovely vacation home in Estes Park, Colorado. We occasionally drove from Omaha to Estes Park to spend several days hiking in the Rocky Mountains, reading, talking and meditating in front of a roaring fire in the evening or having dinner in special restaurants around the canyon country. We made the most of every moment together because we always knew our next visit would have to wait a few months. Bill was a golfer, so when he was scheduled for a golfing trip out of state, Pat was on the phone with me to plan our retreat together especially at those times. I made frequent visits to Omaha and Pat visited me in Nashville occasionally, and at other times at Sparrow Hawk Village where I lived and worked for several years in Tahlequah, Oklahoma. We especially enjoyed our times floating on the Illinois River on huge inner tubes in the foothills of the Ozark Mountains. Our favorite place remained Estes Park with the beauty of nature all around us as we hiked the mountain trails. We could even see the stars at night in the clear indigo sky, and we almost felt that we could reach up and count them by touching them. We liked to go out on the deck at night and look for UFOs, and there were times when we were sure we had seen a few. Pat was writing a book of lessons for her course, *Ageless Wisdom for Today's World*. We spent many of our mornings during one visit to Estes Park meditating, going over the lessons and editing and proofreading which of course stimulated more deep discussions.

On one of our hikes in the Rockies, we were pretty far up a mountain trail when it began to snow. Pat knew the trail well and was ten or more feet ahead of me. She immediately turned around and told me to start running back down the mountain. She explained that the snow so quickly covered the trails we would soon not be able to see them. There was danger of getting off the trail and falling through covered brush into a ravine. Like children, we bounded down the trail, and she was right; the snow came down so fast and in such large flakes that it didn't take long for it to completely cover our trail. With all the unexpected exercise, we weren't satisfied with the fruitarian lunches in our backpacks, so we headed for a nearby restaurant. It was rustic, warm and inviting with a roaring fire in the massive rock fireplace. We sat and enjoyed a leisurely end to our trail adventure with lunch and cups of hot tea. What wonderful memories we made!

One winter, on one of Pat's visits to Nashville, we drove from there to Atlanta where we stayed a few days to visit with friends and colleagues involved in spiritual work. From Atlanta we drove to Asheville, North Carolina where we were able to have some time with Pat's son, Chris, and his wife, Mary Ann. We were staying in a bed and breakfast near Asheville and decided we should have fruit in our room for snacking. We found a natural foods market and stocked up on fruit and nuts. I was the driver, and when we returned to the car with our groceries, one of us said something unusually funny. We both began laughing so hard that we couldn't stop. The laughing would subside and I would start the car and have to turn it off when we burst into laughter again—to the point of tears! This happened a few times before we could calm ourselves enough to get the car started and drive safely back to our bed and breakfast. I can't recall ever having laughed so hard and for so long, and the experience set the tone for a magnificent visit and indelible memories of that trip.

Pat was a lovely petite and energetic woman. Born Patricia Ruth Morey in Palisade, Nebraska on August 30, 1926, she was a *double Virgo*—Sun and Ascendant in Virgo with her Moon in the sign of Gemini. The elder of two girls in her family, she entered nurse's training at Immanuel Hospital in the Cadet Nurse Corps. Upon graduation, and as a registered nurse, she worked in the nursery of the Clarkson Veteran's Administration Hospital in Omaha. We had this profession in common; I was also a registered nurse in earlier years. Pat married Bill, an architect, and they became parents of a daughter and two sons.

Pat and Bill traveled throughout the world with their children and with close friends. I loved hearing stories of their exciting travels: to the pyramids in Egypt; the Blarney Stone in Ireland, St. Andrews Golf Course in Scotland and many other exotic locations. I had my own personal talking travelogue. Pat wanted me to marry again and travel with them. She even played cupid for a friend of theirs and me. It didn't work out but she didn't give up.

Pat was Coordinator and Seminar Chairwoman for Spectra Incorporated, a program which drew well-known speakers and seminar leaders in metaphysical topics to Omaha, and the area became a hub for these programs and activities. She coordinated large Expos of New Age speakers who offered workshops and seminars. She was also an Executive Director on the Paranormal Claims Research Board. She of course coordinated groups of students who studied Pages of Shustah. While Ann Manser was still teaching her classes, she told us that she had spent most of her adult life writing her Shustah lessons and related study material. She emphasized to us, "I've brought the work into material form and now it can be rewritten in an updated form." She asked for volunteers among her students to adapt her writings for specific population categories such as a neophyte work for students who are beginning to take metaphysical study seriously; a children's version of the work which would be written in a form that would teach children principles and laws of life on their levels of comprehension; and the color work, a symbolic language for the principles and laws of life as we work with and are exposed to light and color in everyday living for healing, learning, spiritual values and many other levels of application. I have a manuscript in progress on this color work, and Pat volunteered to write the lessons for neophytes. Her resulting work is in the form of the earlier mentioned study course called *Ageless Wisdom for Today's World*. She bridged the metaphysical concepts with concepts for practical application, with subjects ranging from the *aura, reincarnation and karma, chakras,* to *evolutionary development* and more. She included a study guide and meditation for each lesson. The *Ageless Wisdom Study Course* was published in a three-ring binder and illustrated for added comprehension. A few years later she published a cassette tape album of twelve meditations with background music by Leah S. Wilkins. Pat continued teaching her course in *Ageless Wisdom* until her health deteriorated so she could no longer hold her classes.

Pat worked hard and she played hard. I learned many things from her, but her ability to play impressed me as much as almost anything else. Her mind was busy and creative. She liked to plan and plan and plan. She was a master organizer and investigator. She knew how to get the most out of any situation. I might have had a vague idea of what I wanted from a particular excursion, but Pat knew how to get the very ultimate from the same excursion. She did her homework and she knew almost everything that a place or situation had to offer. Traveling with Pat was always a special adventure. She didn't waste any time getting around. Although I was a bit younger, I had difficulty keeping up with her at times. We had both been nurses and had developed a pretty swift nurse's gait, but Pat had me beat. Even with her shorter legs, she moved quickly. I recall a day when we went to visit her Aunt Lola in a hospital. We started down the corridor side-by-side. In a few moments she was gaining several strides ahead and finally looked around at me, making a vigorous effort to keep up, and asked, "Are you coming?" Panting, I told her to keep going and I would catch up eventually.

Pat, Pioneer Woman

Ann, Medieval Maiden

LeRoy and Pat

Pat on a Rocky Mountain Trail

Ann by a Rocky Mountain Stream

CHAPTER 13

Saying Goodbye, and Hello Again

Death is not the end, it is simply
walking out of the physical form and
into the spiritual realm, which is our
true home. It's going back home.

~ Stephen Christopher

I CALLED PAT ONE FEBRUARY morning for one of our catch-up visits. She was in her early seventies by then, although she never looked nor performed near her chronological age. At the beginning of our conversation, I asked her what she had planned for the day. It was snowing in Omaha, and Pat impressed me with, "Bill and I are going sledding down the hill behind our house in a little while." I loved it—I loved that they were not only able but that they still enjoyed so much doing the things they had always done together. What an inspiration!

Pat and Bill were on vacation in Spain early in the year 2000 when Pat began to experience abdominal pain. It was severe enough to cut their vacation short, so they immediately returned home. Her diagnosis took a while, and in the meantime we wondered about a possible spastic colon or a similar condition. For many years she had been involved in an alternative and holistic lifestyle using natural remedies for any health concerns. We shared that philosophy, too. But even with extra dietary discretion Pat's symptoms and pain increased. She was finally given a diagnosis of ovarian cancer. Throughout her illness, I was ever the optimist. After all, Pat was invincible! She had weathered many demanding challenges before and I was certain she would outsmart this one. We had plans to travel to the British Isles in the summer of 2001, a pretty powerful goal for both of us. We kept it in front of us and were so positive it would happen that we continued to make lists of things we wanted to do on our trip. We would look up records of ancestors in England and Scotland and check out some names given us in past life readings. Pat was using a combination of alternative and allopathic treatment, was encouraged many times and at times was discouraged. Even in one of our last conversations she assured me with, "Now don't give up on our trip; I'm going to beat this thing and we're going to the

British Isles!" She lost ground rapidly and wasn't able to win over the last round of treatment. Pat made her transition on January 24, 2001 with her husband and her sister at her bedside. Reportedly, she was completely conscious when she reached for both of them, gave them a last hug and said, "It's time for me to go," and she departed for her new life in another dimension.

In a beautiful memorial service, her adult children, husband, Bill, other family and friends celebrated her life as she would have wanted in an upbeat review of her loving and productive life on Earth. There were photographs of Pat displayed in various stages of her life, video clips of her years with Bill and their children and the music she loved. Among her favorites were John Lennon's "Imagine," and Pachelbel's *Canon in D*. I had sent her a tape of this canon several years earlier. She told me, after she received it, that it had been one of her favorite pieces of music and that she had planned to buy it when she could find the name of it. I was thrilled that it was chosen for her memorial service.

My closest friend was gone. I couldn't just pick up the phone for our regular visits and catch-up sessions. We weren't going to the British Isles together. No more hikes together on the Rocky Mountain trails. What would I do without my precious friend, Pat?

With every day that passed, I seemed obsessed with wondering where Pat was and what she was doing. I knew she would be busy—she was always busy with something new and exciting! I wanted to know all about it. I bought a lovely treasure chest for the safekeeping of my letters and cards, pictures and gifts from Pat. It filled up quickly. I filled a photo album with pictures and memoirs of our wonderful trips and adventures together. Right away, I began dedicating some time to her in meditation and in what felt like one-sided conversations. I started a journal for my attempts to contact her and wrote notes to her almost daily. I had no doubt that she was receiving my notes and how I wished I could receive responses from her. I asked her for dream visits. About a month after her transition, I began to have memories of dream visits with Pat. The first one came to me on February 27, 2001: Pat came to visit me in my home and told me she was a bit weary from her long journey and that after she had taken a relaxing bath she would like to visit for a while. I was so excited to see her! In the dream I provided her with fine scented soaps, salts, lotions and fluffy thirsty towels, and then I drew a warm bath for her. She soon recovered and was ready to go again. We went shopping at an international market for something Mediterranean and delicious to eat. Pat liked fine foods and exotic flavors. She chose some favorite cheeses and we sat and ate and talked until the dream visit ended. I was not able to recall much of our conversation but the visit was reassuring and comforting.

In March, she came for me in a dream and we made our trip to the British Isles! I didn't recall many of the details, but she seemed proud of herself that she had been able to make it happen. She kept her promise . . . we did indeed have our trip to the British Isles! There were many other dreams, some about being together with her family and then with my family. We went to an outdoor concert, to a musical stage production and took short trips through her old neighborhood in the Regency Park section of Omaha. There were many more dream visits and I shall share only a few that might be more universally significant.

In an early May 2001 dream visit, I was watching and listening as Pat explained something pertinent to my personal spiritual growth. There were convex shaped door-sized windows lined up in a row from right to left. I say right to left because Pat demonstrated her points to me in that direction. There were ten principles that needed my attention, principles such as *security*, *stewardship*, *vigilance*, *release*, *trust*, and five others. As Pat focused on one of the principles and explained the meaning specifically for my work with them, the window with scenes depicting that principle would light up. These are principles that cannot be mastered in a short time but must be learned in depth, gradually, and integrated at the soul level. They are steps and stages having to do with the development of inner consciousness. The windows had dimensions depicted in colors and images that moved and then paused for my reflection. In my waking state, I found that I couldn't work with more than one or two at a time. I wrote each one on an index card in bold letters and on the back of each card I wrote the definitions, intuitions and any other research pertaining to the principle. Insights in the use of each principle are being kept in a journal. I am forever grateful for this kind of guidance and assistance from my forever friend.

A few nights after the dream visit with Pat, in which she explained the visions in the ten windows, I had another dream visit with her. We were among a fairly large group of people sitting around a long dinner table eating a meal together. I asked Pat if she knew anyone there—I didn't know anyone but Pat. She vaguely knew one of the guests, or at least knew who he was. Other than that, they all seemed like strangers to both of us. After dinner was over, a social director stood up, the table was removed and music began playing in the background. The social director announced that everyone was invited to do some folk dancing and we could choose partners if we wished. Pat and I of course chose each other. The music moved more to the foreground and we were taught dance steps to folk music. Pat was dressed casually in khaki pants and a light blue denim jacket. I believe her shirt was red or was trimmed in red. The music and dancing paused for a moment and we resumed our conversation. I was asking her about her new residence there and in fact wondered if she thought it was a beautiful place to be when I suddenly began to withdraw to go back to my physical body. I wasn't ready to leave, and as I traveled through the tube or tunnel back to my own dimension I was actually repeating my question to Pat, "Do you think your new home is a beautiful place to be?" The suction through the tunnel was too strong and I couldn't delay my return. But I could still see Pat until she became a tiny dot in a brilliant light at the other end of the tunnel. I was immediately awake in my own bed with this experience fresh in my mind. As I wrote about it in my journal, I realized I had just shared in a social gathering planned as a part of Pat's orientation process on the other side. Although we conversed while I was with her, I was not sure if we were speaking aloud or communicating by telepathy. Her voice quality sounded the same that it always had on Earth, so I might have been translating her thoughts into audible vocal sounds through an inner mechanism of my own. My inner ears have also heard her voice in meditation and I've recognized the voice quality as being hers.

One evening, I knew I could feel Pat with me as I spoke to her and listened for her in meditation. It was a Thursday evening, and I told her that I knew she could hear me but I couldn't hear her. So I suggested that I would get in touch with our mutual friend, Steve Engel, over the following weekend and see if he could find a way to communicate with her. Steve was a student of Ann Manser for many years and was acquainted with Pat through his sister who had previously lived in Omaha. By the next evening, I had not contacted Steve but when I checked my email there was a message from him. He wrote, "Pat Larson is around me a lot today and I don't know why. Pat and I knew each other, but we weren't close, so I don't know why she has come to me." Excitedly, I wrote my response to him, "I sent her to you, Steve. Please see what she has to say. I've been talking to her but it has been a one-way communication because I can't hear her." Steve agreed to pay attention to Pat and to attempt to make contact with her.

Steve was able to make the contact with Pat. The transmission was a short one assuring us of her well-being, sending her love to us and giving me pointers for my practical everyday living. Once I knew Steve could make the contact, I wrote out questions for another contact which was made two days later. In this transmission she explained something about her own preparation at this stage for making the contact with our dimension. The vibratory frequency has to be compatible enough to make the contact. Our atmospheric conditions also affect the ability to make the contact. "Just as there are different radio frequencies within the same room, different worlds or spheres or planes interpenetrate—from the highest vibrations to the lowest."[1] The receiver on our earth plane needs to make preparation mentally and emotionally and to learn to focus in order to create the compatible line of contact—the channel.

Pat shared that she was studying, writing, going to concerts and art exhibits. She described her place of residence for that time as being a small cottage located in a quiet wooded retreat close to a stream. She was studying and writing her autobiography of this life, just lived on Earth. She was also doing other private journaling and some dialogue writing or question and answer dialogue and was working on a play or drama with esoteric messages. "Some of my writing will be used to help people bridge the communication with animals," she said. "I've had this cottage for a very long time—centuries. I always come back to this retreat." She said she was preparing to teach a class. She also mentioned a work place, a place where she does a lot of her research. The building is what is called a "grand house," two stories with windows and turrets, Arabian in design and built of materials resembling beige sandstone. Her assistant is a dark-skinned man named Najbair who looks Middle Eastern. He helps her file papers, brings material such as scripts and music from the library and "provides me of course with fine food. We know each other from the past." She also mentioned a female entity who helps with her research and cataloging. This description gave me a context for thinking about Pat. It enabled me to see her in my interpretation of her abode according to the description she gave me through Steve.

Pat answered many of my questions, one of which was about her contact with Ann Manser on her side of life. Pat's reply, "Yes, I've had some contact with Ann, especially closer to the beginning of my time here and again in April. Her energy field is very strong and radiant. She has not let me see all of her work. Some of it has to do with other planetary evolutions, setting patterns and molds—a multilevel work. She also teaches classes—very high level students. I will have contact with her at appointed times in the future."

Steve had emailed me a question about the name "Shustah." He had been told one thing about its origin, and I told him that Ann Manser had explained that the name had come from a rabbi with the same name. This question was not meant to be a part of this transmission. However, during the transmission, Pat said, "Tell Ann (West) she is right about Master Shustah being a little rabbi. He is a bit . . . not secretive so much, but his energy doesn't shine out. It's there—he just isn't showy about it. He, too, has students." To this, Steve responded with "So you read my email from Ann West?" Chuckling, Pat replied with "Sometimes." Pat had more to say but suggested that she would like to wait until she could give the information to me directly. She suggested a beginning date for me to sit in meditation and be open to her thought transmissions. The date of our first working session was set for Thursday, May 31, 2001.

This might be a good time to explain some things I have learned about our mental capacity after crossing over into a new dimension. George Meek, in *After We Die, What Then?* states that "Everything in our world, this universe and the Cosmos, results from energy, and energy manifests as vibration at some specific frequency."[2] We have light waves and sound waves, all vibrating at different frequencies. It has been determined through extensive work of research scientists that the brain and the mind are not the same thing; that the brain is the computer-like physical vehicle through which the mind operates. "Even the fanciest computer is totally useless unless there is a programmer—some intelligence separate and distinct from the computer itself. It is only in recent decades, a mere instant in humanity's long evolutionary climb, that science has given us a valuable tool which enables us to understand that the mind is the programmer . . ." Now what does this mean for us when we leave the earth and take up residence in another dimension? For one thing, we're no longer limited by the physical brain. Just as the computer limits the information it can put out, the physical brain also limits the information filtered through it. The mind has access to information far beyond its physical boundaries. This is where meditation can be of great assistance because in meditation we set aside the ego and can move into a space that is infinite in knowledge.

Meek also tells us that it can be extremely difficult for those in higher planes of other dimensions to make contact with us because of technical difficulties. We live in an atmosphere so full of disruptive and dissonant frequencies that those in finer vibratory states have great difficulty adjusting their vibratory rates to a point of compatibility which would let them make their contact in our dimension. Meek relates an experience in which "a spirit with a marked French accent introduced himself as Richet" to a medium with whom he was engaged in some research, "and in the course of conversation with him we learned he was the late Professor Charles Richet, the eminent French physiologist who in 1905 was president of the Society for Psychical Research in London and who was the winner of a Nobel Prize in 1913. He told us that not only must the communicating entity lower his own frequency to the lower one of Earth, but simultaneously he must remember what his voice sounded like in his lifetime and recapture memories of happenings which will give proof of his identity to the person with whom he wishes to communicate. When the professor was asked by a sitter whether he could see and hear people at a séance, he answered that it depended on the amount of concentration he put into the effort to do so. If he focused his mind sufficiently, he could both hear and see people on earth; but he found it simpler to apprehend their thoughts before they were uttered as words."[3]

An analogy used by Meek might help to explain the frequency adjustments needed by both dimensions for conscious contact. If we put a pan containing ice on the stove and apply heat, the atomic particles increase their vibratory action. Thus the vibratory rate of the newly-formed water is higher than that of the solid ice. Applying more heat to the water raises its vibratory rate still more. Then the application of still more heat can cause the water particles to fly into space. The resulting steam represents energy at an even greater level of atomic vibration. Conditions relating to thought, both in this and in the astral world, represent energy levels and vibratory rates far beyond that of steam. Each succeeding higher level of thought in the worlds of spirit represents even higher rates of vibration. These next statements are important ones in attempting to understand the distortions that can result when communicating with the spirit world. Those spirits living in higher mental levels have such a high rate of vibration that direct contact through the mind of a medium could result in damage to the medium's physical brain. "Communications from these higher levels have to be relayed down in steps." Transformers or relay stations can be used to step down the vibratory level and may "cause a loss in content, a loss in quality—and may even represent a gross distortion to what the higher-level being is trying to pass down."[4] This could offer an explanation for messages that we receive from the spirit world which cause us to react with statements such as, "that didn't sound like Aunt

Sally," or "I can't relate to what he's trying to tell me." Our spirit contacts apparently have more success with transmitting thoughts through symbols and pictures. These transmissions do not give us word for word messages but a complete thought which requires the recipient to decipher the symbols. This happens also in our dreams.

In the afterlife dimension, the mode of communication is mental telepathy or thought transmission. This is the way we receive impressions from other dimensions, and as previously mentioned, through visual symbolic language as well. The spirit who wishes to communicate with our dimension is limited by the life experience of the psychic or medium receiving the transmission. If the spirit is speaking of something unfamiliar to the medium, there might be confusion with the interpretation of the message. Because the vibratory frequency is so much higher and faster in the higher dimensions, the medium is sometimes challenged to keep up with the message being communicated.

CHAPTER 14

New Journeys with Pat

Often, spirits have been around you for
much longer than you recognize, just waiting
for you to reach a point of openness that
permits you to know of their presence.

Rita S. Berkowitz and
Deborah S. Romaine

ON MAY THIRTY-FIRST I AWOKE excited about the new journey I would take with Pat. She was going to help me learn to communicate with her in her new dimension. This would become a whole new chapter in my own life! Through Steve Engel, we had set an evening for our first session. This was also the evening of the Commencement Ceremony for one of the schools where I was most involved in my work as an Educational Therapist. One of my clients, an eighth grade student, would graduate that evening. I couldn't miss this special celebration with her. I felt I needed to be quiet and prayerful in preparation for my big experience with Pat, and I also wanted to be cheerful and encouraging for my student as she shared her big moment of accomplishment with me. She had worked hard to get to this point, and I wouldn't disappoint her. I was almost giddy as I moved among the guests at the reception following the ceremony, being friendly, visiting with old friends and congratulating the graduating class. In all the spaces between conversations I was very aware of my little secret . . . that I would soon be working with my precious friend, Pat, on the other side of life.

Driving home, I was in a heightened mode of anticipation, actually trembling with excitement. Now I needed to rid my subtle bodies of the outer world vibrations, so I showered and visualized these vibrations being washed away and replaced by glistening white light. By nine o'clock, the computer was turned on with a fresh page for notation as our session began. The set-up included a glass of drinking water, a shallow clear bowl of water, lighted candles and fresh cut flowers in a vase. These were suggested by Pat to represent the elements and to add to an ambience of tranquility for meditation. I sat, and for a few minutes I read inspirational material to soothing music. Then I began with a prayer and took several deep breaths for total relaxation. I was ready to call upon Pat now. As instructed, I called her name a few times and just waited. She had told me that she could be with me within a few minutes of my call. I was not far into the session when I began to feel a change in my own energy pattern. I could feel a warmth and pulsating action around my heart chakra. At first I thought it was still the lingering feeling of excitement, but the more I relaxed the stronger the pulsations seemed to be. I would soon learn that this was a part of adjusting my frequency to blend it with the higher frequencies I wanted to contact. I felt the contact was being made although I was not able to receive any definite impressions on this first trial. I knew there would be a period of preparation for me and that I must be patient.

During the summer months, I added a session per day after checking with Pat through Steve to be sure she would be available—one in the morning and one in the evening. I so looked forward to these sessions—I was pretty eager. I began to have more awareness of some of the subtle activities during the sessions. One evening, I clearly saw a man standing next to me working with what looked like some kind of electrical equipment with wires hooked to machines and leading to some part of my upper body and head. He was dark-skinned and wrapped in a kind of orange-colored sarong-type garment. He could have been Haitian or East Indian. Then I thought of Najbair, Pat's assistant. I was fascinated with all that was going on. In a later session, I psychically saw a disk, about twenty-four inches in diameter, directly over my head—approximately fifteen to twenty inches above me. It had a bright light under it and reminded me of pictures I had seen of "flying saucers." I asked Pat if there was such an object over my head at that time and she replied, "Yes, it's an *infusor.*" I knew the meaning of infusion but I didn't know about an infusor. So after the session ended I looked for the word in the dictionary. It was not listed in that form in my dictionary.

On October twentieth of the same year, I invited my friend LeRoy Zemke, a very fine and well-known spiritual intuitive mentioned earlier, to join me in my session with Pat. He was in town to lead a seminar and very graciously agreed to observe and participate in our contact session. The room was set up as usual; I was at the computer and LeRoy was sitting at the end of my desk about six feet to my right. Our preparatory ritual included a prayer, an affirmation of Light and *The Great Invocation. The Great Invocation* from the Master Djwhal Khul can be found in Chapter 20 in this book and in some of Alice A. Bailey's publications. LeRoy joined in reciting these with me, and we began our meditation and contact. He agreed to speak aloud his impressions so that I could type them on the computer as the session progressed. The following is a transcript of that session:

L. Z.   I see a spiral of blue light surrounding you, moving down your body to the solar plexus. The whole field is silvery-white. There is throat work being done—a lot of blue, a lot of heat. Pat and her teacher are working together. Pat is standing near you, Ann, with both hands on your shoulders. She appears to be making an effort to integrate into the force field. (Pat turned to LeRoy and asked him to help with the energy around my throat. He instructed me to breathe deeply, to let my mind go blank and watch words being formed). There is a switchboard with switches connected to chemical chambers—to activate bodies and levels. Pat's assistant is working the switches. The bridge has been formed and good channeling work should be taking place in about six months.

Pat: I know why I get to work with her (Ann West). You remember that I was always so impatient about wanting things to happen *right now*. Ann wants this to happen faster than it can. She has to allow the links in the chain to be strengthened—"telephone lines" to be connected. Think of it this way—these links are like chips in a computer. They are in place but they have to be activated.

L. Z.: (Later in session). Pat looks bright.

Pat: Do you think I've changed?

L. Z.: Yes, you look younger.

Pat: (Smiling). I've worked hard to make my appearance be in a way that I'm comfortable with it as it relates to the pattern I held on the earth. I am not going to maintain that always. It will be different. I will be taller (Pat was about five feet tall in her physical body), with a darker complexion—more olive-skinned.

L. Z.: (At end of session). Pat is still standing behind you, Ann, with her hands on both your shoulders. She is now giving you a hug from the back.

Ann: I love you, Pat.

L. Z.: Pat is saying, "Tell her I love her—I will always love her." She's walking over and placing her hand on my forehead and thanking me for being present at her passing. I did not know this; I was not aware I was with her at that time.

LeRoy later described Pat with longer hair, more youthful than when he had known her and dressed in a deep pink or rose-colored two-piece long dress. He also mentioned that there were disks above my head and he thought they had something to do with adjusting my frequency. I told him about the one, the *infusor,* I had seen in June, and he said, "there are more than one—there are several that I can see above your head, a few feet apart."

Weeks, no, months of meditation, serious study, and daily sessions—sometimes two, followed that first week of contact with Pat. Each session made me feel closer to our goal and I had to watch my level of impatience with myself. I was to learn that this was a long-term project. I had read of others who had worked hard for enhanced psychic abilities, and some told of two to three years and more with almost full time commitment. I had to perform reality checks at times and remind myself of just why this work was so important to me. I had no desire to become a medium with public recognition, but I affirmed my desire to be in touch, not only with Pat but with others in higher dimensions in order to bring forward spiritual teachings to be shared with those who are open to working with them.

Allow me to digress for a moment to tell you about a dream I had many years ago—in 1981. In the dream, a woman, perhaps a teacher, came to me and told me she was "looking for someone with a strong hand and wrist." I told her I would be happy to help her look for someone. But she replied, "I want you—you have a strong hand and wrist." I then asked her why she needed me, and she said, "I need someone to do a lot of writing." I wasn't sure I could do what she needed me to do but she seemed confident that I could. I regret to say that I let that opportunity pass me by. I was at a major transition point in my life having just been through a divorce and the emotional adjustment it required. I had moved my youngest daughter and myself from St. Petersburg to Nashville and was in my first year of graduate school at Vanderbilt University studying hard and completing effusive writing assignments for that program. I couldn't imagine how I could possibly fit another demand into my schedule. Of course my priorities in those days were a bit different from my priorities at this stage in my life.

Continuing with my psychic development, I began to have more psychic experiences and my intuition began to sharpen. My awareness of everything around me began to grow as a result of the work I was doing with Pat and her team. I checked in periodically with Steve, and Pat affirmed through him that I was indeed experiencing some of the things I thought I felt. She volunteered much of the information without my having to ask. This was convincing for Steve and for me, too. During the sessions, I continued to have the familiar warmth and pulsating effects around the heart chakra and in addition there were prickly sensations on areas of my face, head, and neck as if a thousand ants were crawling around those areas with a concentration of them in the brow or third-eye area. There was an intermittent ringing in my ears, usually on one side at a time. These sensations were and are always encouraging to me. There were even times during the night when I would wake up from my sleep and feel some kind of unusual activity taking place around my head. Now, some people might be frightened by this kind of project. While there have been a few surprises, I have a background of study in metaphysics that has helped me to create a context for most of this work. I have also been highly motivated by friends as close as Pat and my teachers Ann Manser and LeRoy Zemke and my mother Kathryn who has been very active from her dimension . . . as well as the encouragement of my friends Steve Engel and Bob Murray—very fine and highly developed psychics in this dimension.

In early August 2001, I began having nosebleeds. I had never had them before. They occurred at the most inopportune times, when I was having lunch out or dinner with someone, when I was shopping or driving. In other words, it was not always when I was at home alone. I'm not talking about an inconspicuous incident here, I'm talking about sudden unannounced hemorrhaging that had to be stopped, not with a single tissue but with a handful of tissues. This went on for many months with periodic incidences. I added more Vitamin C with bioflavonoids to strengthen the blood vessels, because I had decided the hemorrhaging was caused by weak blood vessels. The episodes would subside just long enough for me to give up the idea of asking for medical help. I was alarmed at first, and certainly embarrassed at times. Then I realized the inner work we were doing, the adjustments to my vibratory frequency just might have something to do with the nosebleeds. I decided not to seek medical assistance until I had checked with those on the other side who were working with me. When I checked with Pat, through Steve, she told me that her teachers told her they were apparently transmitting too much high frequency energy into my system for me to adjust to at that time. They said they would turn back the voltage to a level that I could safely receive. There was never a problem with the nosebleeds after that, but I noticed that the heart chakra pulsations I felt were much less dramatic, although they were still present and are still occurring.

Pat has used many props and symbols to deliver her messages from her dimension. There are times when I'm in an altered state of consciousness and she will use a large white porcelain board, like those we use in schools and businesses, and dry erase markers to write messages to me. She has given me instructions over the course of our work together, some directly and some through Steve and Bob—the most obvious of which is to be open and receptive, visualizing myself surrounded by a spiritual white light. Exercises before a contact session might include the strengthening of the desire body by visualizing the body drawing into it the color green, a clear emerald green. The desire body can become depleted, when one is under emotional stress, and must be replenished. During one session, a visualization that was suggested was of a large iron door or gate that opens to a village. "You are on the outside of the gate and you have a magical key," Pat said. "The village is yours to explore if you can open the door."

During another session, Pat wanted to tell me that one of her friends in Omaha needed some help. This time she used a symbol, a small Scotty dog which I was able to see at the end of a long tunnel. I asked her if she had something to tell me about the friend whom I thought this symbol represented. She said, "Yes, she is having some difficulty and you might offer some healing words." I named the friend and asked Pat if I was getting the correct name. She answered, "Yes, she needs some words of comfort." I told her to consider it done. I emailed our mutual friend the next morning and found that she had a "fierce cold, the first I've had in several years." In order to increase my sensitivity during our sessions, I made a habit of asking Pat what color she was wearing when she was with me. I wrote down the color of my impression. Sometimes the impressions were very strong and at other times a little weaker. There was no way to verify these impressions. I just felt it was a good exercise for my own development.

In a dream visit with Pat in April 2002, she was preparing to leave for a while. I wasn't clear about where she was going, but we worked together to get some things ready for me to take care of for her until she returned. We were outdoors, both on our knees, transplanting some indoor plants from plastic containers to long clay or ceramic containers. I seemed to know more about this particular process than did Pat, so I was showing her just how it should be done. As we walked indoors, carrying the plants, we talked about how they would grow and eventually burst into bloom over time. At first I was sad about her leaving me, but she assured me that things would be all right and she would return within a few weeks. In this dream, I knew that Pat was able to read my mind and that she knew everything I was thinking before I said it aloud to her. In the spirit worlds, since mental telepathy is the medium for communication between spirit entities, to Pat this was very natural. To the level of consciousness I was utilizing in this dream, it was not a familiar medium and would have been a bit threatening if I had not been with a close friend. My interpretation of this dream experience went something like this: Pat needed to interrupt her part in our work together for a short period of time and wanted me to know this. The plants represented my chakras that were being stimulated for this work. The energy was being deepened and made more permanent and reliable in its function, eventually bringing the chakra functions into fuller bloom. They were in fact being aligned like the plants in the long ceramic containers from their previous random and separate growth in the plastic containers.

When I emailed Steve for another contact, I didn't tell him about the dream until after he had contacted Pat for me. She told me through Steve that she would be away on a retreat for a while. She had received a very special invitation to attend this retreat and assured me that her team would continue to work with me. Sometime in July, I felt her return to our work which I had kept up daily while she was away.

In December of the same year, 2002, I heard Pat's voice on a phone in a dream. Her voice was very clear and the voice quality was definitely hers. She was conveying to me a message she had received during her last year on Earth. It was a message of her acceptance on some level for a particular spiritual work. There have been other phone conversations with her in my dream state.

Dream visits with Pat in the year 2003 were much less often. I missed them but I still felt her presence in our evening sessions and I continued my periodic contacts with her through Steve. This was a difficult year for me because of my mother's transition in February of the same year.

Dream visits with Pat picked up again in the next two years, numbering on the average of one per month. But by the end of April 2006, she conveyed to me the difficulty she often had in slowing down her vibratory frequency enough to make frequent contacts. However she continued with brief visits until the fall of the same year. Of course her visits might be more frequent than I'm able to recall. One day in August, I had been working on the manuscript for this book and decided to take some time out for meditation. I apparently had an out-of-body experience and found Pat standing next to my desk in my library. She looked lovely in blue—an electric blue satin blouse and silvery gray skirt. After a brief telepathic conversation, we seemed to shift to another location—to a stage in a theater. Pat was then wearing a beautiful copper-colored satin blouse and a brown skirt, but she soon disappeared and another woman appeared. We introduced ourselves. Her name was Camille, and she seemed to be serving in some official capacity in the theater. I asked her if she could tell me where Pat had gone. She said she didn't know. This reminded me of a contact made with Mother through Bob Murray. Mother told Bob that Pat visits her sometimes and gets distracted by a thought in mid-sentence and just disappears for a few moments. She said she didn't think Pat was aware that it happens, and Mother just found it amusing. You will hear more about Pat in the story of Kathryn, the next remarkable woman.

CHAPTER 15

A Remarkable Woman Named Kathryn

I think of you often—very often, and
I bless you whenever I see beautiful beings
or noble things, because you are
both beautiful and noble.

~ Kahlil Gibran

On the morning of January, 25, 2001, following my evening news of Pat's death the day before, I walked next door to Mother's house and shared my sad news with her. Mother cried and said, "I can't believe it—Pat was one of the most alive people I ever met—always so full of energy!" We consoled each other and spoke of our wonderful visits with Pat—her visits to Nashville when Mother and Pat had become acquainted. Later that same year, in November 2001, Mother (Kathryn) was diagnosed with pancreatic cancer.

The diagnosis of pancreatic cancer, so often attributed to alcohol abuse, was a shock to our family. Mother only occasionally had a glass of wine. She was very fond of desserts, however, so that fact likely contributed to her failing pancreas. Caroline Myss tells us in her workshop, "The Energetics of Healing,"[1] that this is a third chakra matter and the pancreas is the organ affected by a tendency to feel too responsible for everyone or not responsible for anything. It deals with responsibility to the extreme on one end of the continuum or the other. One's energy becomes trapped in the pancreatic region and manifests in disorders like pancreatic cancer or diabetes. If that problem manifested for Mother, it was at the extreme of feeling responsible for so many others in her life.

After thorough evaluation, it was determined by Mother's oncologist and another doctor, a surgeon, that the risk would be too great if the route of surgery was followed—in part because of her age, 88, and because of the location of the tumor. Surgery would be long and complicated according to her doctors. She chose chemotherapy along with alternative methods to support her immune system and to aid her tolerance of the harsh medications she would have to endure. The alternative methods included a nutritional program, chiropractic and acupuncture procedures, Reiki healing and homeopathic and herbal remedies. We designed a schedule listing all her medications and natural remedies, a checklist posted on her refrigerator, so she could check them off as she took them. She had a wonderful attitude and sense of humor about it all. One morning she said to me, "I'll just sit at my back door with my mouth open and you can come over and drop in anything you think I need to take." She called her herbal tinctures, which came stabilized in an alcohol solution and which she mixed with a little water before swallowing, her cocktails. Because of these alternative remedies she never suffered enough pain to warrant use of pain medication nor did she experience much nausea. For that, we were very grateful!

Mother was amazing! She was not a complainer, so we never knew for sure just how she was feeling. There were days when she could run circles around those of us who were comparatively healthy. She kept up her usual activities until her final weeks, making calls for her church, celebrating family birthdays, and even Christmas shopping. She seemed to enjoy the contact with her church friends, so making the phone calls was her way of continuing that contact and of keeping up with the latest news when she was no longer able to be with her friends socially. She received cards and telephone greetings from many people daily and she was always happy to have visitors.

Eventually there were trips to the hospital for blood transfusions or intravenous fluids. Although the chemotherapy was effective for a while, she became anemic and grew weaker. The last round of chemotherapy proved to be the most devastating of her entire experience. She ended her fifteen month treatment for pancreatic cancer when she made her transition to her new life in the next dimension on February 14, 2003. Although very difficult for her family, I thought her *choice* of Valentine's Day was a fitting one for her transition because the world was so full of love on that day.

Kathryn Young George (Parrotte) was born on June 11, 1913 in Fayetteville, Tennessee. The fifth-born of eight children, she was the daughter of William Cullen and Myrtle Mooney George. Stories of Kathryn's childhood reflect a rural life of work and play on the farm with siblings of all ages. Her most vivid memories revolved around the years the family lived on a three hundred acre farm called *Emerald Meade Farm* located between Lynnville and Cornersville, Tennessee. It is now owned by the Sloan family of the Cain-Sloan department stores and is called *Gone Away Farm*. The original two-story Victorian house has been renovated in recent years. One summer Mother took my sister, my Uncle Ted (her youngest brother) and me on a tour of her childhood homes in that part of Tennessee. When we arrived in front of *Gone Away Farm*, John Sloan was there and graciously invited us to tour his home while Mother provided delightful stories of her childhood there.

Summer and autumn seasons for the George family were full of blackberry picking for scrumptious cobblers, picking apples, gathering nuts, roasting chestnuts and popping popcorn over an open fire. The younger children played such games as Fruit Basket Turn Over and

Blind Man's Bluff while the older brothers and sisters played tennis on their own tennis court and entertained their friends on the front lawn. Mother said she felt she was in a "Fairyland" when the Japanese lanterns were strung and lighted for parties given by her older siblings on their front lawn. She was a shy but inquisitive child—always devoted to her large loving family.

There are many stories about the farm and the farm animals, the old T-model Ford, going to school and church together, churning ice cream and other enchanting memories. Kathryn liked to read, and she recalled reading to her younger brother and sister. She told of the time she read to them from their little red Bible Story Book the story of Joseph and his coat of many colors. When she came to the part about Joseph being sold into slavery by his brothers, they all three cried. She was an excellent student, and she expressed her musical talent at the piano. Her youngest brother, Ted, tells about Kathryn practicing the piano every day after school. He said he didn't care if he never again heard "The Wedding of the Painted Doll." Her love for the piano continued when her own children were old enough to sing along and begin their piano lessons. Music was always important to Kathryn, and she had a lifetime appreciation for symphony concerts, Broadway musicals church music, and popular music of the first half of the twentieth century.

In Nashville, after her graduation from Morgan Preparatory School in Petersburg, Tennessee, she worked and met my father Vestal Frazier. My younger sister, Mary Elizabeth, and I had what seemed to me an idyllic childhood with parents who loved us and whom we adored. This came to an end all too soon with the diagnosis of our dad's brain tumor and his death a few weeks later—one week before my eleventh birthday. Kathryn, only thirty-three years old, became a young widow. Her years as a stay-at-home mom were over, and she spent many of her remaining adult years working for the United States government. Several years after my dad's death, she married again and our little brother, Bobby, was born.

Mother was petite, with a tiny frame, but was a tower of strength for her family. Her blue eyes sparkled with compassion and interest in the whole world. Her smile was always warm, welcoming, accepting and sometimes even a bit impish. When I was in the fifth grade I opened my lunch box at school one day and took a bite out of my sandwich. I couldn't taste anything but bread, so I took another bite. When I opened it there was nothing between the slices of bread. Mother had made our lunches in a hurry and had forgotten to put any filling in mine. I confronted her about it later, and without skipping a beat she said, "Oh, I guess you got the jam sandwich." Before I could explain that there was no jam, she continued with, "Two pieces of bread jammed together!" We both laughed, and that made it all better.

Mother's talents as a seamstress were certainly important to us as children and teenagers. She sewed and made lovely clothes for us. I felt like Alice in Wonderland when she made some of our little dresses with white organdy pinafores to wear over them. Nothing seemed too great a challenge; we wore lovely hand-smocked blouses, pleated skirts, weskits (vests), and coats and leggings hand-made by our mother. But her ultimate sacrifice was her willingness to stay up half the night making beautiful gowns for her two teen-aged daughters to wear to their formal dances—and she was a working mother as well! I had only a fraction of the proper appreciation for what she had done for us until I had my own family. She wanted her children to have all the opportunities available for their growth and development and to experience things she missed in her childhood and teens. Her family was large and her parents were hard-working. She was not always able to take advantage of the experiences and opportunities she could only dream about.

Mother didn't learn to drive until she was in her fifties, so we either walked or took public transportation when we wanted to go somewhere. We walked about a mile or more to church. Try to imagine walking that far these days dressed up and in high heeled shoes. In the summertime Mother picked up a light blanket, made a bag of popcorn and we walked more than a mile to the Reservoir Park where we spread our blanket on a hillside and joined many other families to watch black and white movies on a huge outdoor screen, once it was dark enough to view them. Perhaps this kind of entertainment led to the concept of the drive-in theaters which became popular sometime later. We were privileged to live in a college-university town where so many free cultural events were available. Mother also took us on the city bus to the Peabody College campus to enjoy very professional outdoor musical performances. Two that I recall with great pleasure were "Naughty Marietta" and "Carousel." The staging and lighting were sophisticated for that time, and it was always a special treat for this young widowed mother and her daughters. Only much later did I learn how very fortunate we were to have these opportunities available to us.

Mother taught us to cook and to sew and to take care of our own belongings. As a teenager, in preparation for the next school week, my Saturday mornings were spent washing my dresses and blouses and ironing them after they had dried on the clothesline. We had supper started by the time Mother returned home from work on week days. I enjoyed making some of my own clothes and knew I could have more if I could make them myself. I started out with summer clothes because summer fabrics were easier to cut and sew than the thicker winter wools and corduroys.

Sometime in the summer between my eighth and ninth grades in school I decided to make a couple of outfits. I pinned a pattern on light blue chambray on Mother's bed near her sewing machine. At the same time, I was also listening to a soap opera called "Stella Dallas" on the radio. Few families had television yet. I became so involved in the story that when I had almost finished cutting the fabric I realized that it felt awfully thick for chambray. I had cut out a chenille skirt and blouse from Mother's bedspread at the same time! What would I do? I removed my fabric and pattern and carefully placed all the pieces of the bedspread back together so that at first glance the massacre wasn't obvious. I intended to choose just the right moment to break the news to Mother when she came home from work. I suppose that by that time I was so involved in something else I forgot all about my horrid mistake, and she must have discovered it when she was ready for bed. I waited for her to bring it up the next day, and she didn't. How irresponsible of me! Years later, I asked her why I wasn't disciplined for that awful mistake and my failure to explain it to her. She told me, "I didn't need an explanation. I knew it was an accident when I saw the shapes of the cut-outs. Besides, I hated that bedspread and it gave me an excuse to buy a new one." Kathryn was such a reasonable and practical woman.

Mother was also a compassionate and generous woman. She seemed always available when someone was in need. Her brothers and sisters helped her when she was most in need of their support, and she was certainly available for them in their times of need. Approximately ten years before her retirement, no longer married, she bought a duplex that would house not only her teen-aged son and herself, but she invited her mother and older sister to live on the other side free of charge until they could contribute some payment for the rent. She seemed to always be on call for friends and relatives who needed her to drive them for their various appointments. She loved and was loved by many, young and old alike.

Her Gemini qualities were demonstrated in her quick wit and her curiosity and interest in the world around her. I miss her physical presence in my life tremendously, although her spirit presence is very real to me now. We've had some profound contacts, and I shall tell you more about those a little later.

Kathryn

Mother's memorial service was planned down to every detail by her, including her burial dress and the music. It gave our family some peace of mind to know we were carrying out her wishes for her service. My daughter, Wendi, and I designed and printed a fourteen-page booklet commemorating her life in pictures with messages to her from family members. It contains a short biography, a genealogical list of her parents, brothers, sisters and her own children and our families. It is called "A Celebration of the Life of Kathryn Parrotte," and it has a photograph of her on the cover with the dates of her lifespan. Wendi and I had a good time working on this together, and we had it finished and printed in time for Mother's memorial service. It was received with much appreciation by her family and friends, and it was a great processing tool for those of us who were contributors. I highly recommend such gestures. They can be helpful in your own healing and in that of others.

Memorial Booklet for Kathryn

CHAPTER 16

Contacting Kathryn

*You cared for me with love—from infant to adult
and then became my friend. God has blessed me twice.
Once with a wonderful mother and again
with a cherished friend.*

~ Laura Campbell

AT DIFFERENT TIMES, DURING THE last year of her life, Mother asked me the following two questions. She first asked if I would try to contact her after she was gone. I told her I definitely would do that. She knew that I was involved in the work with Pat—the afterlife contacts with Pat, and she encouraged me to keep up that work. Mother had studied related material for years. I recall being surprised and pleased when I found that she had been studying a correspondence course from Switzerland called *The Spiritual World* for over twenty years. The material was metaphysical, and the teachings were received from the spirit teacher Joseph in the German language through a Swiss medium, Beatrice Brunner. This material was recommended by author Walter Hinz in his book, *The Corner Stone*. Hinz, Professor Emeritus at the University of Gottingen, concludes his book with this statement, "But never forget that the man who is on intimate terms with the world of spirit is forever open to the flow of sacred, healing energies."[1]

Mother and I had both been engaged in a study of the afterlife—I was delighted! This fact afforded us many wonderful discussions about our perceptions of the afterlife—reassuring for both of us. I asked Mother through a psychic medium, after her transition, if those lessons helped her understand her new home now. Her answer was, "Yes, it put me on the right track, but there is so much more than what we read."

Her other question was, "Do you think Pat would help me cross over if I needed her?" I told her I was certain that she would if she would only ask her and if it were within the realm of possibility for Pat to assist her in that way.

I contacted Pat, through Steve, for advice on Mother's care during her treatment for cancer. The suggestions were sound and sensible and were always approved by her doctor. Her doctor was so impressed with the effects of some of the alternative remedies that he sometimes asked us to write them out for him so he could make recommendations to other patients. There were herbal remedies to retard metastases of the cancer, to build the immune system and to prevent pain and nausea from the chemotherapy. Pat gave us guidance on the use of Reiki procedures that were specific to Mother's needs at any given time. She sometimes recommended increased or decreased dosages of certain vitamins or minerals in her diet and in supplement form. Mother of course always had a choice of whether or not to follow Pat's advice from another dimension. She most often carried out the recommendations and felt great benefits. It was amazing to us that we could consistently receive such loving health care from another dimension. Many believe that we do receive that kind of input, and it comes to us through what we call intuition. I often receive this kind of information through my dreams as well.

In February 2003, about a week after Mother passed away, my sister, Mary, and I went to Mother's house to look for her will. We knew there was a will but neither of us had asked about its location. We looked through Mother's desk and in a small black box of valuable papers, but no will was found. We then decided that she must have kept it in a safe deposit box at her bank, but we didn't have a key. We again began our search, to no avail. No key and no will. The next day, I went over to the house and sat in Mother's living room and called her to me. I told her of our dilemma and asked for her help in locating the key. I didn't see her, nor did I hear her. But after a few minutes, I was strongly impressed to look in a chest of drawers in her bedroom. I went through every drawer, and in frustration I stopped and quieted my mind and asked again for her help. I was distinctly impressed with "You're looking in the wrong chest. Go across the room and look in the dresser chest," a smaller chest with a mirror attached. I immediately went to the middle of three drawers and found that this was her underwear drawer. I picked up some things on the left and there I found all kinds of bank documents and some savings books. In the very last savings account book, taped on the inside of the back cover, was the key to her safe deposit box. Mary and I took it to the bank and there we found the will!

Earlier, I spoke of dreams in which I felt I was actually visiting with Ann Manser and Pat. I've learned through the years that there are dreams, and there are actual dream visits. Of course there are many categories within these larger categories. In most of my research into afterlife communication, authors make distinctions between dreams about deceased loved ones and actual visits with them. In the dream state, the conscious mind has less control over our thought processes, allowing many levels of our mind to be more open to new perceptions and experiences. One is in an altered state of consciousness, in other words. Because the ego is not involved, and we are not attempting to control the mind in this state, an opportunity is created for us to have contact with a spirit loved one on occasion. This is a time that is conducive to the reception of messages and reassurance from our deceased loved ones. Bruce Moen, in his writings on his exploration of the afterlife, talks about the purposeful designing by spirit entities of dreams that benefit the dreamer in some way. One example he uses is a dream setting which supplies a "dream player" to bring a man out of a long-term coma. We have frequent dreams which remind us of lessons we need or which deal with our current situations. It is my understanding that some planning is required on the parts of the spirit entities who visit with us in the dream state. Atmospheric conditions must be compatible with vibratory frequencies needed to carry out the dream drama so that it is received clearly, as intended.

Another consideration is the vibratory frequency we create around ourselves before falling asleep. If we are engaged in positive thinking and feeling, we surround ourselves with higher frequencies which make contact with deceased loved ones more possible. There are of course dreams about the loved one in which the spirit might be symbolic of some aspect of oneself or an awareness we need, but it may not be a real visit. The difference might be in the feeling you have about the dream. If the dream is vivid, you feel you've actually been with the person and your senses are involved, such as touch, smell, vision and hearing, it is more likely to be an actual contact.

Berkowitz and Romaine, in *Communicating with Spirits*, state that "You can intentionally invite spirit entities to visit you in your dreams."[2] Before falling asleep, state your intent for a visit with a loved one. Call the loved one to you and make the request for a visit. You might even write the name of the spirit and any information you wish to receive on a piece of paper and place it at your bedside. It is wise to keep a pad of paper and a pen or pencil next to your bed for jotting down key words from a dream immediately upon waking. I usually jot them down when I wake up from a dream in the night, too.

My first dream about my mother, after her transition, came to me two and a half weeks later. In the dream, I was standing in my front yard talking to a neighbor when I saw Mother driving away in her mauve-colored Toyota Camry. It had, in actuality, been her car. In the dream, she drove with confidence and direction. I seemed to know where she was going, so I didn't worry about her.

Shortly before the time of the above dream, I contacted Bob Murray, an excellent psychic and author of *The Stars Still Shine*, and asked him if he would be willing to contact Mother for me. I had read his book the year before and had passed it on for Mother to read. I was impressed with his contact with his son-in-law, Michael, who had been killed by a hit-and-run driver in 1997. Bob didn't know me, so there was a natural confidence in the authenticity of his contact which was made February 23, 2003, just nine days after Mother's transition. Bob's contact with me was by phone, and he was in communication with my mother's spirit as we spoke. It was most rewarding. He began with, "There is someone here by the name of Pat—Patricia—Patsy. She's trying to identify herself. She says to tell you that everything is under control. She further identifies herself by saying *I get all the details down. I make lists, sometimes irritating to people I knew on Earth.*" (Pat Larson was indeed a detail person and an organizer).

Ann: That is my best friend, Pat.

Pat: I took the liberty of helping your mother cross over. She called for me to help her. Your mother is with me. She has been resting in a hospital—a kind of halfway house for those making transition. She had to stay a while this week to get back on her feet. She is awake. There is no pain. She has been introduced to a lot of her relatives. They stayed for a short time. Her brother Bill was here . . . and their mother and father.

Bob: Your mother is awake and wants to say something. She thinks it's very strange to be talking into mid-air. "There is no telephone," she says.

Mother: I am here. I don't know why I'm here in the hospital. I'm okay. I want to send my love to you. I'm having trouble with my teeth—I'm talking with a lisp, and I don't like it.

Bob: Did your mother have implants?

Ann: She had them in the lower gums. They were giving her trouble while she was ill, and she kept removing her lower denture because it didn't fit well anymore. She planned to have the implants built up but didn't feel well enough to keep her appointment with her dentist.

Mother: People have been wonderful here. They're taking such good care of me. Thank you all for being there for me. Don't throw all my stuff out yet. I know I won't use it, but I'm still a little attached to it. On a shelf in my room, here, above my bed, there is one of my favorite dolls dressed in red. I don't know how it got there.

Ann: It must be her little Madame Alexander doll. (Mother loved dolls, bought them and made clothes for them and gave them away or sold them. She had collected a few small Madame Alexander dolls).

Bob: She says it is (a Madame Alexander doll).

Mother: I'm going to be leaving the hospital, and someone is going to make me a house—one that I can live in—tomorrow or the next day. I want you to know I'm still around—still living. I don't know what to call myself yet. I'm so happy to talk to you. I went to sleep and woke up in this hospital. I was fighting—I didn't want to go. I was afraid. I wasn't convinced it would be okay. It's not really what I expected. I knew what other people said they did (in her literature on the subject), but I wasn't sure how it would be for me. I just didn't know. It wasn't painful. Our prayers were answered . . . I'm really okay.

Ann: On the second night after you were gone did you come and fill my room with some lovely perfume to let me know you were all right?

Mother: That was Pat. I wanted her to let you know I was okay, and that was the way she did it. I was so worried that I couldn't tell you all I was okay, so Pat brought the perfume. I feel so light; there is no problem walking now. I feel very young again. I can be any age I want to be. I might go back to about age forty or forty-five. I haven't seen a mirror—I might be an old hag.

Bob: Does your mother have a sense of humor?

Ann: Oh yes, she certainly does.

Mother: Tell Mary (my sister) and Bob (my brother) I love them. I love all of you. I haven't had any review yet; I don't know how that works. Keep up your work with Pat and you'll be successful with it. (Mother says "bye" for now).

Ann: I love you very much and I miss you.

Pat: We must continue our work together. Keep the notes. Look inside your notes—at the beginning is the method we should use—on the second or third page. That's about it. It's a lot simpler than we realize. It's right under your nose. Believe in yourself. Believe in what you're doing. Have faith. Listen to the voice inside your head—it's usually correct. Don't make it as work. The secret here is that there is no secret. Have fun. As we know, life is too short.

Ann: Thank you, Pat. Thank you so much for caring for Mother and for being here today.

Pat: I am so happy to be here. Hearing your voice has made your mother realize that she can get up and do things and move. She is so happy to have this contact, and she wants more of it. She is getting dressed now for the first time. She said something about going to dance.

While Mother was still here on Earth, in the spring of 2002, her deceased husband, Robert, my stepfather, came in spirit through our friend, LeRoy. Robert had been in spirit for almost forty years and was touching in with this message about Mother:

"I have been with your mother in the last month. I want you to know that she's better. She thinks she is going to join us soon, but her place isn't ready yet. If I could, I'd get her to dance again. You tell her that when it's time, and she comes, I'll be there among those who love her to greet her."

These were two different psychics who mentioned dancing. Mother and her husband Robert liked to dance together. My father didn't dance, and she enjoyed having a dance partner in my stepfather. They often danced in our living room when I was a teenager.

It was a great experience to be able to converse with my mother and Pat. There is no way for me to measure the accuracy of this or other contacts. Most psychics do not claim to be one hundred percent accurate, but there was certainly a lot of information to which I could truly relate in this contact, and in LeRoy's contacts, and in those through Steve.

A month later, I asked Bob Murray to make another contact for me. Again, Pat came through with Mother. Mother told of touring a large nursery where young children and infants are taken when they cross over into that dimension, and they stay until there is a person or a family who comes to get them—someone who is related or wishes to adopt them. She met the nurses and caretakers and added that she was also beginning some work with flowers. This made sense to me because she was a very committed flower gardener in our world. She always had lovely flowers around and in her home. Bob Murray says that she teaches children about flower gardening. I have such fond memories of her doing that for me when I was a small child. She helped me plant seeds for colorful zinnias and marigolds. Then she put a short circular fence around them and gave me a child's watering can with a spout. I could hardly wait to get out to my little garden each morning, to water it and admire the beautiful flowers I was helping to grow—all by myself. I took good care of my lovely flowers and took such pleasure in watching them grow. This gave me such a sense of responsibility and accomplishment.

Mother says to Bob, "My cottage changes to whatever I want. If I decide to make a change, someone will help me do that. And if I want other kinds of flowers, I can just think about what I'd like and I'll have those added. It's so much fun."

Mother and Pat proceeded to tell me about their tours and travels. Pat said, "Kathryn and I are on a voyage of discovery. I'm taking some time out for this exploration with your mother. I thought I would have to look after your mother but she's looking after me." They spoke of their excursions to different towns to meet people. I couldn't verify anything because they were sharing only their experiences in their dimension. At some point, Mother mentioned that she'd had a visitor who came to see her with a big portfolio of art work and he introduced himself to her as an artist who knew me. "He said he knew you back when he was an artist and he had studied with a famous artist. He now works with living color. He said he was an artist who lived in the South." At first I thought she was talking about my first art teacher, John Cunningham, with whom I studied at the Carmel Art Institute in Carmel-by-the-Sea, California. John had studied with the famed Hans Hoffman. When she said he was an artist who lived in the South, I had to think a while longer about that. I finally realized that she must have been talking about George Burrows, an artist who studied with and was married to the well-known artist, my teacher, Marilyn Bendell from Long Boat Key, Florida. George and Marilyn later lived and painted in Santa Fe, New Mexico. Bob wasn't able to get his name, or Mother wasn't able to transmit that information to him, but I'm certain now that it was George.

Mother said that she had been doing more with flowers when there was time between excursions with Pat. She said that when they were exploring together, "I didn't have a minute to spare, with Pat in charge. Everything was planned right down to the last detail. I would start to do one thing, and she had something else for us to do." I certainly related to that as would others who knew Pat.

In still another of my contacts with Mother through Bob Murray, Bob asked at one point about a miscarriage. He asked if Mother had a miscarriage at some time in her life. I told him I hadn't been aware of one. He went on with other information, and in a moment he said that Mother was again mentioning a miscarriage. He asked if I had ever miscarried. "Yes, I have," I told him.

Bob: This would have been in 1964 or 1965?

Ann: Yes, it was in 1964.

Bob: Your mother is telling me that a young man who lives next door to her now likes to visit with her and learn about flowers. He's become quite attached to her and visits often. They both have a love of flowers. His name is Stephen, and she has learned that he was the child that you miscarried.

Ann: That was in my fourth month of that pregnancy.

Bob: He told your mother that he was guided to go with another family because of an experience he needed with them for his own development. He wants you to know he loves you and that it was a difficult decision for him. His life was cut short when he had to have a blood transfusion and he contracted the AIDS virus from the transfusion when he was about thirty years old.

On March 31, 2003, about six weeks after Mother's transition, I got up early one morning and as I was getting out of bed I reached over to pick up Mother's camera which I had brought home with me to see if there was any undeveloped film left in it. I picked up the manual and was reading it when my little music box began playing, high on a book shelf in the bedroom. The music box is inside a clown doll given to me by Mother when I was in the hospital after a serious automobile accident in 1991. I had mentioned the clown to her near the end of her life and she had replied, "You still have that silly old clown?" I told her I hoped I would have it for a long time. I later learned that she would use it to contact me when there was a crisis about which I should be aware. This was only the beginning; it has been used several times since then. This entire story is in Chapter 2.

In January 2004, almost a year after my mother's (Kathryn's) transition, I was keeping a regular meditation appointment with her in order to establish a bridge or connection with her for our communication. (See Chapter 17 for the exercise I use for this contact). As usual, I shared with her mentally or verbally and then invited her to share with me. I've had quite a lot of contact with Mother. Our contact has been very strong and definite at times. The following meditation experience was one of those times. On this particular morning, she transmitted visual information to me using symbolic language she knew I would understand. In the first visual frame, I was with a friend in a market place, in a sunny location somewhere, on a holiday or vacation. I was dressed in faded jeans and a yellow sweater and tucking a new purchase into a large tote I was carrying. The feeling was light and full of fun and laughter. Along with other family members, I had taken care of Mother during her illness with pancreatic cancer, tried to process her death and then process my move into her house and suffered the loss of other loved ones all in the same year. I felt that with this symbol she was emphasizing my need to let go and do some traveling to get away and rest the mind, body, and soul—to freshen my perspective on the demands in my life.

The second frame in this transmission was a scene in which I was dragging a large white plastic bag of things from the house. I was releasing those things that I no longer need in my life, and I had the feeling that a part of it was on the material level and another part was emotional. Then I saw the word JOY in large colorful sparkly letters bursting out all around me after I had released the bag.

The third frame showed me playing with my young grandson who was at that time less than two years old. Distance and other circumstances had prevented our being together since he was about five weeks old. I had been frustrated in not being able to have frequent visits with him. I felt Mother was encouraging me to work harder toward that goal and to develop a bonding process with my little grandson. This contact with Mother has helped me to focus on some important goals and, for the most part, they have been carried out. Her symbols were very clear and I had no doubt they were given to me by my mother. Some symbols are more subtle and require more time and effort to interpret. When you're aware that symbols can be used in this type of communication, as they are used in dreams, the communication can make a lot more sense.

LeRoy Zemke had told me in an in-depth reading that Mother was doing some work with children who were crossing over to her dimension as infants, and that she would appear to me at some point and show me a sign related to this work when she had finished her training. A few months later, during our Sunday morning contact, Mother came to me holding a newborn baby whose tiny feet had a bluish tint. I didn't see Mother's face but I saw her arms and hands as she showed me the infant, and I could feel her presence with me. I recalled LeRoy's prediction and realized that she wanted me to know that she had finished her training for receiving and caring for the tiny new arrivals on her side of life.

In a dream at the end of 2003, Mother was packing a bag and going to visit someone south of us—in Alabama. The young woman she was going to see was a teacher with whom I've worked at one of the private schools here. I couldn't imagine why she was going to visit this teacher because I didn't know she knew her. I found out later that the teacher's two-month old son was born weighing just over a pound and was struggling to live. I also learned that the teacher had grown up in Alabama. She might have gone there to her parents for help with the baby. I don't know that for sure. The child is now several years old and is reportedly doing well. The dream was significant to me because I didn't know the actual circumstances in that family when I had the dream. One explanation might be that Mother apparently had access to information about this acquaintance and was trying to pass it on to me—or she might have been involved in working with the child from her dimension. The dream inspired me to pray for the survival and health of the baby.

In many of the dreams I've had about Mother, she was trying to help but letting me know at times that there were invisible barriers and that she could only go so far with her assistance, especially if it pertained to physical crises. There have been dreams of warning and dreams of healing. I had a few dreams in which she put her hand on my back as we were walking on a path or sitting in a lecture hall. In a contact through Bob Murray around that time, he said, "Your mother is worried about your back. She wants you to take care of it." I had in fact strained it a little when I moved some heavy furniture, and it was not feeling very well.

In another dream visit with Mother, I was sitting with her in an outdoor arena about halfway up a hillside on slatted bleacher-like seats. They weren't the usual stadium bleachers, though, because each seat was just a little above the ground on the side of a hill. There were rows and rows and rows of seats above and below us. As I sat in conversation with Mother, on an end seat with my back to the pathway or aisle, I felt someone's arms around me. I turned to find Bertha Zemke, LeRoy's mother in spirit, giving me a big hug from the back. I was so happy to see her. She had made her transition over a decade ago and looked so young and happy. I introduced her to Mother and excused myself to run an errand. I left the two women talking and enjoying each other.

Mother was the organizer of our family reunions on her side of the family. This was a most meaningful biennial occurrence for her and for the rest of the family for many years. Just before the first reunion after her transition, I had a dream about her: There was a motorcade pulling into my driveway. When all the cars stopped, Mother's brothers and sisters and other family members filed out of them. She had brought them all to the reunion. She's still a busy lady! I was so aware of their presence at that reunion that it was difficult to keep it to myself.

One very vivid experience actually happened two days after the first anniversary of Mother's transition. I had late afternoon client appointments but felt I needed a short nap before they began. I fell across my bed, but I didn't really fall asleep. I left my body and soon found myself in a small cozy restaurant. I seemed to enter by a side door into a room with a table set for six, and there were three women sitting at the table. One woman was asking a question about the rest of their party while a server was serving a beverage to them. I immediately realized that Mother was the woman talking at the moment. It was clear to me that I had walked in on a meeting about to take place, and I didn't want to embarrass Mother, but I wanted to acknowledge her. I was so happy to see her, and very surprised, too. I was very aware that I was in the room with her and that I had not actually fallen asleep. Although my body seemed asleep, I felt wide awake and very observant.

Mother was wearing a beautiful light bluish-aqua silk dress with small designs in pale shades of the same color. Around her neck she wore a single string of pearls. She looked younger, perhaps in her forties, with a flawless complexion. She was beautiful! My plan was to work my way over to her side of the table and give her a kiss on her left cheek. After I'd stood in the same place for what seemed like a few minutes, Mother suddenly stopped talking and looked my way in apparent disbelief. She had discovered my presence! This was my chance, and I began walking toward her when I was suddenly unable to move or speak. I felt like a video tape on pause and realized I was withdrawing and traveling back to my body lying on the bed. It was so disappointing to have to leave before I made better contact with her. As I pondered what had happened, I wondered how she perceived the event. Was it like descriptions I had read about spirits from other dimensions materializing and dematerializing on our plane? Was I only partially visible to her? It appears that I just materialized and then faded out. I didn't feel that I had any control over the outcome of that experience. The experience, however, was so exciting to me that it prompted me to learn more about out-of-body experiences (OBEs).

In the 1980s, I went through a phase during which I recorded many out-of-body experiences or astral projections. These were spontaneous projections, not the result of my conscious preparation. I still become conscious during some astral travels and can record my experiences, but I am now working on more conscious projection techniques.

The Monroe Institute is a non-profit educational and research organization dedicated to the exploration of human consciousness. Founded by Robert Monroe, a former successful radio executive, he coined the term "out-of-body experience" to describe his state of consciousness separate from the physical body. He also invented Hemi-Sync. Hemi-Sync is the patented name for audio sound patterns that can have dramatic effects on states of consciousness. Best results are achieved through the use of head phones while listening to Hemi-Sync CDs or audio tapes. Programs at the Monroe Institute include remote viewing, out-of-body experiences, the Hemi-Sync experience and many other opportunities for personal growth and self-actualization.

Bruce Moen was a student of the Monroe Institute and an occasional guest facilitator. He is the author of "Exploring the Afterlife Series," books about his personal explorations in the afterlife regions. In his writings are accounts of his guidance by Robert Monroe himself in the afterlife dimensions. Moen is also the author of the *Afterlife Knowledge Guidebook* with accompanying CD recordings of exercises for afterlife exploration. I recommend this guidebook and CDs for the serious seeker of afterlife contact and information.

For a deep and comprehensive study and new approaches to out-of-body experiences I recommend a book called *Astral Dynamics*, by Robert Bruce. This book is almost an anatomical break-down and explanation of the multidimensional lives we all live and know so little about. He includes information on the many dimensions available to us as well as step-by-step techniques for conscious explorations of the dimensions.

One of the most amazing spontaneous OBEs that I ever experienced turned out to be what I would term a quadri-location experience. I was conscious in four places at once with an extremely heightened awareness of everything I saw, heard and touched. You may have heard of bi-location, being conscious in two locations at once. I've read about this being a natural phenomenon in the spirit worlds, but of course it is a supernatural occurrence in our physical experience. This is not a physical experience but one in which we consciously or spontaneously leave the physical body behind and travel in the astral vehicle.

A group of members from the Temple of the Living God left St. Petersburg one July to attend the meetings, mentioned earlier, of the Spiritual Frontiers Fellowship (SFF) conference in Charlotte, North Carolina. I drove there with my friend, Jane, and our single dorm rooms at the University of North Carolina were next door to each other. There were many exciting workshops scheduled for the conference, and I wanted to experience them all. We had been warned during the orientation program to be selective and not try to do everything on the program. I listened a little, but not enough. There was an evening healing service scheduled, and I learned that Reverend Carol Parrish, our healing instructor from the "Temple," had asked her students to participate in the service. I was beginning to feel some exhaustion from taking in too much of the conference without resting between workshops. The main attraction for the healing service was the world renowned spiritual healer, Olga Worrall. I had read her book *The Gift of Healing*, written with her husband, Ambrose A. Worrall, and I did not want to miss this very special service in which I could be involved as a student of spiritual healing. It was the afternoon before the evening program when I decided to go to my room and take a nap and rebuild my energy supply for the service. As I was falling asleep, I found myself still very conscious in a kind of twilight zone, between waking and sleeping, when I realized I hadn't set my alarm. I was pretty exhausted and certainly did not want to miss this special opportunity, so I opened my eyes and looked at my alarm clock. At the same time, my consciousness was next door in Jane's room. Ben was there making a cup of instant coffee. My sense of hearing was so magnified I could hear each coffee crystal fall into his cup. In the same instant, I was down at the other end of the hall in the ladies' restroom where Jane was explaining the benefits of calcium tablets to a woman for her headache. And at the very same time I was back in St. Petersburg in my own home, discovering Wendi, then six, in her bed crying with a sore throat as her dad stood over her trying to decide how to help her. As I walked through the house to Wendi's bedroom, our little dog, Tammy, barked at me. She was the only one who was able to see me. This all happened simultaneously—and probably in the twinkling of an eye! The same measurement of time in our dimension does not apply in the more subtle dimensions.

When I was able to bring my consciousness back into the material world, the first thing I wanted to do was to check out the other three scenarios that I had just experienced. I knew the clock was there and that I would set the alarm before lying down again for a nap. I grabbed a quarter for the long distance phone call to St. Petersburg and ran out the door into the hallway where I almost ran into Ben. He was coming out of Jane's room with his cup of instant coffee and asked if I would like a cup. I thanked him and told him I might get one later. I turned to my right, and coming toward me in the hallway, Jane was walking with a woman and saying, "I have some calcium tablets in my room. I'll get some for you and you can see if they'll help with your headache." I didn't stop, but ran down the stairs to the first floor where I knew I had seen a phone booth. I put my quarter in and told the operator to reverse the charges. Tom answered immediately saying, "Your timing is perfect! Wendi is in bed crying with a sore throat and I don't know what to do for her." Tammy was still barking in the background. I gave Tom some suggestions for helping Wendi and called back later to check on her. So this experience proved to be more than a figment of my imagination.

The healing service was beautiful and exhilarating. I believe we were all healed that night. What an extraordinary woman, Olga Worrall! What a privilege to serve alongside such a talented and dedicated spiritual healer! As I pondered my other extraordinary experience of the afternoon, I tried to put into words the possibility of such a performance of simultaneous events. How can the mind split off and be totally aware of four events all apparently happening at one moment in time—and with such a heightened awareness? It seemed to be a lesson in, and a tiny glimmer of, what might be termed omnipresence. It gave me only an inkling of the possibilities of the magnificent capabilities of the human mind—if only we were committed to developing them. This spontaneous and enlightening experience helped me to be open to many paranormal experiences to come. For that, I am forever grateful. It has certainly helped me to better understand a fraction of the nature of the dimension where I can find and communicate with my mother and Pat and Ann.

Kathryn and Nova

CHAPTER 17

More Contacts with Kathryn

Every spirit communication should be a healing experience,
and should always be looked at in that way.

~ Rita S. Berkowitz and Deborah S. Romaine

A MONTH AFTER MOTHER'S TRANSITION I had the dream visit with her in a lovely outdoor setting that was mentioned in chapter 5. There were many people present in what seemed to be a picnic area with a lake where some were swimming. We were standing in a shelter or cabana talking with an old friend, Jan, who is in actuality also on the other side. I then realized that this was a kind of mixer or orientation gathering for a group of spirits who had recently crossed over into the same dimension and of which Mother was a member. It was similar to the orientation social that I attended with Pat when she first crossed over.

My first Mother's Day without Mother present for our celebration came all too soon. I was inspired to go alone to a favorite place of ours, Cheekwood Art Museum and Botanical Gardens in Nashville. In solitude, I sat on a bench by a pond just off one of the trails and began to visualize a scene that could have been my mother as a small child walking across the pond on the wooden bridge with an Edwardian lady, her mother, a real "American Edwardian lady." As I sat daydreaming, I felt Mother's presence beside me. Perhaps this was her daydream I was viewing, and she was sharing it with me. I sat for a while longer communing with Mother and the beauty of nature surrounding us, wishing I could see her version of it all—in her dimension.

Later I wanted to tour the trails through the gardens full of lovely spring blooms and invited Mother to join me. As I walked I made comments to her about each colorful garden on display. When I rounded the corner of one of the greenhouses I discovered that I was not alone in the physical, either. Another woman was walking alone, admiring the gorgeous array of colors along the garden path. As she came around the corner of the building, there seemed to be a warm glow about her. We spoke to each other and then she told me she was a visitor from Arizona working on a project that brought her to Nashville for a couple of weeks. She went on to tell me that she had found Cheekwood Gardens listed in our newspaper and decided to spend the afternoon there to honor her mother's spirit. "That is what brought me here," I responded. We talked a bit more, and as I turned to leave I introduced myself, "I'm Ann." She seemed surprised, hesitated, then said, "That is my mother's name. My name is Katharine—people call me Kate." Now it was my turn to look surprised, and I said, "My mother's name is Kathryn." Coincidence? I doubt it.

In *The Celestine Prophecy* James Redfield suggests that as we ponder the spiritual dimension of our existence, opening our minds, we begin to experience phenomena that cannot be dismissed and pushed away.[1] The Swiss psychologist, Carl Jung, called this phenomenon synchronicity, the perception of meaningful life coincidences, and he says that we cannot stop and ponder these occurrences without beginning to see direct evidence of a divine force involved in our lives.[2]

Kate and I agreed that we liked the idea of the possibility that our moms indeed had something to do with our meeting. At any rate, we were convinced that it was definitely beyond coincidental!

Near the end of that first year following Mother's transition there were more and more contacts during my waking consciousness and in my dreams. I was encouraged about my growing knowledge of the afterlife and by what I interpreted as actual contact with Mother and other loved ones. The out-of-body journey to the restaurant scene was particularly impressive for me. I could only imagine how frustrating it was becoming for Mother to attempt to communicate with me only to find my lack of sensitivity to her dimension a deterrent to our communication. That is when I designed a meditation that I thought might help me strengthen the bridge to her dimension of consciousness. Her favorite hymn, for as long as I can recall, was "O Master, Let Me Walk with Thee." I have a CD of the hymn which was arranged and performed instrumentally for her memorial service by Ted Wilson, my nephew and her grandson.

The meditation: I begin our session with a lighted candle, a "Light of Protection" mantram, and "The Great Invocation." Then I turn on the CD, "O Master, Let Me Walk with Thee." I have designed a visualization for the next part, and I use the same one every time. As the music begins, I visualize the Master walking with Mother holding her left hand in His right hand as He holds my right hand in his left hand. This can be the Master Jesus or any Master or exalted Teacher of your choosing. He is walking along a pathway between our dimensions, kind of blending the two dimensions with His energy. At the climax of the music he brings Mother and me face to face, placing his hands on our heads in blessing. He then leaves us to greet each other and to perform the following exercise.

In my vision, Mother and I are facing each other with the intent of constructing a communication channel between us. I see the channels as large flexible etheric tubes connecting us at the brow, throat, and heart chakras. I take a deep breath and send spirals of light through the tubes, simultaneously, as I exhale. Then I bring spirals of light back from Mother's centers in an exchange of Light energy as I inhale. Sometimes the brow tube is almost palpable.

Now of course this contact meditation can be designed and personalized to meet your individual needs. It seems helpful to alert your loved ones on the other side to your plan, giving a specific time if possible. This is a courtesy to their schedule and allows them to slip away from their activities and join you during that window of time. At some point, they might be able to use their bi-location abilities and be in both settings simultaneously. We have many invisible helpers, and whether or not you are aware of them they are on hand to assist you. But you must make your intention clear. When you visualize the channel between you and your spirit friend or relative you might want to visualize him or her seated at eye level just a few feet in front of you. You may even wish to enclose the two of you in a bubble of sparkly rose color—the color of unconditional love. This is a part of making your energy frequencies compatible.

My little clown doll with the music box was mentioned earlier as a channel for Mother's contact with me. She uses the clown when she wants to get my attention, and I take it as a signal to sit and listen for further direction from her. Sunday mornings at ten o'clock were chosen by me to make contact with Mother for our work on our bridge between dimensions. One Sunday morning I overslept and was running behind schedule. I didn't sit down to greet Mother at our appointed time but I was working in that direction. At ten fifteen the little clown began to play its music. Mother had been patient enough and she finally felt a need to give me a gentle reminder. I immediately stopped what I was doing, greeted her, and we began our session together.

It was June 2005, and I had plans to drive to Florida to visit with family and friends there. Things were almost packed and ready for the trip and I was seeing my young clients throughout the day before my departure. While working with Nick that afternoon, around four o'clock, in my home library, I had a very definite contact that I believed was from Mother. On my desk are five photographs in small frames. The one in front is a picture of Mother. Nick and I were busy with his academic work when I suddenly heard a noise from my desk across the room, about twelve feet from where we were sitting. I jumped up to see what had happened and discovered that Mother's picture had fallen on its face. I mentally acknowledged her and told her I would sit and listen to her when Nick's session was over because my intuition told me that she needed to get my attention. After Nick left, I went to the desk and sat and worked with the picture for several minutes. I tried every way I knew to get it to fall face forward again. It didn't matter what I did with the supports on the frame, it was only natural for it to fall backward. It had to be pushed in order to make it fall forward. I was planning to leave on my trip the next morning, so was Mother trying to warn me to wait and go later? I was frantic! The car was partially packed and my bags were almost ready to go. I listened, but couldn't get a clear answer from Mother. Of course when one is frantic it's difficult to even think clearly. I then asked for another sign, one that would clearly tell me what I should do. I believe I had one. As I was falling asleep that night, I psychically saw an auto accident scene complete with an ambulance and patrol cars. That was clear enough for me. I stayed home the next day and left for Florida the following day. On the day I stayed home, I felt out of sync with things, a bit clumsy and uncoordinated, a little mentally foggy. It was a most unusual feeling. But I believe I could have been a potential danger to myself and others on the highway. I thanked Mother for her warning and her clever way to get my attention for such an important matter. If she had used the clown, I might have waited too long to figure out what she wanted me to know. She has often used the clown when someone else in the family needs my attention. The photo method was more dramatic and got my immediate attention.

CHAPTER 18

Communication with Our Pets

Until one has loved an animal, a part of
one's soul remains unawakened.

~ Anatole France

THIS CHAPTER ON ANIMAL COMMUNICATION is important to our goal for making contact with our departed loved ones because the process is similar. If you are interested in communicating effectively with your pets you will learn that this is best accomplished through a telepathic process using mind pictures. The most efficient method of communication with those on the other side, whether you wish to communicate with your human loved ones or your pets, is through pictures and symbols. This way of communicating is natural among those in the spiritual dimensions.

If we list the kingdoms in our planetary system on a scale according to their evolutional consciousness, the main categories would look like this: The mineral kingdom which includes our metals, rocks and gemstones, has a consciousness that is deep and trance-like. The vegetable or plant kingdom which includes our edible plants of vegetables, fruits and herbs, as well as all of our trees, flowers and green terrain has a consciousness of a dreamless sleep. The animal kingdom includes all mobile beings below the human kingdom, and they have a dream-like consciousness. The divisions of the animal kingdom are three. We have the 1) higher animals and domestic animals, such as the dog, cat, horse and elephant. 2) The wild animals include the lion, the tiger and the other carnivorous and dangerous wild animals. 3) The third category is the mass of lesser animals that seem to meet no particular need nor fill any special purpose. A keyword for the animal kingdom is *devotion*. The animals are learning in their domestication the concept of devotion to the human kingdom and love and devotion in the rearing of their young, and marks of intelligence are clearly discernible.[1]

The human kingdom has a waking consciousness. We add the principle of love to the devotion principle that began in the animal kingdom. The Buddha revealed to us the importance of Light or enlightenment and love and compassion. The next great Teacher and divine expression of God was the Christ who introduced the concept of Love, brotherly love, the highest expression of which on our planet is unconditional love. The kingdom of souls is the next category, and the list goes up the evolutionary ladder to the Planetary and Solar levels and beyond.

Yes, animals do have souls. However, until they reach a certain higher stage in evolution they are still guided by a remarkable intelligence called a *group soul or group spirit*. The difference existing between human and animal is that the soul of a human has become individualized. Humans have a creative power and a consciousness of a separate self. Master Djwhal Khul defines the soul as "the subtle coherent sum total which we call the *Personality*, composed of the subtle bodies, etheric or vital, astral or emotional, and the lower mental apparatus. These three vehicles humanity shares with the animal kingdom as regards its possession of vitality, sentiency, and potential mind; with the vegetable kingdom as regards vitality and sentiency and with the mineral kingdom as regards vitality and potential sentiency. The soul is also the spiritual being, or the union of life and quality."[2]

It is the task of humanity to help the animals evolve and lead them to liberation into the next kingdom. As we domesticate our animals, we model for them the human qualities of our own kingdom to prepare them in consciousness for their eventual initiation into the human kingdom. No, in case you are wondering, your child was not your father's pet dog. It does not happen that way. In the evolution of consciousness, it may take eons of time for kingdoms to progress to the next kingdom. Our attention to our pets, their training and their acquisition of higher qualities will bring them to a level of individualization in time. As earlier mentioned, Master Djwhal Khul states that, "The animals which individualize are, in every case today, the domestic animals such as the horse, the dog, the elephant and the cat."[3] The relationship of humans to animals is physical, emotional, and increasingly mental, all levels supporting their individualization or growing self-consciousness. Leadbeater[4] tells us that our duty to the animal kingdom is to train them into a higher and more intelligent state of life. They are "brought to us for affection and help—that we might train them out of their ferocity and evoke in them devotion, affection and intellect. Bailey states that "the outgoing love and interest of the people to which the animal is attached by the bonds of affection or of service" is an important factor in their individualization. This makes me think especially of our service dogs that are trained to assist the handicapped and of course always our horses who have served us through the ages. When I began learning about the developing mental levels of our animals, I began reading aloud to my Himalayan cats as they curled up on the foot of my bed to sleep at night. Ommi was not very responsive but Poppy always offered an opinion if asked.

Until the time of their individualization or self-consciousness, the animals are guided by a group spirit in the subtle dimensions or an invisible guardian that governs its particular species. Heindel tells us that the group-spirit consciousness of animals is that of a "picture consciousness" similar to the human dream state. For example, when the animal in the wild is confronted by an object or another animal a picture is immediately perceived within accompanied by a strong impression that the object is a threat or of benefit to its welfare. If the feeling is fearful, the animal is given a suggestion for escape from the threat."[5] As animals individualize, however, they no longer have the protection of the group-spirit but rely on the human kingdom for their well-being. A good example of the influence of the group-spirit is in the formation and flight of birds, ducks, or geese as they are led to migrate toward southern climates at just the right time each fall. You might experiment in working with the group spirit of the ant species on a picnic invasion of ants. Assume a meditational mode or move into the alpha level of your mind to focus and communicate your desire to the group-spirit of the ants—for them to leave your picnic. There have been stories of great success in this endeavor. One that comes to mind is that of a child's outdoor birthday party where the birthday cake was being trampled upon by an army of ants. Someone at the party who understood the concept of the group-spirit was able to connect with that spirit and march the ants off to another location.

Now that we understand something about the consciousness of animals, let us talk more about how we can communicate with them. We know that some animals can think, although it is not thought to be due to the development of a mental body like that of a human mind. It is because they have been in touch with the human kingdom for many generations and have developed abilities not available to animals in the wild that have not had that advantage. This is based on the "same principle that a highly charged wire will induce a weaker current of electricity in a wire brought close to it. All we do, say, or are, reflects itself in our surroundings. This is why the highest domestic animals think."[5]

In June 2004, there was an article in an Atlanta newspaper reporting research about animal communication being carried out at the Max Planck Institute for Evolutionary Anthropology. The article opened with this statement: "Dog owners who think their pets understand them are getting a hearty woof of support from German scientists. Researchers were amazed with Rico, a nine-year-old border collie, who has mastered a vocabulary of 200 words and is capable of the linguistic *fast mapping* that enables toddlers to learn new words after hearing them once. They were amazed to discover that Rico could pick out items like the *blue dinosaur* and *the little red doll* when told to fetch them from his collection of canine toys. They were more surprised when he was able to repeatedly deduce the name of a new toy when instructed—in the German language—to fetch an item he had never heard of before and to remember the word a month later."

These scientists are assuming that Rico is learning with his sense of hearing and external vision only—resulting in "fast-mapping," but he might have also used his faculty for clairvoyant sight or telepathy, reading the pictures the scientists were creating in their minds as they focused on the objects they wanted Rico to fetch. If you want to train your pet to do something, visualize what you want it to do, not what you don't want it to do. It does not understand the negative expression such as "Don't get on the bed." The word *don't* does not always compute for them. Train the pet instead by saying, "Stay on the floor." Your pet will *read* the picture you are creating with your mind of where you want it to be—on the floor. Pets of course do learn our language—our words—and when the same words are used often along with an action they will remember what they mean. They also pay attention to our voice inflections. A firm "no" will often do the trick.

We sometimes don't give our pets the credit they deserve for being intelligent and intuitive. They often demonstrate to us that they know more about what is going on around them than we realize. Remember now, they communicate telepathically, something we human beings don't make a habit of doing, or we don't often realize we're doing it. A college student, a young woman, rang my doorbell one summer afternoon when she was going from door to door soliciting memberships for Nature Conservancy. It was extremely hot that day, so I invited her to step inside to cool off while she made her presentation to me. My cat, Poppy, heard her come in, and being the social and curious little guy that he was, he stationed himself near where we were standing. As the student spoke, Poppy turned his head toward her and appeared to be listening. When I spoke, he turned his head my way. This behavior continued throughout our conversation. The young woman finally stopped talking in mid-sentence and asked, "Does your cat always do that when you're talking to someone?" I jokingly replied, "Only when he's interested in the conversation." I didn't mention of course that he was probably trying to keep up with our conversation by reading our mind pictures.

When my daughter, Wendi, was a little girl I gave her a Himalayan kitten for her twelfth birthday and we named him Beni. Beni continually amazed us with the things he learned so easily. We had a basket of toys for him in the corner of the living room. Some of them were catnip toys, so he quickly learned that they were his. He played with them throughout the day and by evening they were scattered all over the room. After picking them up and putting them back in his basket a few nights, we decided to teach Beni to put them away. Wendi and I got down on the floor with Beni and crawled around the room picking up each toy, saying "Time to put your toys away, Beni." He watched us put a few toys in the basket and then he joined in the game. It only took one evening to teach him. After that, all we had to do was to say, "It's time to put your toys away, Beni," and he had the task accomplished in record time each evening. Beni was indeed a special kitty. He was a self-appointed "seeing-eye kitten" for our little blind dachapoo, Tammy. The two would sit on the fenced-in patio in the sun together. When Tammy had finished her sun bathing she would walk around the patio hunting for the step up to the deck and back door. Beni responded to her cues immediately, and it was heartwarming to watch him guide her with his own little body, bumping her to give her direction. He was vigilant and attended to her needs for the rest of her life. It was his mission.

My friend, Joan, was visiting Ommi and me. I had an errand to run and left Joan and Ommi alone for a while one day. On the night before, I had complained that Ommi was exhibiting some surprising and destructive behavior. We had just moved into a new home, Poppy had died and left him without a feline companion, and he was in a state of grief over all his losses. He was clawing my Oriental rugs and I was desperately trying to think of a way to deal with his behavior. I even considered, against my better judgment, having his claws removed or having the little claw covers attached to his claws. I didn't want to do this because I know it can cause a cat to feel defenseless and insecure. This idea apparently became an important issue for Joan, too. While I was gone that day she decided to have a conversation with Ommi about it. She told him how I was thinking about a solution to the problem and that if he didn't like the idea of losing his ability to use his claws altogether, he would need to demonstrate his cooperation to me by refraining from sharpening his claws on my nice Oriental rugs. Joan said that Ommi attentively sat and listened as she spelled out his options, mentally. The behavior stopped with that conversation and I never witnessed Ommi's destructive behavior again.

There are many books and stories being published about animal communication. If you can learn to communicate with your pets, you are just a step away from being able to contact your human loved ones in another dimension. You've likely heard of Sonya Fitzpatrick on the television show, "Animal Planet," and from that show and her books you may have learned about her phenomenal ability to communicate with animals. There are animal *whisperers* appearing often in the media nowadays. One such article was in our Nashville newspaper, The Tennessean, titled, "Animal Whisperers: Come Out of the Shadows." This news story focused at one point on Tim Link, a whisperer from Atlanta who was a telecommunications company executive for twenty years before a "Dr. Doolittle moment" he experienced when he attended a workshop on animal communication.

My first experience with an animal communicator was with a very fine intuitive named Beatrice "Bea" Lydecker when she was visiting the Tampa Bay area where I was living at the time. She was most convincing when she was able to tell me about the fears, likes and dislikes of our two cats and our little dog. She mentioned a series of unusual behaviors that were true for our pets but that no one but our family would know about. For example, she said that our little dog, Tammy, missed being dressed up in doll clothes by our daughter, Julie. When Tammy was all dressed up she paraded through the house to hear excited applause and compliments on how beautiful she looked. She loved every minute! As Julie grew older, she stopped putting on the fashion shows and Tammy apparently missed all the attention.

Tammy had a small litter of puppies that soon outgrew her. She was a small dog, a mixture of poodle and long-haired dachshund—a dachapoo. She was allowed out of the house by a workman one day and mated with a neighbor's beagle. We jokingly called her puppies "dachapoogles." Tammy was very proud of her offspring. We found good homes for them when they were old enough to be separated from their mother, but I believe Tammy missed her babies. A few years later, I was showing a box of pictures to a friend. In the cardboard box were some prints we had taken of Tammy and her puppies. Tammy was somewhere else in the house when we were looking at the pictures. As soon as I said, "And these are Tammy's puppies," Tammy came running to us and climbed up to look into the box. I guess she thought we had her puppies in the box. When she didn't see them, she began to sniff around and look behind the furniture for them.

One evening, I was sitting at home reading, alone except for Tammy and Oliver, our smoky gray cat. Tammy was aging, had lost her eyesight and had uremia which made her itchy. She was scratching herself, and I felt so sorry for her because I knew she was miserable. At that moment I had the thought, "It might be time to have Tammy euthanized. She's so miserable so much of the time." She was sitting on the floor at my feet by the sofa. She turned her head as if to look at me with her little eyes that could no longer see. Then she stood up and quietly stole away. I realized at that moment that my little blind Tammy was reading my thoughts. I picked her up and reassured her that I was going to keep her with me as long as she wanted to be here.

When Tammy's time came to depart this life, I had to have the help of her veterinarian. I had been advised by two of my intuitive friends to have her euthanized because of her growing toxicity from the uremia. The reason given was that it would make it more difficult to heal the subtle bodies in the spirit world if they were allowed to become much more toxic. I made the appointment to euthanize her. Then I spent most of that day with her. I gave her a loving bath, held her and sang to her. Then I played her favorite music, Wagner's "Tannhauser Overture and Fest March." She always moved closer to one of the stereo speakers when she heard this particular music. I told her what a wonderful little companion she had been to my family and me. Because she was not very active anymore, and seemed to chill easily, she wore a blue knit doggie sweater all the time. It became a part of her except when I removed it long enough to launder it. When I took her to the animal hospital that afternoon, to be euthanized, the doctor gave me choices for disposing of her remains. I chose cremation and instructed a staff member to leave her blue sweater on her because it was then a part of her.

It was indeed a sad time for me, letting go of my precious little canine companion of eighteen years. I went back home alone and began a meditation for her. I later phoned an animal communicator friend, Marti Klabunde, in Iowa, and asked her to check in on Tammy wherever she was. Marti told me that Tammy had an angel guide and was very happy with her. When Marti asked Tammy if there was anything that I could do for her at that time, she responded with, "I want my blue bed—and I want it now!" I told Marti that Tammy's bed was not blue. It was a large gold-colored cushion on the floor. It later occurred to me that Tammy was talking about her blue sweater. Marti didn't know about the sweater, and I didn't tell her right away. I called the animal hospital and asked if the sweater had been left on Tammy. It turned out that they had removed it and it was folded up on a desk. I asked the staff person to save it for me and I went to pick it up. I held Tammy's blue sweater while I said a prayer for her, then I attempted to contact her telepathically. In meditation, I visualized the sweater *building* on her and imagined her wearing it again. Marti had told me in our initial phone conversation that she would attempt a contact with Tammy again the next day. I called her the next afternoon and asked if she had been able to make the contact. She had, and she said that Tammy said to tell me "thank you for the blue bed." Marti was puzzled and asked if I had done anything about Tammy's bed. I then told her what had happened and what I had attempted to do with the sweater. It had worked! I assumed I had been able to put the sweater back on Tammy in my meditation.

Ann Manser had told me years before this experience with Tammy that spirit animals feed on the essence of food on the earth level after they leave it. She said that when a pet dies it will come back to its regular earth home for quite a while and attempt to eat and drink from its own dishes in a familiar place. It will eventually realize it doesn't need the food and water. She suggested leaving a little fresh food and water in their dishes each day for a week or two after their transition. She also told of how she had followed deceased household pets into grocery stores in her meditations and how she found the stores full of these pets feeding on the essence of the pet food on the shelves there.

Conversation is a two-way communication between two or more beings. As one speaks, another listens. In prayer, the communication is one-way from a person to a Higher Being or God. A two-way communication with God includes listening, as in meditation. Most pet owners use one-way communication, unaware of their own ability to listen to their pets. Marta Williams, a gifted animal intuitive in California, offers us ways to enrich the lives we share with our animals. In her book, *Learning Their Language,* she helps us to learn a new way of talking and listening to our "younger brothers and sisters" on Planet Earth.

When we pay attention to our pets and their signals for communicating we can learn why they behave in the ways they do, why they sometimes get sick, how to possibly find them when they're lost, and about their needs and wishes at any given moment. Marta's books are "must reads" for anyone sharing our planet with pets in the animal kingdom.

Ommi was a Flame-point Himalayan cat whose real name was *Omni*. I brought Ommi home as a companion for Poppy when another cat died. I had trouble naming him and just called him Kitty for a few weeks. Then one night in a dream a very tall and powerful masculine being came to me and bellowed, "The kitten's name is Omni!" I replied, "That's an awfully big name for such a tiny kitten." There was no discussion, but the being repeated, "The kitten's name is Omni!"

The following dream occurred eleven days before fourteen-year-old Ommi's transition to the other side of life. In this dream, I was at home and my front door was open. The screen door was closed, however. I heard a knock at the door and went to answer it. It was a man whose visit I was expecting—a business call of some kind. He stood on the bottom step about three steps from the screen door and reached up and opened the door to come in. I noticed Ommi sitting at the door just waiting for an opportunity to run outside. I quickly called out, "No! Don't open the door until I get the cat!" It was too late, and Ommi bounded out and ran away. I ran behind him as fast as I could go. I couldn't catch him, and I knew he was gone for good—I would never be able to find him. While this was all taking place I was very much aware that Poppy, then in actuality deceased, was lying under a big shade tree in the yard contentedly grooming himself. He had been free for a while and knew how to live in the great outdoors of the afterlife. I also knew that Poppy would look after Ommi and help him to adjust to his new surroundings. Poppy looked so serene and happy and self-confident.

My interpretation of the dream was that because Ommi was being treated for terminal kidney failure and was in a great deal of pain, he was waiting for an opportunity to go through the *door* that would grant him his freedom from a very sick little body. I suspected that Poppy was hovering close to him during his time of need and was assuring me that he would be on hand to help him make his transition.

Ommi's time to leave his Earth life was indeed imminent. I talked with Marta Williams about his illness and she suggested that I watch for signs he would give me when he knew it was time for him to depart. Ommi was always respectful of his boundaries, and especially of my place on a small sofa in my den. He jumped up in my lap only when invited and was never on the sofa when I wasn't sitting there. I came home from work one day and found him sitting alone in my place on that sofa, and I knew right away that he had something important to tell me.

There was one more little client to see that day and her appointment was in my home office in just a few minutes. I didn't want to keep the appointment, but I knew my student was on her way and would arrive at any moment. I wanted to spend this time with my beloved Ommi because I sensed that he was telling me our remaining time together was short. I didn't know what to do. I didn't give my client's parent credit for understanding how important my time with my little cat companion was that afternoon. They had to drive several miles in heavy traffic to get to my home, so I didn't try to contact them. I picked Ommi up and explained that I had just one more session and we could have our time together. I then took him to my bedroom and carefully placed him on my bed.

I was not totally available to my little client for our educational therapy session. All I could think about was Ommi and his desire to spend the last hours of his life with me. I wanted to hold him and tell him how much he meant to me and how I would miss having him in my life and how he would always be in my heart. My decision to put Ommi off robbed us both of a chance to say our goodbyes in a proper and meaningful way. After my young client left I went to my bedroom, but Ommi was not where I had left him on the bed. I looked for him and called his name but he was nowhere in sight. Somehow he had jumped off my high bed and had found a place under it. I tried to coax him out, but he didn't move. His back was turned toward me and I couldn't even see his face. I knew he needed help—veterinary help, so I called the Emergency Animal Clinic because the animal hospital was closed for the day. Through my tears, I explained the situation to the technician on duty. She told me she would make the necessary preparations and the doctor would be waiting for us.

It was urgent that I get Ommi out from under the bed and into the pet carrier, but I couldn't reach him and pull him out without hurting him. As if from another dimension, I heard a soft voice say to me, "Tell him you'll take him to see Poppy." Poppy and Ommi had been inseparable when Poppy was still alive. But Poppy had died about eighteen months earlier and Ommi had almost unrelentingly grieved for him. I got down on my hands and knees again and found Ommi in the same position under the bed. Then I quietly said, "Ommi, come to me and I'll take you to see Poppy." Ommi's head turned so he could see me. I repeated what I had just told him. By then he could barely move, but he managed to drag himself out from under the bed—no longer able to stand up. I carefully picked him up, held him close to me and told him I loved him, and I put him on a pillow in the carrier. His advanced kidney failure was obviously causing him a lot of pain.

At the Emergency Animal Clinic I sat with Ommi during the euthanizing process, expressed my love, said prayers and meditated. I called on the angels, my mother, Pat, Ann Manser and Poppy in other dimensions for help with Ommi's transition. In a seemingly short period of time I had a wonderful sense of peace. When I felt that Ommi was at peace, too, I said my last goodbyes. The doctor and attendants were very compassionate and they allowed me to stay as long as I wished. They also allowed me to give them instructions for the timing of the cremation process, taking into consideration my own beliefs about it—to wait for three days before disturbing his body for cremation.

At home again, emotionally exhausted, totally alone and without a beloved pet for the first time in over twenty-five years, I fell in bed. I was about to fall asleep when I suddenly felt Ommi's familiar jump onto the foot of the bed. He apparently wanted me to know that his journey to the other side—to the next dimension, was successful and that he was pain-free and again "full of life." I sat up in bed and talked to him for a bit, although I wasn't actually able to see him, and I thanked him for letting me know that all was well. When I settled down to try to go to sleep, I felt him walk across my legs and up the bed to nuzzle against the small of my back—as always! He came for those nightly visits for the next couple of years. Even now I'm aware of his presence on many nights. He and Poppy have come together for visits with me. I've been aware of sitting up in bed in my astral body in their dimension and playing with both of them—sometimes even feeding them kitty treats. It all seems so normal when it happens. During the Christmas holidays, I've often heard them snooping in the paper and plastic bags of gifts left on the floor after a shopping trip, just as they did when they were in their physical bodies.

I've often wondered if Mother was taking care of some of my little pets in her dimension. One morning when I was still between sleeping and waking consciousness, in that hypnogogic state, Mother appeared to me holding one of my cats for me to see. I believe she was letting me know that she was indeed taking care of my little cats and dogs. In fact, two of my psychic friends have said something like, "Kathryn always has a lot of little animals around her." They're usually describing something about her other-dimensional home location when they mention it. It makes me feel good to think that they're being cared for by my mother who knows them and loves them.

Marta Williams had communicated with both Poppy and Ommi when they were little physical cats. So I of course wanted to see if she could contact them in their new home on the other side of life. She began her intuitive reading for me with information about Ommi's transition. Although I had not mentioned any of my preparation for his transition, she told me that "Ommi had a bevy of loving beings to greet him as he crossed over." She said that Poppy was there, as I had promised Ommi, and that others included my mother, my friend Pat and angels and several other beings. It has been my experience that if Ann Manser can't respond to my call at any given time, she always sends an angelic representative. It seemed indeed that Ommi received a royal welcome into his new life.

In J. Allen Boone's *Kinship with All Life*, he tells about his struggles in learning to communicate with his handsome German Shepherd named Strongheart. Strongheart was known the world over for his stardom in Hollywood films, but in his heart he was just a dog without human level ambitions. Boone wanted to know more about the inner feelings of his majestic and highly intelligent companion, so he set out to experiment with developing a deeper level of communication with Strongheart. Boone was aware of the dog's ability to understand his thoughts and wishes but he felt that his own intuition was not as highly developed. In his first attempt at conscious two-way communication, he talked heart to heart to Strongheart and told him what his intentions were for their new project. He then asked Strongheart several questions about himself and listened for his answers. He got nothing. Strongheart sat, completely attentive and involved in the experiment, and when in time Boone couldn't seem to receive his responses he would blink his eyes, yawn and turn and walk away thus ending the session. Boone read to him and talked to him in daily sessions, but it was still one-sided. It was only much later when Boone realized that Strongheart had been silently talking back to him. Boone had gone into a blank state of mind and had become open and receptive in a way he had never allowed before. He then realized that he had made the contact. He knew how to listen as Strongheart already knew how to do. His proof was that he had answers to all the questions he had asked Strongheart.

There is a lesson here for communication with all forms of life, on this side and the other side of life. A good exercise for attuning to other life forms is to sit outdoors in a quiet place where you're not easily distracted and attune to the plant life around you. There are nature spirits which inhabit and assist the growth of all the trees, flowers and other growing things from the earth, as well as those connected to the elements of water, air or wind and fire. In Eastern philosophy, the higher forms are called devas and there are other-dimensional fairy-like and angel-like forms who are responsible for the many stages of growth and development of the forms manifested by our elements. There are tree devas, magnificent mountain and ocean devas, to name a few. To make this attunement one must sit quietly, stilling the mind and then being open to lines of communication that follow. With regular practice, the devas learn to trust you, and you will eventually be privy to more and more information about the inner worlds of nature. You might even develop the ability to see them with your inner eyes.

It is this same openness that will help you in your communication with the animal kingdom. Don't expect your responses in words. The thoughts of your pets are more often conveyed in complete concepts or in picture form. Marta Williams in *Learning Their Language* asks you to trust what is given to you intuitively by your pet. "Assume that whatever you receive in impressions, feelings, words, visual images or sensations is information that was actually sent to you intuitively by your animal."[6]

An animal will sense and know the truth of your thoughts and feelings. You can say one thing and feel another. Your animal will respond to your feeling about what you say. Sometimes the discrepancy will even cause confusion for them, and in that case they might not know how to respond. Be honest with them, as they are honest with you.

Death doesn't mean the same thing to an animal that it does to a human being. Animals do not anticipate it as a fearful experience, but they move easily and consciously between dimensions in their everyday existence so that they are somewhat familiar with the process of *stepping* into another dimension. It is more fearful for those being left behind because we don't really know what to expect or how to prepare for letting go of a little animal companion. There are so many decisions to make, especially if there is a long illness and suffering on the part of the pet. Should we help a pet through the use of euthanasia? When is it time to ask for veterinary help? Rita Reynolds in her book, *Blessing the Bridge,* says that "pain and confusion are a part of the process."[7] We might be cutting short a valuable lesson for the pet and the owner if we are too quick to euthanize a pet. Your pet will let you know when it's time to go. Watch for the signs. Ommi was able to let me know, and it is my hope that you will pay better attention than I did. Let your pet know it is all right to go. That is a very reassuring gesture whether it is your pet or a human being. And don't forget . . . if you can learn to communicate with your pets while they are here in the physical, you can continue to do so when they are in spirit.

Beni

Tammy

Poppy

Ommi

PART III

Guide to Afterlife Contact

CHAPTER 19

Our Psychic Legacy

Your mind is a powerful tool. As a bridge between
your thoughts and your spirit, it converts energy
into images, memories and articulations.

Rita S. Berkowitz
and
Deborah S. Romaine

A S HUMAN BEINGS OUR MEMORY banks can be divided into several categories which include short-term memory, long-term memory and active-working memory. In psychology, memory can be identified as conscious, subconscious and super-conscious levels of memory.

Conscious memory is voluntary based on sense perceptions to which we have instant conscious access. Subconscious or involuntary memory is the result of the impressions of one's surroundings recorded on the etheric body. These surroundings are recorded by an individual in the greatest detail regardless of the awareness of the individual. These recordings of the material environment are completely accurate. For example, if you were walking past shop windows full of merchandise, a few items may stand out in your short-term memory or even your long-term memory as you attempt to recall what you saw displayed in those shop windows. If under hypnosis, you attempt to recall what you saw, you would discover that your memory reveals every minute detail of the contents of the display, as in a photograph. Conscious memory and subconscious memory relate only to experiences of the present life. But what of the superconscious memory? This is the repository of all knowledge gained and faculties acquired in our previous lives, sometimes active and sometimes latent in the present life.[1]

We are conscious in our present time in a way that is very different from our earlier existence in evolution. Our physical bodies sleep when we feel the need to restore our energy while our subtle bodies, the mental, emotional and spiritual bodies become active on their own levels of consciousness in other dimensions. We bring back to waking consciousness on the physical level some of this activity in the dreams we recall.

Eons ago, before there was a fully-developed material world with physical bodies, the human consciousness was awake in the etheric body on its own level where it lived among its companions in a sphere of activity, although much below the awareness level we now know. It was something like living in the dream world that we experience during sleep in our current time. When the night of activity on those levels ended and the soul felt the need for rest, it returned to its newly-developing physical body for rest during the day where it became slowly but increasingly aware of the dense world forming around it. Rudolf Steiner places this condition of consciousness sometime during the period preceding the last third of the Atlantean epoch. A soul did not have a consciousness of self; he did not call himself "I" but functioned under the direction of a group soul. Humans gradually matured and developed a consciousness of the individual *self* during the Persian and Babylonian-Egyptian ages. With the development of ego-consciousness came the faculty of sight in the external world. The spiritual world previously open to him was gradually closed to him. The consciousness shifted from the inner and psychically visual world to the external world and our limited physical vision. Steiner tells us that "earlier men saw what the later myths relate: Woden-Mercury, Jupiter-Zeus (and other gods and goddesses of mythology). They saw all these beings at night; they were then among them. The door to these spiritual beings has closed. In their place man has gained the world now surrounding him."[2] The spirit world has not disappeared, but our own focus of consciousness has shifted to the limiting environment of the physical earth plane.

Through our super-conscious memory, the memory of knowledge gained and faculties acquired in our previous lives across the eons of time is still a part of each of us. With this awareness we are capable of re-awakening our psychic abilities. When we fall asleep, our awareness shifts to another level of consciousness and the physical body with its sensations is at rest. Information that we bring back in memory to our waking consciousness on the physical level often seems disconnected and nonsensical. The physical brain is able to process information according to its experience in this lifetime. When experience in dreams or spiritual dimensions are filtered through the physical brain, much can be left out or distorted by a brain to which the experience is unfamiliar. Just because your brain remembers a dream that doesn't make much sense, it does not always indicate that your dreams or visits to the spiritual realms are meaningless. Robert Moss quotes a Seneca Indian healer in his book, *Conscious Dreaming*, who expresses, ". . . the remembered dream is often different from the fuller dream experience."[3] Moss states about this book, "You will read many accounts of how our departed ones return in dreams with vital and life-affirming messages; you will also learn to screen and discriminate among communications from the spirit world.[4] Dreams are very important in many cultures where families greet the new day together and share and discuss their dreams from the night time with each other. Moss also informs us that "With poetic clarity, Yeats explained that the dreams of the living are also the work of the dead who use the living person to complete their life reviews." Moss further states: "Those on the Other Side actively seek out the living in the dreamspace to achieve mutual forgiveness and understanding, to make amends, and to perform family or community service that they feel is now required of them."[5]

The more attention you pay to your dreams, the more dreams you might be able to recall. I've kept dream journals throughout my adult life and a few in teen years, too. If I go for a period of time without recording or otherwise working with and giving attention to my dreams, I don't seem to remember very many of them. As soon as I give them some attention, I begin to recall several in a night. I believe dreams are important messages to the conscious mind from the subconscious or super-conscious minds or from the spirit dimensions. There are many experts in this field to help you sort through your dreams, suggesting ways to work with the dreams and with the symbols they produce. A favorite contemporary authority on this subject is the above-mentioned Robert Moss. I highly recommend his books and workshops to guide you in your spiritual work and your opening to spiritual dimensions.

It is helpful to keep a pad of paper and a pencil at your bedside in case you wake from a dream in the night and want to jot down important words and symbols. A few years ago I decided to set up a small cassette recorder to use for this purpose so I wouldn't need to turn on a light in the night for writing out my dreams. I recorded a dream one night, but the next morning I forgot that I had done so. I proceeded to write out the dream in my journal. A few days later, I needed the recorder for something else. When I checked it, there was something on the tape so I listened to the recording. I discovered that it was the same dream I had written about in my journal a few days before, but the tape held much more detail—details of which I had no conscious memory.

In an enlightening dream visit that took place in an outdoor scene in the afterlife, I found myself standing with a small group of women in conversation about their experiences there. I knew a couple of the women and was aware of their earlier transition and crossing over to another dimension. One woman was sharing her delight with her new ability to materialize objects and settings from her thoughts, often instantly. She asked if there was something I would like to manifest so she could demonstrate her new-found ability. I suggested a lovely garden. She did indeed create a garden, but it was not my idea of a lovely one with colorful flowers and lush greenery. Her garden looked more like a desert scene with sand and succulent plants, such as cacti—a rather dry and muted array of desert plants. I soon realized that our conception of a lovely garden had everything to do with our unique earth experience. She had apparently spent her life in dry regions of the country, and mine was spent in the eastern part of the United States where there are abundant forest areas and areas of rich soil for growing lovely flower gardens.

Many afterlife accounts emphasize the choices we can make when we are on the other side. Wherever we find ourselves in consciousness and whatever we conceive of as comfortable and as beautiful will have a big part in determining our first experiences there.

If you believe that you've lived before, you're in good company. Marcus Tillius Cicero, Julius Caesar, Henry David Thoreau, Carl Jung, Thomas Edison, Albert Einstein, Ralph Waldo Emerson, William James, Walt Whitman, Eleanor Roosevelt and Albert Schweitzer are just a few among many famous people who have expressed a belief in reincarnation. Those who are believers say that most of us come into this earth life with what has been termed earth blindness. How confusing would it be to be aware of other lives while you're trying to live and accomplish your goals for this one? I believe it is possible for memories of other lives to sometimes "bleed" through to our "this life" consciousness. I spoke of one in an earlier chapter when I had some suicidal ideation for a short time. I've had other past-life memories in dreams and spontaneous flashes while I was engaged in some activity that stirred the memory. I have learned over time to trust these little memory flashes. The most thorough and dramatic memory took form over a period of several years following a dream I had consciously programmed to answer an important question. I will tell you that story now.

In the spring of 1984, I was invited to a full moon ceremony that was to take place in a colleague's authentic Native American teepee. The service was conducted primarily by Native Americans with the assistance of some of my colleagues. It was a lovely and meaningful ceremony. Another colleague, Tom, had learned through an earlier conversation that my attitude toward the Native American culture was fairly neutral. I felt no prejudice and I felt no real devotion to the culture as did many of my friends and colleagues. They seemed to have an attachment to the culture that I just didn't feel. Tom came to me after the ceremony and asked if I'd received any insights during meditation regarding my attitude toward the culture, which was not at all negative, just neutral. I hadn't, and I vowed to work with it again at home in meditation and perhaps even ask for a dream of explanation.

When I arrived at work the next day, Tom met me and asked again if I'd had any revelation concerning the Native American culture. I told him "No, I didn't recall a dream about the Native Americans but I'd had a dream about Andrew Jackson." He caught his breath and asked me to share the dream.

In the dream I was a boy of about seventeen years of age living in an earlier century. I was standing in front of a large, beautiful old chifferobe or wardrobe full of very fine wool uniforms and coats. I knew that I was General Andrew Jackson's favorite nephew and that he relied on me to aid him in many ways; I was his personal valet. As I stood in his bedroom in front of his chifferobe, I proudly polished the brass buttons on one of his navy blue uniform coats. It seemed that I knew that it would soon be my turn to serve my country in our army and how proud I would be then to serve under the general, my uncle, in that capacity.

Tom was visibly stunned and responded with, "You were on the other side!" I admitted that I didn't remember the history of that time and asked him to explain. He told me that Andrew Jackson was very much involved in the exodus of the Cherokee tribe of Indians from Georgia and some from the states of North and South Carolina and Tennessee in the early to mid-nineteenth century. A large percentage of lives were lost from illness and exposure during the journey on foot to northeastern Oklahoma, called the "Trail of Tears." I thought about what Tom had said for a long time. I felt such sadness and a genuine sympathy for the Native American Indians who had suffered so horribly as a result of this exodus. Although I had no direct responsibility for this action, I pondered the possibility of indirect or group karma. I did not even know if Andrew Jackson had such a nephew. I recorded the dream, but the memory of it soon faded and became lost in my efforts to complete my academic work. I was involved in an internship for a doctorate in Human Development Counseling at Peabody College of Vanderbilt University.

In the spring of 1986 I received a call from Carol Parrish, a friend whom I knew when we both lived in Florida. She was then living in Tahlequah, Oklahoma where she and her husband Charles Harra had developed a church-related village, Light of Christ Community Church in Sparrow Hawk Village, in 1981. The church and village had grown and as a result a school, Sparrow Hawk Academy, had been founded. The school's founders, a husband-wife team, were going back to their home in Texas to pursue more graduate work and the positions of headmistress and teacher were now open. Carol invited me to fill those positions. I made a visit to the village in July and moved there to fill the positions at the school in the fall.

After a few years of very rewarding involvement in the school, church and village, the school had to close its doors. The older children finished school and there were too few in lower grades to make it feasible to keep the school open. I was left looking for employment. I still needed one more internship for my degree at Vanderbilt and then there would be the dissertation requirements to complete. I took a position as Clinic Director and Psychologist in the Child Guidance Clinic at the Oklahoma State Department of Health. This satisfied my last internship requirement as well as my need for gainful employment.

In the fall of 1991 I was in a near-fatal automobile accident. I was a passenger in a vehicle that hydroplaned on an almost flooded rural highway and deposited the driver and me in a ravine after turning over three times. The driver had minor injuries, but mine were severe. While I was on leave from the Health Department for five months, I contemplated my situation as a resident of a state too far away to visit with my family as often as I wished. Why was I still in Oklahoma? Then the memory of that dream came back to me. Where was I? I was living in northeastern Oklahoma in Tahlequah, the Cherokee Nation Capital where the *Trail of Tears* ended. I was among the Cherokee Indians, descendants of the Indian population for whose exodus from the eastern states Andrew Jackson was largely responsible. It suddenly became clear to me that this was indeed a possible karmic *tour of duty*. Here I was helping many Cherokee families put their lives back together through child and family counseling, educational testing and working with their schools on intervention programs for them. I even had opportunities to meet and do some work for the tribal chief of the Cherokee Nation, Wilma Mankiller. What a powerful yet humble leader! I performed some specialized work with house parents and children, many orphaned, in a rural Indian village (Oaks Indian Center) and facilitated seminars at the Cherokee Nation for teachers of young Indian children. When this profound awakening occurred, I began a whole new level of commitment and work with my clients. I felt a deep sense of mission with them that I had not consciously felt before.

While waiting for Workers Compensation from the accident, I also completed my doctoral dissertation and was awarded a Doctor of Education degree from Vanderbilt University. The following year, with my mission accomplished, I was back in Nashville. After my move back to Nashville, Pat Larson came for a visit. The first thing she wanted to do was visit the Hermitage, home of Andrew Jackson, where we discovered the chifferobe of my dream back in 1984. It was Andrew Jackson's very own chifferobe! We also discovered that Jackson's favorite nephew and personal valet was Andrew Jackson Donelson, so we included a visit to his home, Tulip Grove, on adjacent property.

Now I cannot prove that I am Donelson reincarnated, and I do not wish to be in a category with the many who believe they are Napoleon or Cleopatra. But you'll have to admit that there were many significant signposts along the way that would make a very good case for some truth to my story.

CHAPTER 20

You Can Contact the Afterlife

We don't need a go-between to talk to the deceased.
We can have direct communication with our departed,
in timely and helpful ways, especially if we are willing
to pay attention to our dreams and learn the arts
of active conscious dreaming.

~ Robert Moss

IF THERE IS RELUCTANCE TO developing our psychic abilities it may come in large part from the historic time of the witch-hunters who burned people at the stake if they revealed any indication of psychic ability. Even now there is some skepticism surrounding the whole arena of extrasensory perception and its development. The skeptics seem to be in the minority in recent years, however. Skeptics seem to think in terms of probabilities rather than possibilities and perhaps need to have at least one personal psychic experience that just *blows them away* in order to become a believer. "The whole history of the Bible, as well as many other ancient histories, revolves around the importance of visions, prophecies and dreams."[1] Sometimes such an experience is so subtle that we don't pay attention or give it any credibility. We are all psychic. It's just a matter of developing our psychic ability in order to make it more useful to us. Many of you are already well-developed, psychically, and the process outlined here will be a natural one for you. "One thing you'll discover when you begin to activate your sixth sense is that what you're truly doing is nurturing your most authentic self, your spirit. Nurturing intuition is actually the art of discovering and honoring who you really are."[2]

If you have any doubts about whether you really want to make contact with those in other dimensions, take a moment to think about how you might feel if your transition were imminent. Would you want your loved ones to remember you and attempt communication with you? Think about how you might feel if you tried to contact your loved ones on Earth and you were unable to get any response. In his book, *Heaven and Earth*, James Van Praagh states that "One must also realize that someone who has recently passed on is now in a completely unfamiliar world. A spirit may be a bit confused at first because the physical laws to which it had become accustomed no longer exist. Once a spirit recognizes that it is not dead, but very much alive—more alive than ever before—it learns that it lives in a world of thought. Thus a spirit must begin to understand how to use thought to create what it wants." He also says that when spirits have adapted to their new home they become more aware of our grief and sadness. It can become extremely frustrating to them when they cannot communicate to us that they are still a part of our everyday lives and "we just don't get it."[3]

In preparation for contacting other dimensions it is helpful to know something about how things work on the other side of life in the higher or spirit dimensions. It has been proven scientifically that everything is energy, energy vibrating at different frequencies on a continuum that spans not only our physical dimension but dimensions below and above and beyond the Earth frequency. In my research into the process for making contact, I have concluded that those in spirit always *hear* us when we focus our thoughts on them. They can hear our messages telepathically, however it takes a lot of effort on their part and ours to get their messages to us. Those from the spirit realm must learn to lower their vibratory frequency in order to be compatible with our frequency which is considerably lower. We on the earth plane must learn to raise our vibratory frequency and attempt to blend the two frequencies to cause a coalescing of energies from both sides of the veil.

"In concentrating the mind on any one spirit person, you are sending out real, live, active forces. These forces pass through the air in precisely the same way as electrical waves do, and they never miss their mark. You concentrate on Mr. A in the spirit world, and immediately Mr. A is conscious of a force coming to him. Thought communication is the closest link between the two worlds, but it must be well-ordered and well-trained brain action."[4]

In *The Blue Island,* Stead spoke of going to a building in his part of the spirit world where there were spirits who help newcomers transmit messages to their loved ones on Earth. He learned about travelers who worked close to the earth frequency and who were able to sense the people on Earth who could receive spirit world transmissions. I believe I met my mother in a dream visit in a place like the one Stead described. I arrived at a large station or depot and disembarked from a monorail car into a very spacious room leading to a junction of hallways. I had a choice of going straight, down a wide hallway to my right or into another large room on my right. I chose to take the hallway on my right. I knew I was to meet someone important, but I didn't know who it was at that time. As I turned into the hallway, I suddenly found out who I was meeting. It was my mother! I was overjoyed to see her and ran to her and threw my arms around her. She had a message for me, so she didn't hesitate to deliver it. I was aware that we can't always "hold the frequency" as long as we'd like, so business had to be conducted before I might be pulled back into my body asleep on my bed. I recall actually pinching her gently and saying, "No one will believe that I've actually seen you and touched you. This is as real as it gets!" She smiled, and our meeting was over. I noticed that she was wearing a nice navy blue suit and a white blouse which was familiar attire for her over the years.

I have also read about signals of spirit lights indicating receivers on Earth. Some say that there is a kind of spirit light in the aura of persons who are open to developing or have developed the ability to contact the spirit world. This is a signal, to the spirit wishing for contact, that one is ready to listen and to receive messages from the other side. Stead speaks of his attempts to make contact with his daughter, Estelle, to let her know he was all right after his death in the Titanic tragedy of 1912. His official guide took him to a room of two or three people on Earth discussing the disaster. They were holding a séance, and Stead's official guide showed him how to make his presence known.

Stead was told that "thought" was the controlling force and that he should visualize himself there with the people in the room, standing in the center of the room with a strong light shining on him. He was to create a picture of himself there and hold the visualization very deliberately and in great detail, staying focused on his actually being there, with the people in the room consciously aware of his presence. He said he failed at first, but after a few more attempts he succeeded and they did see him.[5]

For our purposes here, we won't dwell on spirit materialization but more on learning communication using meditation techniques to develop clairvoyance or seeing with our inner vision; clairaudience or hearing with our inner ears; and clairsentience or an inner knowing.

There is some basic preparation for those who are serious about designing a systematic program of discipline to develop methods of contact with the spirit world. This preparation includes paying attention to your health, physically and mentally; cleansing or clearing your channel for receiving; energizing your "desire body;" loosening your subtle bodies; learning to relax and focus your mind, and becoming acquainted with your subconscious mind and *Low Self*, the latter being a very important key to making the contact. You may say, "But that sounds like a lot of work." For some it might be too much to ask; others may already be ahead of the game because they are already naturally in condition for this kind of work; and for still others it will be a labor of love to know you can actually do something to make contact with your loved ones a reality. Don't forget, you can ask for the help of angelic presences, your own guides and loved ones on the other side, as well as parts of yourself such as your *Low Self* and your *High Self*.

The following are suggestions and they may be modified to suit your individual preferences:

Physical Health:

1. Exercise, in fresh air when possible, is important for increasing circulation and forcing you to breathe deeper, therefore taking in more oxygen. Find time also to relax and let go of stress.

2. Increase your water intake and decrease your salt intake. Water is a great conductor of electrical forces and our cells need hydration in order to conduct the electrical forces of communication with other dimensions. Drinking pure water will not only lubricate your cells but will deliver to them the nutrition that keeps them in good health. Some people report enhanced psychic ability while showering or bathing.

3. Foods that have a lot of life-force will aid you in clearing and vitalizing your chakras for meditation and contact with other dimensions. In particular, eat mostly fresh vegetables, fruits, and grains, with a minimum of (or no) sugar, caffeine, or red meat which tend to clog the chakras, according to Doreen Virtue. Alcohol and drugs will lower the vibratory frequency making it difficult to synchronize your frequency with the subject of your contact. You should allow twenty-four hours to pass, after using alcohol, before attempting afterlife contact. For details on eating for health and for spiritual work, I recommend Virtue's book, *Eating in the Light*.[6]

4. Fasting will hasten the cleansing process. Consider a juice fast to let your digestive system rest and cleanse toxins from major organs. There are many kinds of fasts that can be used: vegetable juice, fruit juice and water fasts seem to be the most popular. If you use a juice fast, consider juicing your own fruits or vegetables to avoid sugar and sodium added to many bottled juices. If you use bottled juice, buy natural juices without additives. It is a good idea to work toward a liquid fast with a couple of days of eating only fruit, mixed fruit or all the same fruit, such as only bananas or only apples or grapes. One of my favorite fasts is one that uses only grapes and grape juice. There is enough natural sugar in grapes so that developing headaches during your fast will not be likely. I like to eat grapes for a day or two then juice them for another few days. It is best not to mix a fruit and vegetable juice fast. Along with any juice fast, drink plenty of pure water and take Vitamin C. Dr. Andrew Weil advises leaving all other supplements off during the fast, if possible. He says you may want to add herbal teas to your fast.[7]

Mental Health:

Meditation for any reason works better when we are rested and calm and free of mental-emotional clutter and fears. It is easier to focus when our minds are not busy with so many distractions. If you are new at meditating, consider starting with five minutes in the morning and five minutes in the evening—just sitting and being aware of your breathing. When you feel ready, add five minutes at a time until you have reached the length of time that feels normal for you—twenty, forty, sixty minutes daily.

Cleansing and clearing your channel for receiving:

A simple approach to clearing your channel for meditation and receiving transmissions from the spirit world is the use of light and color. I use a visualization of the violet flame to clear my whole energy field before sitting down to meditate. It can be performed standing, sitting, or lying down. The violet flame will be included later in this chapter in the section on exercises for meditation and contact. This is a good purification exercise. All of the exercises can become automatic when you have used the image of each regularly and with intention for a while. Use the violet flame before meditation and before sending healing to someone.

To continue the clearing of your channel, a spiral of sparkling, brilliant white light may be used—spiraling clockwise downward around and through your body and into the earth.

Grounding:

Many sources that teach meditation do not mention grounding techniques, but grounding oneself is important because it will prevent a feeling of being scattered during and after the meditation. You will be able to bring down to the physical level higher concepts and expressions of creativity that can become practical and useful in your everyday life when you are able to ground them. A favorite grounding technique is to visualize a column of brilliant white light coming from high above your head through the crown, down through your subtle and physical bodies, filling every cell with light and exiting through the soles of your feet deep into the earth. More grounding techniques will be given later in this chapter.

Low Self Contact:

In a contact session through Steve Engel, I asked Pat Larson some questions about making contact with her. She told me to "Have a conversation with your subconscious mind (Low Self, Basic Self). Tell him/her you need this to come forward. Your subconscious can play a key, vital role in this."

In psychology we learn about three main levels of the self called the subconscious, the conscious and super-conscious minds. Sigmund Freud, Austrian psychiatrist and founder of psychoanalysis, called these levels the id, ego and superego. Max Freedom Long uses the terms Low Self, Middle Self and High Self in place of the psychological terms. These are the terms to which I shall refer here. The Low Self in this case is the Self which is under the dominion of the Middle Self and High Self.

Max Freedom Long was a teacher who moved from California to the island of Hawaii in 1917 to teach elementary school. He became aware of healing methods being used on the island that appeared to him to be like "magic." He eventually became convinced of the value of these methods and devoted the rest of his life to research into the origins of the methods and the native Polynesians, called kahunas, who originated them and passed them down through the generations to the few who practiced them and kept them sacred. The word kahuna can be literally translated as "keepers of the secret." Long eventually named his teachings "Huna," a shortened version of kahuna, meaning "hidden secret." He categorized the Huna teachings as a science and not a religion. Huna suggests that harmonious living is created by being aware of our three selves and of the cooperation among them. "For all practical purposes, the goal of man is the full union of the THREE SELVES to form a complete man or woman."[8] In Long's research, he concluded that the Low Self represents the subconscious, inner, emotional and intuitive levels of the self. The Middle Self represents the waking consciousness and rational self, the self we rely on for logical choices and decisions. And the High Self is the connection with the divine or the personal God part of the self.

The Low Self must be trained by the Middle Self. There are many ways to accomplish this, but it is important to keep in mind that repetition is needed. Think about how you would train your pet to do something. Use the same words consistently or perform the same actions repeatedly. That is how the Low Self forms a habit. It takes the meanings of your words literally, so be careful of the way you express them. Use the most positive form of a thought possible, leaving out negatives such as *not* and *don't*. At times it is also helpful to perform some kind of physical act to emphasize and to ground specific commands or requests. For example, if you write out a list of personal bad habits that you'd like to remove from your life you might let go of them by burning the list and creating an affirmation of positive actions to replace them.

The use of affirmations is an effective way to train the Low Self. For example, "I give thanks for the ability to contact higher dimensions," or "I am now able to make clear contact with Aunt Meg and Uncle Will." You can say the affirmations or write them two or three times a day or as often as you think about it, always using the same words. If you are writing them, you might want to write them out ten or more times a couple of times a day. As you say or write the words, visualize the action for the Low Self as if it is already happening for you. For example, visualize yourself sitting opposite Aunt Meg having a lively conversation with her as you repeat the affirmations.

Another way to establish communication with your Low Self is to use a pendulum. A simple beginner's chart might be a circle with a horizontal line crossing the middle of the circle and a vertical line drawn through the middle of that line, forming a cross. This gives you a visual chart of pathways for your pendulum. You can take any small object such as a ring, a small crystal or small pendant on a chain, a cord or a piece of thread. Some use a fishing sinker or metal washer—not too heavy though. Hold it between your thumb and first finger in the hand that feels most comfortable for you, leaving about two to three inches of cord between your fingers and the pendulum. Point your thumb and finger down toward the chart. You can rest your elbow on a table. Just hold the pendulum over the center of the cross without moving it. You are now ready to establish the pathways for your yes and no answers.

Tell your Low Self that you wish to communicate with him or her and you would like to know which direction the movement of the pendulum will always indicate a *yes* answer. Then do the same thing to establish the *no* answer. It might swing back and forth for one and side to side for the other. Or it might follow the circle clockwise for *yes* and counterclockwise for *no*. If it doesn't soon move on its own, move it in a direction and say, "This is a *yes* answer." Then move it in another direction and say "This is a *no* answer." Then check it out with yes and no questions that you can confirm. You will want to designate a pattern for *I don't know* and *I can't tell you that* answers, too. My Low Self uses the vertical swing for *yes* and the horizontal swing for *no* She uses a clockwise circle for *I don't know,* and a counterclockwise circle for *I can't tell you that.* Practice this daily, and it won't be long before you'll be able to rely on its accuracy. When I began my contacts with the other side, I sometimes checked them out later with the pendulum. For example, "Was I really making contact with my friend Pat?" Remember, the Low Self learns through repetition.

You might want to name your Low Self and call her or him by name during your sessions together and at any other time you wish to teach her something. Ask for a name in your meditation. Your first impression is usually right, and it could be a very unusual name or a pretty common one. You might find yourself using the pendulum for questions concerning your health or for decisions you need to make. There are many chart designs in books devoted to pendulums and dowsing. Sid Lonegren has published a book as a part of a kit called *The Pendulum Kit* which includes a pendulum.[9]

Two more preliminary considerations for serious contact are the exercises for strengthening the desire body and loosening the other subtle bodies to facilitate easier contact between dimensions. These exercises are especially helpful for people who tend to be too mental, who have difficulty getting into a feeling, intuitive place in their consciousness.

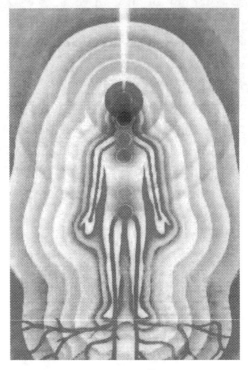

Subtle Bodies

Those who choose to develop their extrasensory perception (ESP) or psychic ability can develop the ability to see these subtle bodies. These bodies surround and penetrate the physical body. We want to remain grounded when we're involved in the outer world, so it would be a good idea at the end of your contact session to imagine that you are *pulling* those bodies back close to your physical body.

Those of us on the physical plane of Earth have physical bodies. These are the bodies that use the five senses of sight, hearing, smell, touch and taste. At this particular time in our evolution of consciousness, we can be aware of twelve bodies—the physical body, the lowest in vibratory frequency, and eleven more, each level having a higher or finer frequency than the level below it.

Dimensions of consciousness, sometimes called planes, are divided into twelve levels of consciousness as found in Ann Manser's teachings of the *Holy Kabalah* and *Pages of Shustah*. These twelve planes have seven divisions or sub-planes. They begin with the Plane of Divinity and descend to the Earthen planes, our material world and the lowest, densest point in consciousness, for example a black hole.

Listed in descending succession of vibratory rate and corresponding colors, they are:

Divinity:	Light
Spiritual Memory:	silver
Spiritual Motion:	violet
Abstract Mental:	indigo
Concrete Mental:	blue
Upper Astral:	green

<BRIDGE>

Lower Astral:	yellow
Etheric:	orange
Physical:	red

There are three more planes called Regions of Chemical Change, Contact and Integration. The planes named above are enclosed within these Regions. They are the Universal Unconscious which is a repository of all the memories of universal knowledge and experience, sometimes called the Akasha or Akashic Records. They are:

Region of Chemical Change:	russet
Region of Contact:	rose
Region of Integration:	cream

Between the Upper and Lower Astral Planes there is a separation or bridge connecting the lower group to the upper group of planes. We build our bridge between the two worlds by right thought and action. This bridge is sometimes referred to as the Antahkarana.[10]

Pulling in "green" to strengthen the Desire Body:

Green is the color of the Desire Body, one of the bodies in consciousness that we all have. Like the physical body it can be altered, it can be injured and it at times can be damaged or depleted. When this body becomes depleted through emotional stress, for example, a medium shade of emerald green is a good color to wear and to think about in order to balance and heal the body. Steve Engel, a friend and very fine intuitive, suggests the following exercise:

"You can strengthen your Desire Body by sheer will power. Imagine green coming down to you from above. Let it surround you. Feel the vitality of green around you. Then lock it in. Imagine the green being hooked in much like one would bring down clamps on a pressure cooker. It may help if you clench your fists as you do the visualizing. Visualize the green becoming locked in place in your consciousness. Doing this exercise three or four times in an interval of several minutes will make a considerable difference in your energy level."[11]

Loosening Bodies for Psychic Awareness:

Engel suggests that by tightening the subtle bodies one becomes more grounded. But if you reverse the process you become more open to psychic and intuitive impressions. Imagine your invisible subtle bodies expanding, reaching outward from your physical body, sharing your energy and inviting higher lines of communication into your expanded energy field. You are opening other levels of your consciousness to communication with beings in other dimensions. See the exercise for protection later in this chapter.

Meditation:

"Meditation is a process of inner blooming, a process of charging your vehicles with spiritual energy. This energy regenerates your body, cleanses your emotional vehicle and purifies your mind, and as a result your physical body looks younger and becomes radioactive, your heart enters into peace and your mind gets sharper and more inclusive."[12]

"With the eyes closed and concentrated on the spiritual eye, the devotee knocks at the gates of heaven. When the eyes are focused and still, and the breath and mind are calm, a light begins to form in the forehead. Eventually, with deep concentration at the point between the eyebrows, the dual positive and negative currents flowing from the medulla into the two eyes reunite and the meditator beholds the *single* or spiritual eye."[13]

It is suggested that cleanliness and loose clothing are important considerations when preparing for meditation and that the air in the room should be fresh. If possible, meditate before a meal or wait at least an hour after a meal. Schedule your meditation for the same time and place using the same format each time. If you want to follow a ritual for the meditation, below is a sample ritual to follow. Drink a glass of water about fifteen minutes before you are ready to begin your meditation ritual.

1. Light a candle and burn incense if you wish. The incense should be light, not heavy and oily. If you like, begin playing some quiet meditative music.
2. Surround yourself with the violet flame for about thirty seconds.
3. Relax with deep breathing, releasing all tensions and worries.
4. Use your grounding exercise here.
5. Say a prayer for intention and protection.
6. Imagine yourself being surrounded by white light to create an environment of high vibratory frequency for contact with higher beings or your loved ones. You might want to visualize a column of white light entering your crown chakra and flooding your body, lighting every cell and descending through your feet into the earth below you.
7. Recite the Great Invocation or the Awakening Prayer or some positive passage to lift your own vibration and to give positive energy to the world.
8. Concentrate on your breath, breathing deeply from the abdomen in a circular motion from inhale to exhale. This will soon become automatic. Just watching your breath in meditation for a couple of weeks before beginning an intentional meditation may help you to concentrate—to focus.
9. When the breathing slows down and you feel relaxed, with both eyes looking inward, find the place of the third eye. As a guide, you might want to touch the area on your forehead just above the place between your eyebrows. Rest the tip of your tongue on the ridges just behind your upper teeth to close the circuit.
10. Now begin to visualize a tiny point of bright light in the third-eye area and expand it a little at a time. Breathe into this area with your rhythmic breath.
11. If this is a contact meditation and you are ready to end your session, say a prayer of blessing, give thanks for your visitor(s) and indicate your desire to meet with them on a continuing basis. If you can meet at the same time on a certain day, express that, too. Then snuff out the candle flame to indicate that the session is over.

The above model will assist you with developing your inner vision. If you are getting signals that your strength is in clairaudience rather than clairvoyance you might want to alternate and direct your breathing to the throat area some of the time. With some practice in the use of color and light in the exercises above they will become automatic when you state your intentions. Yogananda taught that meditation is the most effective way to spiritualize the body.

When you are feeling comfortable with your routine meditation technique you might feel more capable of making contact with your loved ones. Invite the help of your Low Self to make contact with the spirit being you have chosen for communication. With your focus still on the third-eye area, visualize your spirit friend seated in front of you face to face. To aid you in this visualization, you might have a photograph of the person as you knew him/her or a piece of jewelry or other item that belonged to him/her. Look at the picture, noting every detail, then close your eyes and begin your visualization. If you are holding an object of his/hers, be open and receptive to the energy you are able to feel from the object. Think of times when you felt happy or felt a lot of love for this person with the intention of making that kind of connection again. Send love to him, to her. If you want to use color for this part of the contact, the color of unconditional love is rose. Unconditional love is the most powerful force in the Universe. It is the link with our loved ones in the afterlife. Some meditators use visions of lovely rose-colored roses or hearts being sent toward or surrounding the loved one. You may not be aware that the contact has been made the first time you attempt it, nor the second. It might take some practice. But the secret is to capture in your own imagination the times you were feeling very close to each other or when you felt a deep appreciation for that person and concentrate on those times with the intention of strengthening your bond, your connection. Remember, you are trying to match vibratory frequencies here. You might want to visualize a kind of spiraling cord—you can make this a rose color, too—from heart-to-heart becoming stronger and more alive between you with the energy being exchanged in this way.

You are, in essence, building a bridge between the two of you. Be open to any impressions you have during your attempted contact and afterward. Even if you are not immediately aware of the contact, your spirit friend might have given you some seed thoughts that will become clearer later. You will eventually become more aware of thoughts that did not originate with your own thinking. Many of our thoughts, solutions to problems and *Aha* awareness come from those in another dimension who feel committed to helping us when we need it. They are waiting to hear us ask for assistance. When they can help us it helps them to progress, too. It is helpful to keep a journal of your experiences including your impressions and feelings. You can track your progress, and this action reinforces the seriousness of your intent.

When I asked Pat if there were things I could do to "set the scene" for our contacts, she said that nothing in the outer world was necessary but that it might help to play soft music, light a candle and have a shallow bowl of water and a cut flower or flowers nearby, "but mainly be open." She suggested that I visualize a very soft golden yellow light surrounding me with a funnel-like vortex of light moving clockwise above the crown of my head where she could transmit symbols and messages as I let my mind relax and be clear and quiet. I recall that at first she sometimes used a white porcelain board and colored markers for her messages. I was able to see these in my mind's eye. She also suggested that I might "visualize a big iron door leading to a village. You are on the outside and you have this magical key . . . yet it is a practical key. The village is yours to explore if you can open that door." I worked with this for several sessions and I was finally able to enter the village. It was much like a secluded valley as I entered, with grassy hills and trees and flowers. The road, or more like a pathway, led to a small friendly village full of kind and happy people and shops of all kinds.

Very soon after we began our sessions together, I moved to my computer so I could type out any thoughts that might come to me. I headed a page on my word processor with the date and Pat's name and began a filing system of my sessions with her, making a new file for each month. Eventually, I was able to experience very good contact with her at times. I asked her questions, and some of her answers surprised me, or I received answers that I had never heard before. For example, when I asked her about the lighted disc above my head, she told me it was an *infusor.* It made sense, but I couldn't find the word in a dictionary. The word *infusor* was confirmed by Steve Engel when he asked Pat about the lights above me. I realized that my accuracy level was probably not very high, but I also knew that with practice it would improve and I believe it has.

"Information from spirit is completely controlled by levels of energy vibration. The quality and clarity of the energy channel is fundamental to the accuracy of the transmission between the transmitter and the receptor."[14]

Medium, Muriel Williams, expresses the belief that: "Cosmic disturbances around our planet can interfere with the quality of the communication, almost like static on a radio frequency can interfere with transmission."[15] She goes on to say that if the receiver's energy is low or below par in any way it would be difficult for resonance of the energies of the sender and receiver to take place, and that one who is still grieving would have difficulty being open and receptive to spirit communication.

Our loved ones do try to contact us; they reach out to us in many ways. They don't want to frighten us so they often wait until they know we are ready to open up to their contact. I mentioned earlier that my first contact with my mother outside of the dream state was through the little clown music box that she had given me many years before. She has knocked over a picture of herself and another time she rolled a basket across a shelf. Sometimes a spirit will greet you with certain familiar scents of flowers, perfume, a favorite food you shared or even tobacco smoke if they were smokers. The night after Mother made her transition, I was sitting in bed reading as usual when I began to smell a scent of perfume. Because of Mother's asthma she couldn't wear perfume in her later years, so I was a bit puzzled. I still thought the scent was somehow related to Mother and I was later assured that it was. During my first contact with her, through Bob Murray, I asked about the perfume. Her answer was that she had asked Pat to do something to let me know she was all right. So Pat infused my room with the perfume. I did feel better about her that night and the perfume was a pleasant scent. I have felt her touch on my cheek many times in meditation or at other times when I was quietly reading or working at my computer, and I've heard her voice speak my name.

Exercises and Meditation Tools:

"Students of meditation must learn to imagine more. The use of imagination in these matters is of real importance and develops a connection between that faculty and its higher counterpart, the intuition."[1]

The Violet Flame:

While standing or sitting, visualize a cool violet flame rising from beneath your feet and enveloping your entire energy field and physical body. Watch it grow higher until it forms a peak two or three feet above your head. Hold this image about thirty seconds. The violet flame will transmute any negative energies in or around you. After you have used this exercise consistently and built the image over time, it will form automatically at your command.

Relaxation and Breathing:

There are many approaches to relaxation, and when you have practiced it consciously for a time you will learn to give your body the cues it needs to relax more quickly.

A standard relaxation technique is to begin at the toes and be aware of any tension, breathing deeply and releasing the tension in every area as you move up the body, down the arms to the hands and fingers, to the back and shoulders, to the face and then to the top of the head. You might need to tense some areas of your body and then let go of the tension for maximum benefit. Feel your body melting into the chair or bed or wherever you have chosen to meditate. I have suggested to my young students that they pretend at the end of the exercise that they are rag dolls.

My friend and Author Advocate, Patrika Vaughn, shared her original discovery with me called:

A Virtual Massage: Make yourself as comfortable as possible. Imagine that you have at your service a masseur or masseuse, a master of the art. As you feel the touch of his or her hands moving and massaging from your toes upward, experience every movement of the hands. As the hands move from a part of your body, imagine yourself letting go and feeling a warm glow in that area. When the hands get to the soft spot on the top of your head, feel a magnificent surge of bright, powerful energy entering your body, flooding it with even more of the warm glow you felt as each area was massaged. Remember to breathe deeply as you are relaxing your whole being. This is also a helpful exercise to perform if you sometimes have trouble going to sleep at night.

Grounding:

Technique number one: Visualize a golden cord attached to your feet and your coccyx or sacral chakra at the base of the spine. Follow this cord through the layers of the earth and attach the other ends to large rocks to anchor you to the earth. Bruce Moen uses large crystals which give an elegant image.

Technique number two: Visualize roots growing from your feet and sacral chakra downward through the layers of the Earth to its center. Release your tensions and negative emotions through these roots. When this is completed, visualize the nourishing Earth energies traveling back up through the roots to ground you and make you feel safe.

Prayer for Protection:

Torkom Saraydarian, spiritual teacher and author, teaches that "the whole secret of protection is the harmonious development of the three vehicles of man. A disciple must pay attention to his physical and etheric body, keep them clean of any pollution; give them the needed rest and relaxation; enjoy nature, the woods, the mountains and the ocean; be in pure sunshine and in clean air. In addition to all this, care must be given to the emotional body by exposing it to great music, to great art of any kind, and by expressing positive emotions—peace, joy, and love."[17]

These are suggestions, but you may want to compose your own prayer of protection.

I am the Light.
The Light is within me.
The Light moves throughout me.
The Light surrounds me.
The Light protects me.
I am the Light.

—Consuella Newton

Another passage that is often used is *The Prayer of Protection* by James Dillet Freeman. Reprinted with permission of Unity, original publisher:

The light of God surrounds me;
The love of God enfolds me;
The power of God protects me;
The presence of God watches over me.
Wherever I am, God *is*, and all is well.

The Great Invocation

From the point of Light within the Mind of God
Let Light stream forth into the minds of men.
Let Light descend on Earth.

From the point of Love within the Heart of God
Let Love stream forth into the hearts of men.
May Christ return to Earth.

From the center where the Will of God is known
Let purpose guide the little wills of men—
the purpose which the Masters know and serve.

From the center which we call the race of men
Let the Plan of Love and Light work out—
and may it seal the door where evil dwells.

Let Light and Love and Power restore
the Plan on Earth.

For more information on this third stanza of The Great Invocation, reprinted with permission of Lucis Trust, I refer you to *The Externalisation of the Hierarchy.*[18]

The Awakening Prayer: Ascended Masters Saint Germain and Kuthumi offered this prayer to more than 200 people at the 1990 Global Sciences Congress in Denver, Colorado. Group and individual meditation of the Awakening Prayer encourage a heightened spiritual consciousness and Cellular Awakening.[19] To see the original prayer, refer to *Points of Perception by* Lori Adaile Toye.[20] or to Lori's website: http://www.iamamerica.com/media/awakeningprayer.pdf

Invoking the Light to Prepare for Meditation and Spirit Contact:

In this exercise, previously given, with your eyes closed, use your inner sight to visualize a shaft of brilliant, sparkling white light coming down from high above the crown of your head. Let it pass through and surround your body, filling every cell of your body with light and reaching below your feet into the earth.

If you have difficulty achieving a higher frequency for contact, you might want to employ a method such as visualizing yourself stepping into an elevator and watching the numbers go up as you ascend. Or you might identify with a radio with a dial you can use to increase your vibratory frequency. As you use either of these exercises, visualize yourself filling your body with brilliant light at the same time.

Do not be discouraged if you cannot make spirit contact right away. A lot of things need to happen to make it a successful two-way communication. The bridge or connection will take time to strengthen. If you have been very closely involved with the transcended spirit of a friend, mate, parent, child or in others on the earth plane, you are already ahead of the game. There is already a strong bond upon which to build this kind of connection. Work with it regularly, with love and positive emotion. Anne Gehman, noted medium, says that it is not something we can do in a workshop, or a weekend, but it takes commitment over time.

Those on the other side are honored each time you acknowledge them in special ways. You might want to have a private ceremony or celebration of their birthdays, Mother's Day, Father's Day, Christmas, Easter, an anniversary or any other special time that you spent together. I still do that for my closest loved ones. I put out pictures on a table, light candles and sometimes I burn incense to cleanse the atmosphere. If there were special times you spent together with family or in travel or any occasion that was happy for both of you, put out pictures of those occasions and talk about them. I sometimes read passages that I know were special to my loved ones, or I play a CD of some music they liked. You can have a kind of *show and tell* if you wish. If there is something you want to share, bring it to the table and talk about it. After I have talked and shared, I tell my friend or relative that I will sit and listen for a bit. Then I sit as if in meditation and listen and watch for a response. When I made a contact with Pat Larson through a psychic friend, he said, "By the way, Pat said she really appreciated your private celebration of her birthday. She was so pleased that she invited others to join her." Then he mentioned a special object I had selected just for that occasion. This was a real confirmation for me.

My first Mother's Day without my mother was a rough one for me. She loved Cheekwood Art Museum and Botanical Gardens and having lunch at their Pineapple Room. I went to the Cheekwood Gardens that day and sat alone on a bench by the pond and talked with her. Then I walked the trails and through the gardens and made comments about the beauty I saw and

I thanked her for sharing that afternoon with me. I couldn't see her nor did I hear her voice, but I felt her presence and I believe it meant as much to her as it did to me.

At Christmas, I was visiting my children in Florida. My two daughters and my granddaughter and I set up a coffee table with candles, pictures of Mother and a special angel ornament and had our visit with her. We each related to her something about a special remembered time we had shared with her.

You have the idea. Even if you don't get immediate feedback on your efforts, do know that they are appreciated by your loved ones on the other side of life. Giving a gift in their name or doing something special for someone in their name means more to them than we can imagine. It means so much to them to still be considered a part of our lives because they are definitely involved although invisible to most of us. They try to get messages to us telling us that they know of our successes and our trials and they are able to send their good wishes, congratulations, and condolences when needed. Prayers for them are very much felt by them. Those in the spirit world are apparently very sensitive to the thoughts and feelings they receive from our dimension. They feel the love we send in prayers or thoughts as *warm fuzzies* or hugs, as encouragement for their progression. Think of them often and think about what you would like if the positions were reversed for you and your loved ones, remembering that they are now unconditionally loving. Our outer worlds are distracting to us and we get caught up in the tasks at hand. In the spirit world there is much to do, too, but their mode of communication is through telepathy, so they are instantly aware of our thoughts when we are focused on them.

CHAPTER 21

More Contacts

Dreams are . . . illustrations from the book
your soul is writing about you.

~ Marsha Norman

The path of the soul after death is the same
as the path of the soul in dreams.

~ Lakota Saying

Look to your experience in dreams
to know how you will fare in death.

~ Tenzin Wangyal Rinpoche

WHEN I AM READY TO make the spirit contacts in a more formal or focused way, I have a different vision or task that I use for each spirit I want to contact.

With Mother (Kathryn), I have a beautiful CD of her favorite hymn, "O Master, Let Me Walk with Thee," arranged and performed by her grandson (my nephew), Ted Wilson, Jr. As the music begins to play, I visualize the Master Jesus taking my mother's left hand in his right hand and taking my right hand in his left hand. This can be the Master Jesus, the Master Kuthumi, Master Djwhal Khul, Paramahansa Yogananda, or any spiritual Teacher of your choice. I then see and feel him walking us down a path where the two dimensions are blending—hers and mine. I feel a powerful transfer of energy from his hand and his presence, and I'm aware that Mother is on his right. As the music builds, I feel us getting closer and closer to the point where the Master stops and brings Mother and me face to face. He places a hand on each of our heads in blessing, and we are now ready to work on our part of the contact. Sometimes we remain in the same standing position where we were left and at other times she is seated just in front of me. I greet her and thank her for being available for the session, and we then carry it on in a direction of our choice. I sometimes ask questions and then I listen for answers. We've had success with her transmitting pictures and symbols, but I don't feel limited to them.

When I am ready to make contact with Pat I play one of Mike Rowland's CDs, "Within the Light," which was recommended to me by our mutual friend, Colleen, in Omaha. Colleen and Pat were in a meditation group together that used Rowland's music, in Omaha, so I knew Pat was familiar with it. It is a beautiful, serene and meditative selection.

At first, I effortlessly climbed a lovely crystal staircase to ascend to her dimension or somewhere between our dimensions. When we met, we immediately transported ourselves to a small chapel where we could visit and converse. This has worked well for us, and we change the location or scene occasionally. When Pat and her teachers began their work with me, at the computer, I didn't seem to need the visualizations as often.

When I first began to build the channel of consciousness between Ann Manser and myself, I used the vision of a bridge across a small body of water, like a very large mountain stream or a narrow river in the moonlight. Ann waited on the opposite side of the arched bridge. I could ascend to the top of the bridge and see Ann, but I couldn't seem to get past that point and go to her. The vision would fade before I could reach her on the other side.

Ann was finally able to get through to me, in a dream, and give me another symbol for my approach. In the dream I boarded an elevator in a large glass building with a very high dome. Inside the elevator, I pushed the button for the eleventh floor (eleven being Ann's special number). Now, when I use the elevator to attempt to boost my vibratory frequency to that higher level, I'm aware of the lights above the door which indicate the levels I'm passing. When it stops on the eleventh level, the door opens into a lovely outdoor garden. I step out onto a natural path between green plants and bushes. The path turns to the right and straightens out and leads me to a larger path lined with white dogwood trees in full bloom. I feel like I'm suddenly in a Disney movie. I don't walk far on the path before I come to a park bench on my right, and there I find sitting and waiting for me, my friend and Teacher, Ann Manser.

When I was using the bridge as a symbol of crossing from my world into hers, I visualized her as a woman a little younger than she had been when I first met her. She has recently given me, in my mind's eye, an image of herself when she was much younger. So that is the image I always use when I want to call on her. These images that I use for all of the contacts are often shown to me in meditation. If you have an image, try using it. If it doesn't seem right, just ask for one that will work for you.

Dream Visits:

Dreams were very important and sacred in many ancient cultures. Many saw their dreams as messages from the gods, some positive and some negative in tone. Long states that "dreams are the open door to premonition."[1] He goes on to say that the research in the area of dreams has disclosed the fact that we are given dreams almost every night regarding our future. When we don't remember our dreams, we remain unaware of those glimpses into the future except through the vague promptings of the Low Self that reveal some inner sense of what is about to happen.

Robert Moss, dreamer, storyteller, teacher, scholar and author shares with us from his personal experience in *The Dreamer's Book of the Dead,* "The dead are alive in our dreams, and for many of us this is our first direct evidence that soul and consciousness survive physical death. It can also be the source of considerable confusion. People who are alive on the *Other Side* may not understand they are dead (in the sense that they no longer have physical bodies), while their survivors may not understand that the dead are alive somewhere else."[2] Moss also tells us that an important reason we have visits from our deceased loved ones is to prepare us for our own crossings, to reassure us that we'll have friends to escort us when it is our time to journey to the other side.

Bruce Moen talks about the appearance of discarnates or spirits who use the dream states and scenes of those still on the earth plane to influence them to carry out their soul patterns or to be aware of future events in their lives. They use imagery and symbolism to urge their loved ones to pay attention to their thoughts, actions or patterns. They sometimes come to us to warn of the consequences of our actions or of psychic attacks against us when we might need extra protection. They often come to thank us for our help with an important event in their journey.

My former husband, Tom, and I eventually became close friends again after our divorce many years ago. He was a victim of cancer and made his transition in March 2010. During his illness he had more time than ever before to reflect on his life and his limited future in this lifetime. His attitude was positive from the time of his diagnosis until the very end of his life. However, at some point he had to shift his perspective regarding his future. Until close to the end, he was confident that he could overcome the cancer, and when things ceased to look so hopeful he was able to approach the end of his physical life with a level of optimism and courage not always seen in a dying man.

Tom had been a successful college professor of psychology whose faith was strong in God, in other people and in himself. Somewhere along the way he began to search for spiritual meaning in his life that expanded his faith into areas beyond the boundaries of his early traditional understanding. He knew I was working on the manuscript for this book and asked me if I would share some chapters with him. I was honored that he had made the request and saw it as a multilevel benefit for both of us. I would receive his expert feedback and he would receive a better understanding of possible future scenarios for his life after death. It was indeed a successful and rewarding exchange. He pointed out my need for clarification of concepts in the manuscript and a need for references in some instances. In return he received comfort and anticipation of possibilities in his new life to come. We had deep and meaningful conversations about what he might expect in the afterlife, and he shared that he had no fear about what he was facing and was in fact looking forward to the adventure ahead of him. Our daughters were with him at the time of his transition and reported a calm and peaceful experience for him. For that, we are all grateful. Since that time I've had many dream visits with Tom beginning on the eleventh day after his departure. I believe the dream that follows was related to our exchanges stemming from his reading of the first ten chapters of the manuscript for this book.

Dream: Tom and I were in the process of moving from the house we shared. He was looking for a set of hidden keys that he knew I could access. I was busy working on something in a large room and he was standing in a darkened hallway and seemed vision-impaired in some way. I knew exactly where the keys were hidden so I stepped through the doorway just barely into the hall and reached up and took them off of a nail almost at the top of the door frame. I handed them to Tom and said, "Do you think you will be able to use them at the new house?" He assured me that he would, and then he thanked me and left. He moved on to our new home, and I knew I would be there later.

I felt this dream had to do with the spiritual keys he received through reading the manuscript I was writing about the afterlife; I had stepped just outside of my dimension to access the information, the keys, and presented them to him on the first level of his new dimension where he had not yet quite developed his vision for his new home. He was thanking me for the keys that I had provided to help him make a smooth transition.

Dream: Eleven days after Tom's transition, I found myself in a dream state visiting him in an inner plane hospital or health center. I was downstairs in the waiting room with our adult children. We were waiting to be told when we could see Tom. I could actually see him in a hospital bed on the level above us. The wall was made of glass or some transparent material. I asked a nurse if we would have to wait much longer to see him. She said, "Oh, you can go on up now, if you like." The children asked me to go and check with him and to let them know when they could see him. I walked up the stairs and knocked on the door. A male nurse walked by and said, "You can go on in." I did, but Tom was not in the room. I went back into the hallway and found the nurse and reported that he was not in that room. The nurse said, "They just moved Tom to another room," and he directed me there. The door was open, so I stepped inside. Tom spotted me right away and smiled from ear-to-ear and said, "I'm so glad to see you!" We had begun talking about his new experience when a young man walked into the room through a side door. I couldn't hear what he said to Tom, but I recognized him as having been a student of Tom's many years ago. The young man was followed by a technician who began wheeling Tom's bed out of the room. Tom turned to me and shrugged his shoulders, apologetically, and explained that it was time for a treatment, a color healing treatment, I think.

The above dream visit was real, I believe. When a person has endured months of illness, malnutrition because of the illness, weakness and unrelenting physical pain and myriad medications for all of the above, the subtle bodies are adversely affected, too. To bring the spirit being back into balance and harmony in the new dimension, the bodies must go through a process of healing. Of course, on those higher levels, non-invasive techniques for healing are used. There are treatments using light and color and other energetic means for balancing the vibratory frequencies in the bodies. If you'll recall, in Chapter 10 I related a story about Ann Manser and the "healing matrix" in the desert. I believe this is a common theme for those who cross over after an extended illness.

In their book, *Love Beyond Life,*[3] Martin and Romanowski give some pointers for recognizing dream visits as opposed to ordinary dreams. They say that dream visitations stand out from other dreams and are clearly significant or meaningful. They are more vivid, persistent and real than the usual dream. Deceased loved ones often appear as they did in life, although they seem the picture of health no matter what their physical state was at their death. The message that dream visitations convey is usually simple and to the point. Communication within dream visitations seems to occur telepathically and usually serve a purpose. Generally speaking, most direct contacts first occur within two years of death but they can happen any time. They are often verifiable and leave subjects with a feeling of well-being or peace. If your loved one had been able to talk openly and freely about her/his approaching death you might have been able to make plans for your communication after death. You might have chosen a symbol, a touch, a code word or some other way of recognizing the visit from the spirit world. Sometimes spirits will give you a symbol of their presence. It could be a butterfly, a coin, a bird or any other animate or inanimate object. This sign or symbol can be physical or psychic. Sometimes it can be an action of some kind, like a picture falling from the wall or a television turning on *by itself.* Ann Manser showed me a red bird, a cardinal, so when I psychically see a red bird I know she is present. This was somewhat confirmed when I later ran across an email that I received from Steve Engel a few years ago. He told me that a friend of his could hear birds chirping when Ann was present.

Pat has shown me coins, but not at times when I'm working with her in contact or meditation. I've called upon her at times when I was shopping and looking for something in particular and I've found pennies—sometimes more than one along the way. This began when a magazine published a story about her son, Chris, a very fine architect. He had designed and built a beautiful home using all natural materials, and his story and pictures of his lovely family in their new home in the woods earned six pages in the *Natural Home* magazine. When I learned about the article, I set out to find the magazine. I went to a couple of stores and they were out of them. I started into another store when I suddenly saw a penny on the floor. I bent over to pick it up and an image of Pat flashed into my mind. I decided the penny was from Pat and that she wanted to lead me to the magazine. It made me stop and listen anyway. I clearly received her message to go to another store a few miles away. I called the bookstore first and made sure they had the magazine. They did. There have been a few more *coin meetings* since that evening. In another instance, when I was having a little difficulty with something, I found a Nebraska quarter. Pat lived in Nebraska during the years we were friends. Finding the quarter, again made me slow down to listen and receive her guidance on something when I needed it. I always acknowledge the presence of the contacting spirit and thank him/her for their help.

Kathryn (Mother) has used objects around the house to dramatically get my attention. I was in an auto accident several years ago in another state. While I was in the hospital, Mother came to see me and gave me a little clown doll (pictured in Chapter 2) with a music box inside. Earlier, you read the story about the little clown music box. The little clown has greeted me many times since then, and at times it has alerted me to a need by someone in the family. When I hear it, I always check out that possibility first. Otherwise, I treat it as a greeting and a sign that she's around sometimes and doesn't want to be forgotten.

There is one more story I would like to share with you, one involving Tom West again. It had been an unusually taxing Saturday sometime in the summer after his transition. I was exhausted by evening and decided I wanted to relax in front of the television and watch a movie. I didn't find anything listed that I really wanted to see, so I looked through the free "on demand" movies provided by my cable service. The choices were still limited, but I found a movie I thought might be interesting called "Speak" starring Kristen Stewart, a favorite actress in the "Twilight" movie series. I did not realize the heavy tone the movie would convey or I might not have chosen it; but then I really do believe in divine order. As I watched the character, Melinda, go through the emotional trauma in her life, keeping it a secret from her family and friends, I was touched on a very deep level. Although I had not experienced the kind of trauma she'd experienced, this story brought up emotional trauma from my *failed* marriage that I thought I had faced and had somewhat resolved. Apparently I had not completely dealt with it or the secrets around it that I'd kept for all of these years. At this point in my life, I do not have a tendency toward feeling depressed, however that night I allowed these feelings from the past to emerge and dominate my mind and emotions. I found myself in a most emotionally uncomfortable place. I felt it was healthy to bring the feelings to the fore, face them and deal with them, but I found myself not really knowing how to do that. It was then that I realized how stoic I had allowed myself to become!

Feeling helpless about controlling the old tapes that kept playing, I decided to follow my usual nighttime routine. I got ready for bed, picked up a book I was reading and relied on the contents of the book to again cover up the years-old trauma. I soon found myself reading the same sentences over and over again. It wasn't working, so I turned off the light, said my prayers and hoped I would be able to go to sleep and deal with the churned up effects the next day. I lay on my right side facing the rest of the room, almost asleep but still conscious of this world. I was in a hypnogogic state, a kind of twilight zone. I'm accustomed to occasional visits from my little furry friends from the other side when I turn out my lights and get still and quiet. I suddenly felt something larger than those little furry friends climb up on the bed. It climbed over me, accidentally hitting my knee, and settled down behind me. For some reason I had no fear. I didn't want to open my eyes or move because I knew I could lose the twilight consciousness and miss out on this other-dimensional experience. It moved again, and I heard a familiar sniffle—it was Tom! He had a characteristic nervous sniffle that occurred when he was a little unsure of himself. I smiled and greeted him and thanked him for being there— for comforting me. I fell asleep in his arms and all was well. During the following year, he has appeared in many of my dreams each week. We seem to be working out the problems we faced in our marriage and our family many years ago. We sometimes discuss the things we're working on, and at other times we're acting them out, often with our children involved. The result has been that of much happier memories of our time together—a truly healing effect.

Our spirit loved ones do care about us and they do whatever they can to let us know they are there when we need them, even when we don't know we need them. The admonition here is simply to pay attention. When we are able to pay attention to these signs, we eventually become more observant of everything around us. That, in turn, makes us much more aware human beings.

CHAPTER 22

Conclusion

Dreaming is not fundamentally about
what happens during sleep. It's about waking up.

~ Robert Moss

T HERE WERE LATE AFTERNOON APPOINTMENTS on my schedule, but I felt I needed a short nap before they began. I fell across my bed but I didn't really fall asleep. I left my body, traveled in my astral body and soon found myself in a small cozy restaurant. It was immediately clear to me that I had walked in on a meeting about to take place and found my mother speaking to two other women at her table.

The above scene took place in another dimension a year after my Mother's transition. My ability to do this did not arrive all at once, but the capacity was always there as it is in all of us. I'm not a medium. I'm not a psychic. I am sensitive as are many of you and, like you I have "lost" loved ones to so-called "death" during my lifetime. The time came when I wanted to know where they had gone and what was happening in their new lives elsewhere. By that time, through study and investigation, I had developed concepts and ways of thinking about the possibility of an afterlife far beyond my child-like visions of angels sitting on clouds playing their harps for eternity. I became open to new thoughts on the topic, creating an invitation to those on the other side of life to appear to me in some way. Primarily, my visions and visitations have been spontaneous during meditation, in dreams and often at times when I least expect it. I've found that an important condition for this inter-dimensional contact is openness and a willingness to meet the unknown. Geoffrey Hodson, Theosophical teacher and author, has said that we have all the faculties necessary for complete knowledge of the visible and invisible universe.

Good-byes don't have to be permanent. Life is not limited to any one dimension. Life goes on. As young people, we learned in our science classes that all physical matter is the result of a vibratory frequency. If you amplify the frequency, the structure of the matter will change. If seen on a continuum of vibratory frequency, the physical body is vibrating at a lower frequency where our five senses contribute to our awareness of Earth. As the frequency vibrates at a higher rate, your five senses are no longer adequate to access what is beyond the physical dimension. Therefore, at the end of your life on Earth, your body must be shed in order to make the transition that will enable you to continue to live in dimensions compatible with the frequency of your more subtle bodies such as the astral, mental and spiritual bodies. In those dimensions, you will be able to see with your inner eyes which can also be developed while you're in your physical body.

In the first chapter of this book, you were taken on a hypothetical journey of a possible day in the life of one who has just made the transition to spirit life in another dimension. It is only one of many possible scenarios based on my own experiences in meditation and dreams. There are many different cultures the world over and therefore many different scenarios and experiences possible.

Once we understand more about other dimensions and the possibilities of making contact with those we love and who have been such an important part of our lives on Earth, we will find the methods of contact that work for us and our loved ones. Some methods that have been mentioned are meditation, dreams, out-of-body experiences (OBEs) or contact through professional psychic mediums. It takes time and commitment, but if you are sufficiently motivated it can be a successful and rewarding endeavor.

Those in the spirit world are around us and are aware of our daily activities and like to be acknowledged especially on special occasions that they've been a part of in the past. It takes a lot of energy on their part to make contact with us. Contact for them is easier when atmospheric conditions are clear, when we are calm, quiet and receptive and when we are not grieving. Grieving is necessary for those of us left behind, but it causes an emotional congestion that clouds the astral body and makes it difficult to transmit thoughts from the subtle levels. So prolonged periods of grieving may interfere with the communication we are so eager to experience.

When someone makes the transition to the spirit realms, the next dimension, there are new laws to learn. Things that took so long to do on the earth plane can be done instantly in the higher dimensions. Travel is instantaneous as it follows the thought of a destination. You can manifest your desires there. If you want a lovely garden or a house to live in, all you need to do is to have a clear picture of it in your mind and it will build before your eyes. Thoughts are things. The same rule applies in our physical dimension—just not as quickly, and often with a bit of elbow grease.

Among the questions I had, when I began my search for information about the process of death and the destination of the soul after death, were the questions about what happens at the time of death to the physical body. Among my findings, I concluded that it is necessary for the atmosphere surrounding the dying person to be quiet, calm and free of distractions so that the departing spirit can attend to the panoramic life review that takes place as the permanent seed-atom in the heart is released. The seed atom contains the memories of this life and is released by way of the brain to the higher vehicles or astral bodies. These bodies are connected to the physical body by a silver cord. The rupture of the seed-atom causes the heart to stop, however the cord remains intact until the life review is finished. This initial life review is shown to the person backwards in time while it is being transferred to the subtle bodies. This is done without emotional effects. Another review will take place at some point in the new life dimension, and at that time it will be experienced with all the feelings that attended the events when they actually happened over the span of the earth life. It is generally reported through spirit contact or near-death-experiences (NDEs) that there is no pain in death. When the spirit leaves the body, it leaves the pain behind. The process of going to sleep is similar to the death process. The silver cord connects the spirit body to the physical body. It is not a physical cord, so it cannot be broken until other aspects of the death process have taken place. There is always someone to meet us when we're ready to make our transition. If there are no loved ones available, there are always spirit helpers on hand to greet new arrivals.

In Part II of this book, I shared my personal journey beginning with the time in my life when I was led to give up outgrown beliefs and dogmas and awaken to new perceptions regarding my spirituality and religion. When I became open to new ideas and ways of honoring my inner spirit, significant teachers appeared in my life and a whole new level of my journey began. I had some rather dramatic experiences to enlighten me and show me the way. Not everyone experiences a spiritual awakening in such a dramatic way. The experience is uniquely our own. Three weeks after the transition of my spiritual teacher, Ann Manser, she was able to take me for a visit to an area of her afterlife dimension. This journey was an out-of-body experience and it forever changed my perception of death. I knew without a doubt that there was no death, except that of the physical body. I have been able to continue my spiritual studies with Ann periodically over the years in the inner planes, in her dimension.

There have been many remarkable people in my life, and it was from the three remarkable women whose lives I shared with you that I have learned the most about the life we all have waiting for us in other dimensions. In addition to the wonderful contacts I've had with Ann, there are also those I've experienced with Pat and with my mother, Kathryn. I visit with them often in the dream state when I've left my ego behind and my mind is clear, away from physical life demands and concerns. There are other times when I have contact with them in meditation or through some meaningful sign during my daytime activities in this world.

Occasionally, I call upon my psychic friends, LeRoy or Steve or Bob, and ask for answers to specific questions about a concept I'm studying, or a life situation I want clarified, or just to say "hello, how are you doing?" The three remarkable women have each in their own way encouraged me and helped me to trust my intuition. I am assured of their presence in my life and know they are always by my side when I need them. I also know they like to be asked for their assistance. There are laws on their side of life that prevent them from interfering with our lives unless we invite them to lend their energy. There are many times when those on the other side help us through their mental impressions when we've asked for help.

Our pets are in the next dimension waiting for us, too. Actually, they may be around us here on Earth for a long time after they've made their transition. To our pets, we are *their people*. Sometimes we're the only people they know during their lifetime. When they have to leave us, through death, they are still emotionally attached to us. For a week or so they will come to their familiar surroundings to be with us and will look for their food and water. They don't eat the food but they ingest the essence of the food until they realize they don't need it anymore. Learning to communicate with your pet while it is still in a physical body will help you to know how to make contact with it when it is no longer physical. Because your pet communicates telepathically, mostly through picturing, you will need to learn to listen to it mentally. This is also a good practice for learning to communicate with the people you know in the spirit world. Because the vibratory frequency is so high in that world, it is sometimes difficult for someone in our world to keep up with the rapidity of transmitted language. So symbols and whole thoughts are often easier than a string of words in sentences for transmission across dimensions.

Remember the origins of the taboos (such as the witch hunts) for being psychic and don't let them deter you from your goal of developing your psychic abilities. We are now in the 21st Century and it is time for us to awaken our sixth sense and to use it wisely for obtaining knowledge of the higher worlds and for making contact with those who reside in those worlds. If you are on track with your spiritual development, psychic development will come to you more easily. It is a natural by-product of spiritual development. Remember, also, that the key to making contact with the higher worlds is achieving a higher vibratory frequency. Suggestions for this can be found in Chapter 20.

Another important key is to make friends with your Low Self. Have a conversation with him or her, programming it to carry out your wishes for making the contact. For example: "Victor, I wish to contact Aunt Susy. I need this to come forward. Will you please help me with this?" In the meantime, you will be holding a picture of the spirit in your mind and building the connection through feelings of love. The bonds of love will build the bridges to your loved ones in the afterlife.

Remember, love is always the answer! May blessings and grace be yours on your own exciting journey!

APPENDIX A

Afterlife Beliefs of Major Religions

The soul of all is one soul, and the truth is one truth
under whatever religion it is hidden.

~ Hazrat Inayat Khan

DEPENDING ON YOUR RELIGIOUS ORIENTATION, you will have varying opinions about making contact with those in the afterlife. Our major religions have many beliefs about death and the afterlife as well as certain rituals which are important and meaningful within their traditions. Let us explore some traditions of the major religions in the world that have led many of us to our current beliefs.

Hinduism: Hinduism is considered by many to be the oldest living religion in the world. Its focus is on the recognition of the divinity within us and self-development to become a "Divine Self." Like Buddhists, the Hindus believe in karma and reincarnation or rebirth. Classical Hindu metaphysics states that "No Hindu really fears death, nor does he look forward to it. Death for the Hindu is merely transition, simultaneously an end and a new beginning."[1]

For the Hindu, when the lessons of this life are learned, the soul leaves the physical body and "the awareness, will, memory and intelligence continue to exist in the soul body." It is believed to be a natural experience, one not to be feared. "It is a quick transition from the physical world to the astral plane, like walking through the door, leaving one room and entering another."[2] The physical body is left behind and the soul continues evolving in the inner worlds in our subtle bodies until we can again take on a new life. The Hindu does not think of himself as the body in which he lives, but as the immortal soul which inhabits many bodies in its journey through the evolution of consciousness. It is the soul body which reincarnates, creating around itself new physical and astral bodies, life after life.

This soul body is a pure being, indestructible, "created by God, maturing its way to Him in final merger." "The body of the soul is constant radiance. Its mind is super consciousness, containing all intelligence, and is constantly aware, does not sleep and is expanding awareness as the soul body matures."[3] In this sense, one is a soul wearing a body, rather than a body with a soul.

When a Hindu dies, her consciousness is transferred to the astral and mental bodies and it predominantly lives through those bodies in the astral dimension. It is with these same subtle vehicles that we experience dream or astral worlds during sleep every night. It is painful to the astral body to have the physical body cut or disturbed seriously within seventy-two hours after death. The soul can see and feel this, and such an experience detains her from moving on. One soon realizes that the astral body is now her body for this new dimension and the physical body is released effortlessly. When all karma has been expiated by the individual, one can have hope for unity with God.

Buddhism: Buddhists believe that the universe is composed of different qualities or conditions of consciousness which can translate to degrees of truth. In the case of the gods, they are highly evolved forms of consciousness, according to Manley P. Hall.[5]

The name "Buddha" means enlightenment, and Buddhists teach that the universe is filled with an essence called *self*, an essence the Christians call *spirit*. The perfection of every created thing is achieved by its re-absorption into the universal self or spirit. "The purpose of life is to wear out or overcome the illusions which result in separate existences. Only the self remains, eternal and unconditioned."[6]

Buddhism states that "it requires many millions of years to kill out illusion in the heart of man. It is quite impossible for him to accomplish this in a single life. Therefore Buddhism explains the mystery of the inequalities and inconsistencies of life by means of two inflexible and immutable laws—reincarnation and karma."[7] The good or evil we do in one life returns to us as fortune or misfortune in the next. "So we continue, incarnation after incarnation, until the doing of evil dies out within us and wisdom takes the place of ignorance."[8] Hall also offers that "the principal purpose of the Buddhist organization is to perpetuate the simple truth that suffering is the result of wrong action, and happiness and security are the rewards of right thinking and virtuous living."[9]

In Tibetan Buddhism, the soul or spirit of the newly dead begins a forty-nine day process of adjustment which is divided into three stages called *bardo*. At the conclusion of the bardo, the person (soul) either enters Nirvana or returns to Earth for rebirth. Buddhism does not believe in an immortal soul, one that continually reincarnates in different bodies and earth situations. They seem to subscribe to a "concept of a kind of continuing false self, or a bundled semblance of self-identity, comprised of many of the characteristics known to psychology (such as memories, desires, dispositions, attitudes and sensations). As these fall away over the course of many lifetimes and the self is no more, "one may unite with nirvana, an abode of pure nothingness and lack of individual awareness."[10]

Zen Buddhists don't believe in an afterlife, but do believe there is a constant continuation of energy and a connection to a higher source that continues on.

Islam: "Islam, youngest of the great religions, is in many ways the simplest and most explicit. Its founder, Mohammed, was neither savior nor messiah: merely a man through whom God spoke. Islam is not just a religion—it is a way of life. The word, *Islam* means *submission*—to God's will. Islam is as concerned with man's life on earth as with the hereafter."[12]

A Muslim is a follower of the religion, Islam. Although one of the youngest, it is also one of the largest populated religions of the world. Among the large religions, over 300 million members, are included Christianity, Islam, Hinduism and Buddhism.[13] The many denominations of the Islamic or Muslim religion subscribe to the same fundamental beliefs. Muslims surrender or commit to Allah and believe their souls enter a place or state called the Barzakh or Partition after death and before judgment and remain there until the Day of Judgment.

Islam's doctrine holds that there is a human existence which continues after the death of the human body in the form of spiritual and physical resurrection and that conduct while on earth determines the kind of life one is given beyond the present one. The belief is that a Judgment Day will come when everyone is judged fairly and will enter Hell or Paradise.

Having faith in life after death is one of the six fundamental beliefs required of a Muslim, and rejecting this belief renders all others meaningless. The dead have a continued conscious existence of a kind in the grave. Muslims believe that, on dying, a person enters an intermediate phase of life between death and resurrection.

The end of the world will precede the resurrection at which time a magnificent angel will be commanded by God to blow the Horn. The first time it is blown the inhabitants of the heavens and the earth will fall unconscious except those spared by God. "The earth will be flattened, the mountains will turn to dust, the sky will crack, planets will be dispersed and the graves overturned."[14] The Horn will blow again and "people will be resurrected into their original bodies from their graves" and enter the third and final phase of life. The deeds of the people will be weighed and disclosed. Those who receive their records in their right hands will have an easy judgment and will happily return to their families. Those who receive their records in their left hands will be thrown into the Fire.

"Paradise for the Muslim is the eternal garden of physical pleasures and spiritual delights. Suffering will be absent, and bodily desires will be satisfied. Palaces, servants, riches, streams of wine, milk and honey, pleasant fragrances, soothing voices, pure partners for intimacy; a person will never get bored or have enough. The greatest bliss, though, will be the vision of their Lord of which the unbelievers will be deprived."[15]

Hell is an infernal place of punishment for unbelievers and of purification for sinful believers. Torture and punishment for the body and the soul: burning by fire, boiling water to drink, scalding food to eat, chains and choking columns of fire. Unbelievers will be eternally damned to it, whereas sinful believers will eventually be removed from Hell and enter Paradise.[16] According to many interpretations of the passages addressing this problem of heaven and hell in the Qur'an, "Muslims can be sent to hell (the hottest fire one can imagine), but may be able to leave it eventually, unlike non-Muslims, who never escape."[17]

Judaism: The Torah says, "And the Almighty formed the man of dust from the ground, and He blew into his nostrils the SOUL of life" (Genesis 2:7). In this verse, the Zohar states that "one who blows, blows from within himself," indicating that the soul is actually part of God's essence. Since God's essence is completely spiritual and non-physical, it is impossible that the soul should die."[18] Although there appears to be no clear concept recorded, the afterlife is a fundamental of Jewish belief.

"When a person dies and goes to heaven, the judgment is not arbitrary and externally imposed. Rather, the soul is shown two *videotapes*. The first video is called *This Is Your Life*. Every decision and every thought, all the good deeds, and the embarrassing things a person did in private is all replayed without any embellishments. It's fully bared for all to see. That's why the next world is called Olam HaEmet—*the Word of Truth*, because there we clearly recognize our personal strengths and shortcomings, and the true purpose of life."[19]

"The second video depicts how a person's life could have been if the right choices had been made, if the opportunities were seized, if the potential was actualized. This video—the pain of squandered potential—is much more difficult to bear. But at the same time it purifies the soul as well. The pain creates regret which removes the barriers and enables the soul to completely connect to God."[20]

One rabbi explains that Gehenom is a "hospital for the soul." It is apparently a painful experience for the soul. But it is seen as an act of kindness for the good of the soul. The way to avoid Gehenom altogether is to monitor and atone for our mistakes while we're still on Earth. This is difficult for most, but making the supreme effort to do so in this world will ultimately lessen the greater pain in the next. It is believed that heaven is where the soul experiences the greatest possible pleasure—the feeling of closeness to God. The degree to which this is experienced is different for all souls.[21]

Jewish belief also says that the people we have left on earth can increase our share in the *World to Come* and enable us to earn a better place there. For example, "in memory of loved ones, people often give to charity, name babies, learn Torah in their merit and perform other acts that have everlasting spiritual ramifications. When we do something in someone's memory, we are saying: Because of this person that I loved, I am living my life differently. He may be gone, but he is not forgotten. He continues to be a source of inspiration in my life. His life mattered, and his legacy will continue to make a difference."[22]

Some, of the Jewish faith, take a thirty-day period, ideally the first thirty days after the funeral which is called the *shloshim*, and do something concrete in memory of the departed.

For some it could be placing a coin in a tzedakah (charity) box each day and reciting a simple prayer. Souls in the next world have awareness. They know what goes on here. By choosing to honor them, you are making an impact far greater than you will ever know." (Excerpted from "Remember My Soul," by Lori Palatnik.[23]

Taoism: "Taoism (Dow-ism) is a fundamental Chinese concept that implies a *way* or *path* which one should follow." It is "the final resting place for the Taoist's soul; it is perfection and immortality. It's akin to the Buddhist's interpretation of Nirvana. Taoism believes there is survival of the spirit after death. It doesn't die but migrates to another life. This process, the Taoist version of reincarnation, is repeated until Tao, a transcendence of life, is achieved."[24]

Native Americans: Native American cultures all seem to view the idea of death a bit differently. In the past, most Native American tribes believed that souls of the dead passed into a spirit world and became part of the spiritual forces that influenced every aspect of their lives. For some there were certain superstitions which determined their rituals. In the present day, many believe that what happens after death depends on status in life. There is a special place for special people like warriors who die in battle, or for religious leaders. Those who *sin* might end up in a less satisfying realm. Reincarnation is still an important belief for most Native Americans. Many of their beliefs are still nature-based. However, today there is a strong Christian influence in their beliefs about an afterlife.

Christianity: There are many denominations of Christianity, and beliefs change from one denomination to another. Some Christians believe that the soul is judged immediately after death and is sent to heaven or hell. The Catholics add to this an intermediate state called purgatory where one is purged or cleansed of sins committed in order to enter heaven. The belief is that those who have committed a less serious, or *venial* sin and have not received absolution, go to purgatory. The Catholic Church believes that those baptized in the Church and whose sins have been forgiven, go to heaven, and those who have committed a serious, or *mortal* sin and have not received absolution, go to hell. Other denominations believe the body and soul enter a deep sleep and await a day of judgment when all will arise and be judged at the same time. Some denominations believe that we simply disappear and cease to exist in any form. Each Christian denomination appears to base its beliefs on what it regards as true interpretation of key biblical passages, supported by church tradition, reason and personal experience.

Paramahansa Yogananda came to America in 1920 as a delegate to the International Congress of Religious Liberals in Boston. His mission was to spread worldwide the ancient soul-science of yoga meditation and to reveal the "complete harmony and basic oneness of original Christianity as taught by Jesus Christ," and original Yoga as taught by Bhagavan Krishna, and to show that these principles of truth are the common scientific foundation of all true religions.

In Luke 16: 19-31 in the Christian Bible, there is a parable told by Jesus of the rich man and the beggar. In relating his interpretation of this parable, Yogananda tells us that Jesus is alluding to the different vibratory regions of the astral world to which the virtuous and the wickedness-encrusted souls are attracted after death according to their self-earned merits or demerits:

> The helpless beggar—a virtuous soul, though apparently forsaken by all—after death was conveyed by divine vibrations of the Holy Ghost (angels of God) into the high astral regions where spiritual souls are received by advanced beings and liberated prophets—*Abraham's bosom*. But the rich man, who lived riotously with no effort to cultivate God-consciousness found himself in the after-death state in the darksome vibratory region of the lower astral world where the wicked of materially desirous souls undergo the torment of restless nightmares after the oblivion of astral sleep that is the first stage after death.[25]

In some of my conversations with Christians, on this topic, myriad beliefs and philosophies have been expressed. Many seem to have some vague idea that they will spend eternity with God but have no visual context for their beliefs, and they prefer that it remain a mystery rather than to delve into the unknown for possible answers. Others have a strong belief that life will continue on in much the same way as their life here, but in another dimension. Some with a more scientific orientation identify with a materialistic view and believe that when their life here ends they'll go back into a "state of oblivion from whence I came." Others involved in science are "certain" there is a dimensional region beyond what science is equipped to reveal at this point in time.

Metaphysical: Metaphysics begins where physics leaves off. Everything is movement; everything we can touch and analyze, all things in the physical world or the world of form exist in a certain rate of vibration and are an effect of thought. That vibration becomes more subtle and refined as it leaves the world we experience through our physical senses. It continues into the higher levels of our emotional, mental and spiritual levels of consciousness at which point it becomes metaphysical, or beyond the physical. Metaphysicians believe that we create our own realities; that we live in a world created by our collective thinking and therefore *thoughts are things*. They believe a world beyond the physical is created for the most part by what we imagine it to be as well as the degree of refinement of our vibratory frequencies through right thought and right action.

"It is very hard for us to realize how very partial our sight is—to understand that we are living in a vast world of which we see only a tiny part. We must beware of falling into the fatally common error of supposing that what we see is all there is to see."[26] As we human beings grow spiritually, metaphysical belief says that we refine our levels of consciousness therefore preparing ourselves for the higher realms in the afterlife. It has nothing to do with religious belief on Earth. A person makes for him or herself an astral body determined by desires and passions during earth life that is used in the astral dimension following the death of the physical body.[27]

Metaphysical thought includes many ancient theories which all seem to dovetail in their beliefs but use different approaches or follow different mystery schools developed over many centuries and epochs of time. Their beliefs are now termed *new thought* or *new age*, but they are based on esoteric teachings from very ancient times and brought forth with methods for practical application in the world today.

Metaphysical belief holds that everyone goes to *heaven*. No one is left behind. There are many levels or planes in the afterlife, each having a vibratory frequency higher than the level below it. Heaven is a state of being where most people find themselves after their life is over on the Earth plane. There is not a place called Hell, but there is a state of being which some might refer to as hell because of the suffering they have brought upon themselves. Metaphysicians believe in an evolution of consciousness through which the soul unfolds over time through its reincarnation into a material form which affords the soul the life lessons it requires to develop and refine itself. The metaphysical point-of-view regarding the afterlife is discussed more fully in Chapters 4 and 5 in this book.

Appendix B

Research into the Existence of an Afterlife

*The most beautiful and profound emotion we can experience is
the sensation of the mystical. It is the power of all true science.*

~ Albert Einstein

"AFTER MANY YEARS OF SERIOUS investigation I have come to the conclusion that there is a great body of evidence which, taken as a whole, absolutely and without a doubt proves the case for the afterlife. The discoveries of serious scientists working to prove the afterlife have been misreported, distorted and censored with the result that members of the general public know very little about the great body of scientific research that has been accumulated."

The above statements were made by Victor James Zammit, author of *A Lawyer Presents the Case for the Afterlife*.[1] Using his professional background as an attorney and his university training in psychology, history and scientific method, he has very carefully selected aspects of psychic research and afterlife knowledge that would constitute objective evidence. He further states that "this evidence would be technically admissible in the Supreme Court of the United States, the House of Lords in England, the High Court of Australia and in every civilized legal jurisdiction around the world."

When scientific method is used to measure evidence it is termed *empirical evidence*. This empirical evidence of objective knowledge means that the same cause-effect connection can be demonstrated over time and space, and when the variables are kept constant the results will be the same. Victor Zammit makes a point that it is the reader's choice to believe or not to believe the evidence presented, and I would make that point as well. He uses an example of Galileo and the refusal of clergy to "accept science because it conflicted with (their) personal religious beliefs." "When Galileo showed the Pope the telescope and told him that it would prove Galileo's view of the universe, the Pope called the telescope the *work of the devil* and refused to look through it.[2] Many beliefs become a part of the emotional makeup and are *hard-wired* into the nervous system. These beliefs become very hard to shift," he states, and "even if information is scientific, we initially tend to reject it if the information is too advanced—if it challenges our *boggle threshold* by being too far ahead of our existing knowledge, especially if the information is not consistent with our secular or religious beliefs, history, culture, values and traditions."

Some of the brilliant scientists named by Zammit as among the first to investigate the afterlife, he called "open-minded" skeptics, such as Sir Arthur Conan Doyle, Arthur Findlay, Professor Charles Richet, Alfred Russell Wallace, Professor Albert Einstein, Professor William James, James H. Hyslop and many others. Sir William Crookes was considered to be the greatest scientist of his time, having discovered six of the chemical elements. His extensive investigations into levitation and physical mediumship phenomena were recorded in photographs, and the absence of fraud and trickery in them were verified by other leading scientists of that time.[3]

In 1882, a group of academics from Trinity College, Cambridge, founded the Society for Psychical Research (SPR) as a first attempt to study psychic phenomena scientifically. Among the fifty-one presidents through the years were nineteen professors and other famous scientists renowned for their work in psychology, physics, astronomy and biology. In 1885, the American Society for Psychical Research was founded by another group of top intellectuals which included renowned Harvard psychologist and philosophy professor William James and Professor of Logic and Ethics at Columbia University, James H. Hyslop. As a result of their scientific inquiry these learned men all became convinced of survival after death.

Professor William MacDougall, after accepting the chair of the Department of Psychology at Duke University, established the first university-based laboratory for psychical research. MacDougall saw mind as nonphysical and published his book *Body and Mind* in 1911. It remains a classic study of the mind-body relationship. He made clear, informally, that "the principle aim of the Society for Psychical Research is to obtain, if possible, empirical evidence that human personality may and does survive in some sense and degree the death of the body. Professor MacDougall and Joseph B. and Louisa Rhine of Duke University sought to bring psychical research out of the real world and into the laboratory in order to obtain evidence likely to gain scientific acceptance.

David Fontana, a Fellow of the British Psychological Society, a Distinguished Visiting Fellow at Cardiff University, professor of transpersonal psychology at Liverpool John Moores University and past president of the Society for Psychical Research, has authored a book titled *Is There an Afterlife?* He points out to us that a group that has opposed survival research is a body that should, in theory, be among its strongest supporters, namely established religion. Religion has equated the existence of communications from the beyond with witchcraft and the powers of evil and the "work of the devil." No one other than the ordained had the right of direct access to the Divine or to other worlds. We live in an age where, for many people, faith and belief are no longer enough. Such people have nothing to put in their place except materialism and short-term consumerism. Little is taught about the nature of the afterlife.

Death is still a taboo subject among the general public. We are the first generation in recorded history that is insulated from reminders of our own mortality. This is largely due to immunizations, antibiotics and improvements in public health and in medicine generally. Consequently, there is an unspoken resistance to any talk of leaving this life and of what might happen next. This attitude ignores the possibility that our present lives have a meaning and purpose greater than ourselves and that we are not simply biological accidents driven by our own genes. There seems to be a growing recognition that science cannot provide us with answers to life's fundamental questions. The search for greater meaning in life may therefore become more important.

In her book, *The Wheel of Life*,[4] Elisabeth Kubler-Ross tells of her intuitive guidance to visit an old friend while on her way to a lecture in Seattle. On being welcomed into the home of her friend and her husband, what she thought might be an afternoon visit over tea turned into a channeling session with her friend's husband being the channel. The message to Elisabeth from the spirit being channeled was, "Your work with death and dying is completed. It's now time for you to begin your second assignment. It's time for you to tell the world that death does not exist." To this point, Dr. Kubler-Ross, a world-renowned medical doctor, psychiatrist and thanatologist was known for her work with children and AIDS patients. She brought the hospice movement to the United States. Now she was told she must teach that there is no death. Her lectures and workshops took new paths and gained in popularity. People were more than ready to accept life after death. Many people shared that they were having out of body experiences and traveling toward a bright light and they were relieved to have their experiences confirmed.

In the late 1980s, I was privileged to hear Dr. Elisabeth Kubler-Ross give a lecture at Northeastern State University in Tahlequah, Oklahoma where I was living at the time. The auditorium was packed with students, faculty and staff from the university and many interested townspeople. People began to check their watches when the program hadn't started at the appointed time. Finally, a young man stepped onto the stage and explained that Dr. Kubler-Ross had a flight connection delay and that she would be there a bit later. We were asked to be patient and to wait for her arrival. She arrived thirty to forty minutes later. Breezing across the stage gasping for breath, she apologized for the delay and for her attire. She was wearing her travel clothes, jeans and sneakers, with her shirttail hanging out over her jeans. The audience loved her! She was authentic and had broken the ice and created a truly relaxed and empathetic atmosphere. There was no pretense. The focus quickly shifted to the topic of the lecture. We were mesmerized by her mastery of knowledge about death and dying, by her charm and by her obvious sense of mission.

Dr. Kubler-Ross shared an experience that night that she said had made the afterlife a reality to her, a professed skeptic. She told of a time when she was presenting seminars on death and dying at the University of Chicago and was at a point of making a decision to leave the university. She was talking with a colleague in the hallway when she noticed a woman standing in front of the elevator. She recognized the woman but couldn't recall how she knew her. Her colleague entered the elevator and the woman walked over to Dr. Kubler-Ross and said, "Dr. Ross, I had to come back. Do you mind if I walk you to your office? It will only take two minutes." She then recognized the woman as Mrs. Schwarz, a woman she had worked with and who had died ten months earlier. Mrs. Schwarz opened the door for Dr. Kubler-Ross and said, "Dr. Ross, I had to come back for two reasons: One, to thank you and Reverend Gaines—to thank you and him for what you did for me. But the other reason I had to come back is that you cannot stop this work on death and dying, not yet."

Dr. Kubler-Ross had trouble making sense of it all. She knew Mrs. Schwarz had been buried for ten months, and this went beyond the comfort zone of her belief system. She then found herself touching everything *real* to her—her desk, her chair, her pen, but the woman was still there. She was real, too. The scientist in her wanted proof that Mrs. Schwarz was in actuality there in front of her and she said, "You know, Reverend Gaines is in Urbana now. He would just love to have a note from you. Would you mind?" She handed Mrs. Schwarz a piece of paper and a pencil. Mrs. Schwarz took the paper and wrote a note. Then she got up and on leaving said again, "Dr. Ross, you promise." She didn't want her to give up her work just yet. Dr. Ross promised, and Mrs. Schwarz disappeared. Dr. Kubler-Ross kept the note to remind her of her personal proof of the reality of life after death.

Dr. Charles Tart, professor at the Institute of Transpersonal Psychology in Palo Alto, California works to bridge science and spirituality. In his December 2007-February 2008 article in *Shift: At the Frontiers of Consciousness*, a magazine publication of the Institute of Noetic Sciences, he talks about "What Death Tells Us About Life," and how love is the most important lesson we are here to learn.[5]

Tart tells us that after forty years of studying the evidence for survival of consciousness he admits to being afraid to die, and goes on to qualify his statement by explaining that he is of course speaking about his ordinary conscious self. He adds, "There is also a part of me that is looking forward to death and thinks it is going to be a great adventure. At some deeper level I am not at all afraid, and that lack of fear in some other part of me is data—and data are more important than theories and beliefs when we practice science. Death really reminds us how little we know and at the same time how important it is to try to understand."

Think back in a time in your own life when you may have had some pretty close calls, some close brushes with death. Can you recall how you felt in those moments you thought might be your last? I can, and in each case I felt a sense of surrender. There seemed to be an absence of fear as though I knew I was in the hands of a Being far greater than myself. A sense of calm, an *other-dimensional* feeling of safety seemed to take over and there was a knowing that the outcome would be in divine order.

It was mid-winter, and I was fulfilling a developmental counseling internship for my doctoral program at Vanderbilt University. I conducted group counseling sessions on two evenings each week at the Try Angle House, a group home sponsored by the YWCA for young women ages fourteen through eighteen. The group home offers a family atmosphere and counseling for those who have had to leave their families of origin for whatever reasons.

It was always such fun to work with the girls, usually a group of twelve or more. We worked in a comfortable lounge area in the basement of a large house situated in a nice residential neighborhood. Because we were without windows on the lower level, I was not aware of the snow storm building outside. I love the snow and was excited to discover an inch or two of accumulation already on my car when I opened the door to leave at the end of our session that evening. At the same time, I wasn't too keen on driving home through the city in the snow, and it was falling heavily by then. Try Angle House was located in West Nashville, and my home was in Brentwood over ten miles away via the interstate. The route I chose to the interstate took me in front of the Belmont Mansion, the main building of Belmont University. A driver suddenly pulled out in front of me, and to avoid hitting his car I instinctively stepped on my brake pedal which made me skid. I found myself traveling up onto and across the front lawn of the university, unable to stop without crashing my car into the building. I felt helpless. I knew there was a retaining wall at the end of the lawn, about three or four feet high, I'm guessing. Beyond that there was a sidewalk and a curb to the street that ran by the side of the building, perpendicular to the direction I was traveling. It was all happening so fast, and there were no more choices to make. As I flew through the air over the wall, I recall saying "Well, this is it!" I became very calm, there was no fear. Right there, in mid-air, the most amazing thing happened! My vehicle made a right-angle turn. Now, we know that isn't possible—right? How can a car make a right turn when there is no pavement or solid surface to offer resistance for the wheels? It happened in spite of the physical laws that were ignored. There were cars parked along the curb with one empty space waiting for my car. My car was plopped down perfectly between two cars by the curb, as if parked by a professional. I bounced for what seemed like a long time. Before the bouncing even stopped I heard knocking on my window. A nice college-aged couple, a young man and woman, were standing there still shocked at what they had just witnessed. I was still shaking, but I managed to roll down my window. The young woman said, "Are you all right?" I told her I thought I was all right. Then she said, "We've never seen anyone do what you just did!" I told her I had never done what I just did, either.

After assuring them that I was fine, they left, chattering away, and I sat in the car until I felt stable enough to get out on the road again. I was soon on the interstate and then safely at home. I hadn't been home five minutes when the phone rang. It was Mother asking, "Are you all right?" *Why was she asking me that? How did she know to call?* I told her I was fine and asked her, "Why do you ask?" She said, "I just had a very strong feeling that something just happened to you and I had to be sure you were okay." I thanked her for checking out her feeling and then told her my amazing story. We decided we did believe in angels and my belief was certainly reinforced after that dramatic experience! As I reflected back over the whole experience, I realized that when faced with total helplessness and what could have been a tragic outcome, I had made a spontaneous shift in my own consciousness where there was no fear, where I surrendered to a Higher Power and just knew that I would be protected. This feeling was present at other times when I found myself possibly near death's door; once in an automobile accident, once when a friend and I were trapped on a railroad trestle with a train whistle blowing around the bend, and at another time I knew I was losing consciousness when I was ill with spinal meningitis.

Currently, Dr. Gary Schwartz is out in front with his groundbreaking experiments in scientific evidence of life after death initially inspired by a question from Dr. Linda Russek, a clinical psychologist attending a conference in Florida, "Do you think it's possible that my father is still alive?"[6] Linda's father, Dr. Henry I. Russek, had been a distinguished cardiologist and scientist and had passed in 1990. Dr. Schwartz found himself compelled to share a secret that he had kept to himself for many years because of its controversial nature. When he was a professor at Yale University he had discovered an hypothesis about how systems store information. It had forced him to recognize the possibility that consciousness might survive after death. When he later agreed to team up with Linda in this research project he had to face possible ridicule from his colleagues at the University of Arizona. Here was a man who had built a highly respectable reputation as a professor of psychology and psychiatry at Yale University, director of the Yale Psychophysiology Center and co-director of the Yale Behavioral Medicine Clinic. He is currently professor of psychology, medicine, neurology, psychiatry and surgery at the University of Arizona, and serves as director of its Human Energy Systems Laboratory.

Dr. Schwartz and Dr. Russek kept their initial investigations secret. In 1995, Dr. Schwartz met Susy Smith, a well-known medium and author who founded the Survival Research

Foundation for the collection of scientific evidence for the survival of consciousness beyond physical death. Susy knew her life was nearing its end and told Gary and Linda that she had publicly "offered a $10,000 reward to the first person who successfully received the *secret message* she would attempt to communicate after she died. This message, if received correctly, would decipher a code left in a bank vault in Florida."[7] In a process that would assure Susy that her own work would be taken seriously after she was gone, Gary and Linda set about to create a more scientific design for her code experiment. He published an article on his work with Susy's code in the *Journal of Scientific Exploration* in 1997 and soon gained approval from the head of his department to not only bring the questionable research openly into the university but was granted approval to create the Soul Science Research Campaign to raise funds for expanding this research to other related areas. His research continues with extraordinary experiments and breakthrough scientific evidence of life after death with prominent mediums to prove or disprove the existence of an afterlife. Susy Smith died in 2001, at the age of 89, and her code has yet to be deciphered through the afterlife experiments conducted by Dr. Schwartz. The motto of his Human Energy Systems Laboratory is "If it is real, it will be revealed. If it is fake, we'll find the mistake."[8] Following the publication of his book with William L. Simon in 2002, *The Afterlife Experiments*, he published another book in 2005, *The Truth about Medium*, also with Simon. The latter is an account of "extraordinary experiments with the real Allison DuBois of NBC's "Medium" and other remarkable psychics." Anne Gehman, a well-known medium and a participant in Schwartz's laboratory experiments says that many people have spontaneous experiences with contact from those who have died: "It may happen only once in a person's lifetime—at that moment they're a medium."

Windbridge Institute for Applied Research in Human Potential is an independent research organization consisting of a community of scientists with varied backgrounds, specialties and interests. Julie Beischel, Ph.D. is a cofounder and the director of research at Windbridge Institute. She received her doctorate in Pharmacology and Toxicology from the University of Arizona and was the first recipient of the William James Postdoctoral Fellowship in Mediumship and Survival Research. She also recognizes the public's growing fascination with survival and mediumship in the demand for recent popular television shows. Some of the most popular media productions include television shows such as *Medium* and *Ghost Whisperer* and movies such as *White Noise, The Sixth Sense, Hereafter,* and *Rumors of Angels* as well as dozens of books on this topic. Dr. Beischel agrees with Dr. Schwartz that bringing the study of mediumship into the "regulated environment of the laboratory allows for the controlled and repeated examination of the mediumship process." "Before participating in formal research, each prospective medium is screened over several months using an intensive screening and training procedure."

Dr. Archie Roy, Scottish Professor Emeritus of Astronomy at the University of Glasgow, points out that "most mainstream scientists are simply unaware of the evidence for the afterlife. They have never done psychic research and have never read the evidence." And Victor Zammit goes on to say that "without exception, I have found that the materialist closed-minded skeptics who oppose the existence of psychic phenomena and the afterlife are still grounded in outdated scientific paradigms and just have not done their homework." Dr. Fontana excuses what he calls "ignorance of this kind" because "most scientists have a hard task keeping abreast of developments in their own fields and can hardly be expected to wade through the extensive data on survival of death" (his personal library has over six hundred books on the evidence for survival alone). "A cardinal rule in science is that you familiarize yourself with the evidence before making judgments on it."

Zammit emphasizes that some of the leaders in the scientific research of life after death are extremely intelligent and astute medical doctors who began their investigation as skeptics. Among them, Dr. Glen Hamilton, a highly respected physician and member of the Canadian Parliament known for his photographs of apparitions taken in his laboratory under strictly controlled conditions, and Dr. Melvin Morse, a pediatrician and a recognized world leading authority on dying children, and his extensive study of the literature that led him to conclude that some aspect of human consciousness survives death.[10]

Then there was Dr. Carl Jung, Swiss psychiatrist, known the world over for his profound influence on almost all aspects of our modern culture: medicine, religion, philosophy, literature, art and psychoanalysis. He was a believer in the afterlife and regularly attended séances as an official participant or a private observer in Zurich, and once told Sigmund Freud, "I have been dabbling in spookery again." He also wrote and told him he had been "named an honorary fellow of the American Society for Psychical Research because of his *services as an occultist*."[11] He asked Freud's opinion of this sort of research, but Freud didn't reply.

Laboratory research with mediums is only one aspect of this growing body of scientific investigation into the possibilities of an afterlife. Near-death experiences (NDEs), coined in the 1970s by psychiatrist Raymond Moody, are being reported with greater frequency and being taken more seriously than ever before. These reports are made by those who are pronounced clinically dead but are resuscitated, and by people involved in accidents or in illnesses and are feared to be near death. Some who are actually dying are able to describe their deathbed visions in their final moments. A classic story is that of Betty J. Eadie, author of *Embraced by the Light*, an extraordinary near-death-experience (NDE) that has changed Eadie's life profoundly.[12]

A victim of bacterial meningitis in 2008, neurosurgeon Dr. Eben Alexander, III had dismissed near-death experiences as explainable by the hard wiring of the human brain. The deadly infection put him in a coma. He was so changed by his own near-death experience, which he described as "even more psychedelic than most," that he wrote a book about it, *Proof of Heaven.* "Having trained at Duke University and taught and practiced as a surgeon at Harvard, he knows brain science as well as anyone. And science, he said, cannot explain his experience."[13]

Bruce Greyson, M.D., is known as "The Father of NDE Research." Formerly a professor of psychiatry at the University of Connecticut, he is now the Bonner-Lowry Professor of Personality Studies in the Department of Psychiatric Medicine at the University of Virginia in Charlottesville. He has been researching and conducting studies on near-death experiences (NDEs) for over 25 years and has written an abundance of articles on the subject for leading medical journals, including *Journal of Scientific Exploration, Journal of the American Medical Association* and *American Journal of Psychiatry.* Dr. Greyson also wrote an overview of NDEs for the Encyclopedia Britannica and since 1982 has been the Editor-in-Chief of the highly respected *Journal of Near-Death Studies.*

Greyson says, "I think the most important thing for people to realize, for the average person to realize, is that having a near-death experience is a very common, very normal experience. They happen to everybody. They happened to presidents, they happen to psychotics, religious people or atheists. They are a normal part of living. They have nothing to do with mental illness. They're nothing to be afraid of or worried about if you have them." He further states that when people lose their fear of death they also lose their fear of living life to the fullest because they're not afraid of taking chances anymore.[14]

Dianne Arcangel, a former hospice chaplain at the Texas Medical Center and former director of the Elisabeth Kubler-Ross Center of Houston and author of *Afterlife Encounters* sees "the ability to experience discarnate individuals as a natural *eighth sense* that can be scientifically studied." She explains that we may be able to use any combination of our senses or just the eighth sense of *knowing* or sensing something is there. According to Rupert Sheldrake, English scientist and author, the seventh sense is a connection such as telepathy between the living. So Arcangel asks, "If the seventh sense is the connection between the living, could the eighth sense be a connection between the living and the deceased?" Arcangel has assembled the world's largest database of case studies involving contact with the other side.[15]

The body of research on the topic of the afterlife and on spirit contact is expanding all the time. Humanity as a mass is at a point of development in consciousness that is calling for answers to the mysteries of life and death. Over the last few centuries, science has had a leading role in organizing research into the possibilities of life continuing after the death of the physical body. Two prominent scientists to watch are Dr. Amit Goswami[16] and Dr. Lisa Randall.[17] Both are revolutionary theoretical quantum physicists who are exploring and attempting to validate the existence of the spiritual dimension within a multidimensional universe.

Do Not Stand at My Grave and Weep

Do not stand at my grave and weep
I am not there; I do not sleep.
I am a thousand winds that blow,
I am the diamond glints on snow,
I am the sun on ripened grain,
I am the gentle autumn rain.
When you awaken in the morning's hush
I am the swift uplifting rush
Of quiet birds in circling flight.
I am the soft star-shine at night.
Do not stand at my grave and cry;
I am not there; I did not die.

~Mary Elizabeth Frye

END NOTES

Introduction

1. Boyer, Peter J. "Little Boy's Death Was Just a Walk into Another Galaxy," in *St. Petersburg Times*, 1978.
2. Chopra, Deepak. *Life After Death.* (New York: Harmony Books, 2006), 97.
3. Hodson, Geoffrey. *The Kingdom of the Gods.* (Madras, India: The Theosophical Publishing House, 1976), xii.
4. Borgia, Anthony, *Facts: They That Mourn.* (www.angelfire.com/newviews/facts.html), 3.

Chapter 3: Afterlife Beliefs of Major Religions

1. Lee, Leonard. *The Metaphysical View of Death and Life After Death, Part 3.* (www.positivearticles.com)
2. Ibid.

Chapter 4: What Happens When We Die?

1. Ray, Sondra. *Celebration of Breath.* (Berkeley: Celestial Arts, 1983), ix.
2. Dalai Lama. *The Art of Living.* (New York: Gramercy Books, 1995), 39.
3. Hodson, Geoffrey. *Hidden Wisdom in the Holy Bible—Vol. I.* (Wheaton, IL: Quest Books, 1993), 40, (Matt. 5:48).
4. Ibid., 41.
5. Ibid., 40.
6. Haich, Elisabeth. *Initiation.* (Palo Alto, CA: Seed Center, 1974), 81.
7. Hodson, Geoffrey. *Hidden Wisdom in the Holy Bible—Vol. I* (Wheaton, IL: Quest Books, 1993), 43.
8. Heindel, Max. *The Rosicrucian Cosmo-Conception.* (Oceanside, CA: The Rosicrucian Fellowship, 1969), 98.
9. Ibid., 98
10. Bailey, Alice A. *The Consciousness of the Atom.* (New York: Lucis Publishing Company, 1973), 60.
11. Ibid., 60.
12. Heindel, Max. *The Rosicrucian Cosmo-Conception.* (Oceanside, CA: The Rosicrucian Fellowship, 1969), 103.
13. Besant, Annie. *Death—and After.* (Wheaton, IL: The Theosophical Publishing House, 1999), 96.
14. Borgia, Anthony. *More About Life in World Unseen.* (www.rait.airclima.ru/books) 1951, 5.
15. Borgia, Anthony. *Life in the World Unseen.* (http://anthony3741.tripod.com) 1951, 2.
16. Barborka, Geoffrey A. *The Divine Plan.* (Wheaton, IL: The Theosophical Publishing House, 1980), 390.

17. Borgia, Anthony. *More About Life in World Unseen.* (www.rait.airclima.ru/books) 1951, 7.

18. Borgia, Anthony. *Life in the World Unseen.* (www.angelfire.com/ne/newviews/hereafter1.html) 1951, 1.

Chapter 5: Other Dimensions

1. Randall, Edward C. *The Dead Have Never Died.* (New York: Alfred A. Knopf, 1917), 245.

2. Manser, Ann C. *Pages of Shustah—Lecture 12.* (Omaha: Study Course, 1974), 75.

3. Bailey, Alice A. *Esoteric Healing.* (New York: Lucis Publishing Company, 1977), 444.

4. Randall, Edward C. *The Dead Have Never Died.* (New York: Alfred A. Knopf, 1917), 77.

5. Ibid., 101.

6. Yogananda, Paramahansa. *The Second Coming of Christ.* (Los Angeles: Self-Realization Fellowship, 2004), 203.

7. Ibid., 203-4.

8. Barborka, Geoffrey A. *The Divine Plan.* (Wheaton, IL: The Theosophical Publishing House, 1980), 383.

9. Brofman, Martin, Ph. D. Image. (http://www.healer.ch/Chakras-e.html)

10. Yogananda, Paramahansa. *The Second Coming of Christ.* (Los Angeles: Self-Realization Fellowship, 2004), 820-22.

11. Ibid., 1577.

12. Ibid., 416.

13. Farnese, A. *A Wanderer in the Spirit Lands.* (Scottsdale AIM Publishing Company, 1993), 197.

14. Ibid., 60-61.

15. Chopra, Deepak. *Life After Death.* (New York: Harmony Books, 2006), 73, 77.

16. Randall, Edward C. *The Dead Have Never Died.* (New York: Alfred A. Knopf, 1917), 149-152.

17. Baker, Douglas. *The Opening of the Third Eye.* (New York: Samuel Weiser Inc., 1978), 45.

18. Ibid., 49.

19. Rafferty, Fred, Editor. *Spirit World and Spirit Life.* (Los Angeles: J. F. Rowny Press, 1922), 49.

20. Ibid., 49.

21. Ibid., 52.

22. Ibid., 54.

23. Ibid., 55.

24. Ibid., 55.

Chapter 8: A Remarkable Woman Named Annabelle

1. Manser, Ann C., Cecil North. *Pages of Shustah, Inc. Divination and Meditation Cards.* (Omaha: Paragon Printing, Inc., 1974).

Chapter 9: Closing a Chapter

1. Alder, Vera Stanley. *Initiation of the World, 1972), 40.*

Chapter 10: A Visit to Another World

1. Larson, Patricia R. *Ageless Wisdom for Today's World.* (Omaha: Study Course, 1989), 7.
2. Zammit, Victor James. *A* www.victorzammit.com *Lawyer Presents the Case for the Afterlife, Fourth Edition.* (www.victorzammit.com), 2006, 230.
3. Jung, Carl J. (Psychology Today, www.psychologytoday.com.blog).
4. Browne, Sylvia. *Conversations with the Other Side.* (Carlsbad, CA: Hay House, Inc., 2002), 60.
5. Farnese, A. *Wanderer in the Spirit Lands.* (Scottsdale: AIM Publishing Company, 1993), 197.

Chapter 11: More Contacts with Ann

1. Manser, Ann C. *Pages of Shustah, Inc.* (Omaha: Study Course, 1974), 84.

Chapter 12: A Remarkable Woman Named Patricia

1. Manser, Ann C. and LeRoy E. Zemke. *Evolution of Consciousness.* (Omaha: Study Course, 1974).
2. Dinshah, Darius. *Let There Be Light.* (Malaga, NJ: Dinshah Health Society, 1985).

Chapter 13: Saying Goodbye and Hello Again

1. Zammit, Victor James. *A Lawyer Presents theCase for the Afterlife, Fourth Edition.* (www.victorzammit.com), 2006, 229.
2. Meek, George W. *After We Die, What Then?* (Columbus: Ariel Press, 1987), 11.
3. Ibid., 121.
4. Ibid., 122.

Chapter 15: A Remarkable Woman Named Kathryn

1. Myss, Caroline. *The Energetics of Healing.* Boulder, CO: Sounds True, 1997, 2 DVDs.

Chapter 16: Contacting Kathryn

1. Hinz, Walter, Ph. D. *The Corner Stone.* (Suffolk: Neville Spearman, 1977), 176.
2. Berkowitz, Rita S. and Deborah S.Romaine. *Communicating With Spirits.* (Indianapolis: Alpha Books, 2003), 210.

Chapter 17: More Contacts with Kathryn

1. Redfield, James. *The Celestine Prophecy.* (New York: Warner Treasures, 1994).
2. Storr, Anthony. *The Essential Jung.* (New York: MJF Books, 1983), 26.

Chapter 18: Communication with Our Pets

1. Heindel, Max. *The Rosicrucian Cosmo-Conception*. (Oceanside, CA: The Rosicrucian Fellowship, 1969), 74-86.
2. Bailey, Alice A. *Esoteric Psychology I*. (New York: Lucis Publishing Company, 1979), 56, 259.
3. Ibid., 259.
4. Leadbeater, Charles W. *The Inner Life*. (Wheaton, IL: The Theosophical Publishing House, 1978), 133.
5. Heindel, Max. *The Rosicrucian Cosmo-Conception*. (Oceanside, CA: The Rosicrucian Fellowship, 1969), 83.
6. Williams, Marta. *Learning Their Language*. (Novato, CA: New World Library, 2003), 151.
7. Reynolds, Rita. *Blessing the Bridge*. (Troutdale, OR: NewSage Press, 2001).

Chapter 19: Our Psychic Legacy

1. Heindel, Max. *The Rosicrucian Cosmo-Conception*. (Oceanside, CA: The Rosicrucian Fellowship, 1969), 92.
2. Steiner, Rudolf. *Life Between Death and Rebirth*. (Hudson, NY: Anthroposophic Press, 1968).
3. Moss, Robert. *Conscious Dreaming*. (New York: Crown Trade Paperbacks, 1996), 28.
4. Ibid., 29.

Chapter 20: How You Can Contact the Afterlife

1. Alder, Vera Stanley. *The Finding of the Third Eye*. (York, ME: Samuel Wieser, Inc., 1981, 87.
2. Van Praagh, James. *Heaven and Earth*. (New York: Pocket Books, 2002), 77.
3. Stead, W. T. and Estelle Stead. *The Blue Island*. (Washington, D. C.: ESPress, Inc., 1979), 53.
4. Ibid., 51.
5. Virtue, Doreen, Ph. D. and Becky Prelitz, M. F. T., R. D. *Eating in the Light*. (Carlsbad, CA: Hay House, Inc., 2001.
6. Weil, Andrew, M. D. *Spontaneous Healing*. (New York: Fawcett Columbine of the Ballentine Publishing Group, 1995), 215.
7. Long, Max Freedom. *Growing Into Light*. (Marina del Ray, CA: Devorss Publications, 1955), 21.
8. Lonegren, Sid. *The Pendulum Kit*. (New York: Simon & Schuster, Inc., 1990.
9. Larson, Patricia R. *Evolutionary Chart of the Planes and Bodies in Ageless Wisdom for Today's World*. (Omaha: Study Course, 1989).
10. Engel, Steve A. (E. Charles).
11. Saraydarian, H. *The Science of Meditation*. (Sedona: Aquarian Educational Group, 1981), 21.
12. Williams, Bill, Muriel Williams and Ian Currie. *Life in the Spirit World*. (Victoria, BC: Trafford Publishing, 2006), 81.
13. Ibid., 39.
14. Bailey, Alice A. *Letters on Occult Meditation*. (New York: Lucis Publishing Company, 1972), 195.
15. Saraydarian, H. *The Science of Meditation*. (Sedona: Aquarian Educational Group, 1981), 233.

16. Bailey, Alice A. *The Externalisation of the Hierarchy.* (Lucis Trust Publishing company, 1957), vi.
17. Toye, Lori Adaile. *Points of Perception.* (Payson, AZ: I Am America Seventh Ray Publishing and Distributing Co., 2008), 197.

Chapter 21: Other Contacts

1. Long, Max Freedom.
2. Moss, Robert. *The Dreamer's Book of the Dead.* (Rochester, VT: Destiny Books, 2005).
3. Martin, Joel and Patricia Romanowski. *Love Beyond Life.* (New York: Dell Publishing, 1997), 245.

Addendum B: Afterlife Research

1. Zammit, Victor James. *A Lawyer Presents the Case for the Afterlife, Fourth Edition.* (www.victorzammit. com), 2006, 7.
2. Ibid., 10.
3. Ibid., 12.
4. Kubler-Ross, Elisabeth. *The Wheel of Life.* (New York: Touchstone, 1997), 209-10.
5. Tart, Charles T. "What Death Tells Us About Life." *Shift: At the Frontiers of Consciousness.* No. 17, December 2007-February 2008.
6. Schwartz, Gary E. and William L. Simon. *The Afterlife Experiments.* (New York: Pocket Books, 2002), 3.
7. Ibid., 26.
8. Ibid., xv.
9. Gehman, Anne. 2006 IONS Teleseminars. (www.noetic.org).
10. Zammit, Victor James. *A Lawyer Presents the Case for the Afterlife, Fourth Edition.* (www.victorzammit. com), 17, 18.
11. Bair, Deirdre. *Jung, A Biography.* (Boston: Little, Brown and Company, 2003), 135.
12. Eadie, Betty J. *Embraced By The Light.* (Placerville, CA: Gold Leaf Press, 1992).
13. Kaufman, Leslie. "Readers Join Doctor's Journey to the Afterworlds' Gates," in *The New York Times,* November 26, 2012, p. C1.
14. Greyson, Dr. Bruce. Essentials of Noetic Sciences Series.
15. Arcangel, Dianne. 2006 IONS Teleseminars. (www.noetic.org)
16. www.amitgoswami.org
17. www.physics.harvard.edu/people/facpages/randall.html

Glossary

1. Barborka, Geoffrey A. *The Divine Plan.* (Wheaton, IL: The Theosophical Publishing House, 1980), 378.
2. Ibid., 31.
3. Alder, Vera Stanley. *The Secret of the Atomic Age.* (New York: Weiser, 1974), 40.

4. Lumari. *Akashic Records: Collective Keepers of Divine Expression*. (Santa Fe, NM: Amethyst, 2003), 8.

5. Larson, Patricia R. *Ageless Wisdom for Today's World*. (Omaha: Study Course, 1989), i.

6. Parrish-Harra, Carol E. *The New Dictionary of Spiritual Thought*. (Tahlequah, OK: Sparrow Hawk Press, 2002), 22.

7. Larson, Patricia R. *Ageless Wisdom for Today's World*. (Omaha: Study Course, 1989), i.

8. de Alberti, Lita. *Channeling*. (New York: Weiser Books, 2000), 6.

9. Bailey, Alice A. *The Consciousness of the Atom*. (New York: Lucis Publishing Company, 1973), 99.

10. Heindel, Max. *The Rosicrucian Cosmo-Conception*. Oceanside, CA: The Rosicrucian Fellowship, 1969), 74.

11. Hodson, Geoffrey. (*The Kingdom of the Gods*. (London: The Theosophical Publishing House, 1976), 12.

12. Engel, E. Charles (Steve). *Esoteric Definitions*. (Portland, OR: Angel Estates Publishing, 1992), 12.

13. Alder, Vera Stanley. *The Fifth Dimension*. (London: Rider & Company, 1983), 56,67.

14. Engel, E. Charles (Steve). *Esoteric Definitions*. (Portland, OR: Angel Estates Publishing, 1992), 12.

15. Parrish-Harra, Carol E. *The New Dictionary of Spiritual Thought*. (Tahlequah, OK: Sparrow Hawk Press, 2002), 170.

16. Ibid., 84.

17. Ibid., 85.

18. Manser, Ann C. *Pages of Shustah*. (Omaha: Study Course, 1974), 95.

19. Parrish-Harra, Carol E. *The New Dictionary of Spiritual Thought*. (Tahlequah, OK: Sparrow Hawk Press, 2002), 102.

20. Long, Max Freedom. *Growing Into Light*. (Marina del Rey, CA: DeVorss Publications, 1955), 45.

21. Manser, Ann C. *Pages of Shustah: Holy Kabalah* (Omaha: Study Course, 1974), 1.

22. Bailey, Alice A. *Glamour: A World Problem*. (New York: Lucis Publishing Company, 1971), 21, 101.

23. Parrish-Harra, Carol E. *The New Dictionary of Spiritual Thought*. (Tahlequah, OK: Sparrow Hawk Press, 2002), 132.

24. Bailey, Alice A. *The Rays and The Initiations*. (New York: Lucis Publishing Company, 1972), 341.

25. Parrish-Harra, Carol E. *The New Dictionary of Spiritual Thought*. (Tahlequah, OK: Sparrow Hawk Press, 2002), 132.

26. Larson, Patricia R. *Ageless Wisdom for Today's World*. (Omaha: Study Course, 1989), ii.

27. Collier, Robert. *The Secret of the Ages*. (Tarrytown, NY: The Book of Gold, 1948), 136.

28. Engel, E. Charles (Steve). *Esoteric Definitions*. (Portland, OR: Angel Estates Publishing, 1992), 26.

29. Parrish-Harra, Carol E. *The New Dictionary of Spiritual Thought*. (Tahlequah, OK: Sparrow Hawk Press, 2002), 169.

30. Ibid., 172.

31. Engel, E. Charles (Steve). *Esoteric Definitions*. (Portland, OR: Angel Estates Publishing, 1992), 27.

32. Parrish-Harra, Carol E. *The New Dictionary of Spiritual Thought*. (Tahlequah, OK: Sparrow Hawk Press, 2002), 200.

33. Manser, Ann and Cecil North. *Pages of Shustah Divination and Meditation Cards*. (Omaha: Paragon Printing, Inc., 1974), 3.

34. Larson, Patricia R. *Ageless Wisdom for Today's World*. (Omaha: Study Course, 1989), iii.

35. Chopra, Deepak. *Life After Death*. (New York: Harmony Books, 2006), 29.

36. Alder, Vera Stanley. *The Initiation of the World*. (New York: Samuel Weiser, Inc., 1972),

37. Parrish-Harra, Carol E. *The New Dictionary of Spiritual Thought*. (Tahlequah, OK: Sparrow Hawk Press, 2002), 213.

38. Heindel, Max. *The Rosicrucian Cosmo-Conception*. (Oceanside, CA: The Rosicrucian Fellowship, 1969), 565.

39. Parrish-Harra, Carol E. *The New Dictionary of Spiritual Thought*. (Tahlequah, OK: Sparrow Hawk Press, 2002), 277.

40. Dinshah, Darius. *Let There Be Light*. (Malaga, NJ: Dinshah Health Society, 1990), 71.

41. Parrish-Harra, Carol E. *The New Dictionary of Spiritual Thought*. (Tahlequah, OK: Sparrow Hawk Press, 2002), 282.

42. Hall, Manley P. *Lectures on Ancient Philosophy*. (Los Angeles, CA: Philosophical Research Society, Inc., 1984), 358.

43. http://en.wikipedia.org/wiki/Theosophy

44. Neufeldt, Victoria and Andrew N. Sparks, Eds. *Webster's New World Dictionary*. (New York: Warner Books, Inc., 1990), 627.

45. Parrish-Harra, Carol E. *The New Dictionary of Spiritual Thought*. (Tahlequah, OK: Sparrow Hawk Press, 2002), 301.

GLOSSARY

Adept: A highly developed personality; similar to the rank of Master. An advanced Initiate considered to have taken the fourth Initation. One who has discovered the secret of the sevenfold principles in nature and awakens his/her dormant powers.[1]

Akashic Record: An individual Akashic Record is a record of all of the memories of the soul. On a larger scale, it is the memory repository of all of evolution. In the Christian Bible, Luke 12:6-7, "even the very hairs of your head are all numbered."[2] Vera Stanley Alder tells us in *The Secret of the Atomic Age* that of the four types of ether that surround us, the Reflecting ether is the most refined. "Its inconceivably tiny atoms are said to be photographic and to store records of all that has taken place. They provide the mystery called memory, and are the medium through which thoughts make impressions on the brain."[3] The author, Lumari, speaks of the Akashic Records as "Collective Keepers of Divine Expression, a group of beings who gather and contain and share everything that has happened and unfolded in the universe and within that, all thoughts, explorations, intentions and their actual, probable and possible results."[4]

Antahkarana: Bridge between the World of Illusion and the World of Reality. It serves as a communication link between the higher and lower minds, and is built by the conscious effort of the individual.[5]

Aspirant: One who is on the probationary path and consciously seeks acceptance to the spiritual path. The initial stages of conscious spiritual growth.[6]

Astral Body: Subtle or rarefied Body of the next higher vibration above the physical and etheric bodies that we use when we leave our physical body and travel the astral plane; for example, while we sleep and for a period after we die. Visual equivalent of the physical body in the next dimension.

Aura: The force-field of energy surrounding the soul and the four lower bodies on which the impressions, thoughts, feelings, words and actions of the individual are registered. It has been referred to as the L-field, which some scientists say controls the manifestation of the *physical body*. In her work, Ann Manser referred to the invariant aura which is the most permanent part of the auric field, each color reflecting the principle for which it stands. To some, it is known as the karmic aura and should not be confused with the mood or health colors of one of the auxiliary auras as seen by most clairvoyants.

Basic Self: A separate entity that works with the subconscious mind in controlling the functions of the physical body, the emotions, the psychic doors, intuition, memory and habits.

Bodies: Vehicles or sheaths of the Monads that are formed upon lines of Cosmic Force within each Monad. They are constructed from the Planes as the Monads descend during Involution and expanded as the bodies ascend the Planes during evolution.[7]

Chakra: The word *chakra* is Sanskrit, and signifies a wheel; the literal translation is *the turning of the wheel of the Law*. The use of the word *chakra* with which we are concerned is its application to a series of wheel-like vortices which exist along the etheric spine of the individual. They are force-centers and points of connection at which energy flows from one level or body to another level or body of the individual.

Channeling: The means by which one can make a direct connection with a non-physical or discarnate being. Channeling can be distinguished from mediumship in that the focus for mediums is to prove the existence of life after death. The focus of channeling is to receive guidance.[8]

Clairvoyant: The ability to perceive things not visible to the physical eyes. Extended vision or sight.

Consciousness: The word *consciousness* comes from two Latin words: *con*, with; and *scio*, to know; and means literally "that with which we know."[9] States of consciousness in the kingdoms throughout the process of evolution: trance-like; dreamless sleep; dream consciousness; waking consciousness.[10]

Conscious Self: The part of the mind/soul that projects personalities onto the Earth for experience in a Physical Body. It has the faculty of reason and the power of will. It guides the subconscious mind and basic self or low self.

Deva: Sanskrit word meaning "shining ones" referring to their self-luminous appearance. Winged beings. They are regarded as omnipresent, super-physical agents of Creative Will, as directors of all natural forces, laws and processes, solar, interplanetary and planetary. They also apply to Archangels, angels, and nature spirits.[11]

Desire Body: The relay body between Higher Forces and the lower conscious bodies. The desire body is sometimes referred to as the astral body. The color in the aura is bright green.[12]

Dimension: The word *dimension* comes from the Latin *dimension*, meaning measuring. The first measurement is simply the shortest distance between two points, and gives us a straight line. This corresponds somewhat to the *first dimension*, which is the first elementary movement through space in one direction only. First dimensional existence expressed the primal urge or push forward of life. The *second dimension* is found when a line or direction can be taken at an angle to the first flat plane or straight line. The important aspect of two-dimensional life would be that of intersection. After the primal urge, the *will* to live of the first dimension, followed by the *attraction* and cohesion due to the second dimension, *physical life* appears in the third dimension as rotation and vibration. As we travel upward through the dimensions, the vibration becomes higher and higher. We have the power to travel in time and space through the electrical part of the human mind at fourth-dimensional speed. Each dimension becomes finer and higher in vibratory frequency.[13]

Discarnate: An entity that is not incarnated in our physical world; a discarnate. While having no physical body, it does have the fullness of personality. A discarnate may be on the inner planes between lives or be a personality who no longer incarnates and resides permanently in other dimensions.[14]

Djwhal Khul: "The Tibetan." A teaching Master of Ray 2 who has provided humanity with nearly 10,000 pages of teachings through his amanuensis, Alice A. Bailey, with whom he was in subjective communication from 1919 until she died in 1949. His telepathic dictations conveying esoteric thought were subsequently published in 20 volumes by Lucis Trust, NY.[15]

Embodiment: One lifetime in a Physical Body within an incarnation or series of lives.

Entity: A discarnate, or spirit being without a physical body, that can be seen or recognized by some, undetectable by others, that continues to live in dimensions other than physical incarnation with some overlap between planes—physical and nonphysical.[16]

Esoteric: The Greek root *eso* means "within." That which is hidden, unseen, secret, inner, or out-of-sight—the meaning behind the meaning.[17]

Etheric Body: Sometimes called the *etheric double*. A replica of the Physical Body made up of finer matter. Its function is to convey vitality to the body by way of the nervous system. It is not a separate vehicle of consciousness.

Etheric Plane: The Plane of next highest frequency above the Physical Plane. It penetrates the Physical Plane and is the Plane of records.

Evolution: When concerned with the Monad, evolution is the moving through eons of time, developmentally, from the density of the Physical Body into space by traveling up the Planes; discarding the subtle or rarefied bodies that were built in involution at a time when they are no longer needed. "Evolution is composed of each challenge, each problem that has to be resolved within the personality of each Monadic Life."[18]

Godhead: An impersonal term for the Source of All; a recognition of the Creator of life from which All flows.[19]

Group Spirit:	A guardian spirit governing a tribe of animals or plants from without. Instinct is suggestion of group spirit responded to by animal.
Hierarchy:	A group of spiritual beings on the inner planes of the Solar System. These beings are the intelligent forces of nature and they control all evolutionary processes, including angels, Masters, Chohans and Lipika Lords or Recording Angels. They control and evolve the world by working through their disciples here on Earth.
High Self:	The spiritual part of one's consciousness. It is the eternal part of you that does not incarnate. Every individual has a High Self that is usually at a distance from the body though always *on call*.[20]
Holy Kabalah:	A mystical Teaching concerning the Hebrew Scripture. Hebrew theology is divided into three parts called the Law, the Soul of the Law and the SOUL of the Soul of the Law. The Law, the Torah, was and is taught to all the children of Israel. The Mishnah, the Soul of the Law, is revealed to the Rabbins. The SOUL of the Soul of the Law, which is the Holy Kabalah, is said to be concealed from all but the Adepts and Initiates of the Arcane Wisdom, as only They are given Its secret Principles. Three great books written on the Kabalah are *The Sephir Yetzirah,* which is the key—the book of Formation; *The Sephir Ha Zohar,* which is called the Book of Splendor; and the *Apocalypse* or the Book of Revelation found at the end of the New Testament in the Christian Bible.[21]
Illusion:	The soul is submerged in the illusion of the manifested world and fails to see with clarity until such time when it has learned to pour the light of the soul into the mind and brain and to develop the intuition through which discrimination and discernment become apparent.[22]
Incarnation:	Soul embodiment.
Initiate:	One who is dedicated to the study and mastery of the mysteries of the science of self and has made him/herself ready for the Path of Initiation.[23]

Initiation: Initiation is a process whereby the spiritual person within the personality becomes aware of him/herself as a soul, with soul powers, soul relationships and soul purpose. It is a process of spiritual awakening. Every step upon the Path of Initiation increases group recognition. The disciple on the Probationary Path starts off on his quest for the door of Initiation. Initiation admits the aspirant into membership in the Hierarchy.[24]

Inner Planes: Higher or hidden frequencies of each plane not recognized while conscious in the physical, waking state. Not a product of the subconscious; not a dream, but an experience of another dimension which may be imprinted on the memory and recalled by the conscious mind.[25]

Involution: Process of the Monad moving through eons of time from space into the density of the Physical Body by building subtle or rarefied Bodies commensurate to the Planes through which they are traversing, descending from the Godhead for experience through incarnation.[26]

Karma: The Law of Cause and Effect. It can be positive or negative, but is never intended to mean punishment. It is a balancing of experience for the education of the soul. For every act there is a reaction in the same measure.

Law of Attraction: Back of everything is the immutable law of the Universe—that what you are is but the effect. Your thoughts are the causes. The only way you can change the effect is by first changing the cause.[27] One's vibratory frequency will attract to it situations of a like vibratory frequency.

Low Self: A separate entity that works with the subconscious mind in controlling the functions of the physical body, the emotions, the psychic door, intuition, memory and habits.

Lucid dreaming: Conscious dreaming.

Materialist: One who regards death as final because he/she sees life only in the physical body. Some claim that denying the afterlife is scientific, but in fact it merely indicates a belief in materialism.

Master: A highly evolved personality—one who has taken the fifth initiation. The identity of the master usually remains a secret. The focus of their work depends on their evolution. Masters are involved in various fields of science, human behavior and metaphysics. They tend to have a rainbow-like aura of twenty colors or more.[28]

Maya: The world of appearance. The phenomenal universe; unreality; all that is finite, subject to decay and change; all that is not eternal and unchangeable.[29]

Medium: An individual who allows his or her personality vehicle to be receptive to temporary habitation by an intelligence without form.

Meditation: A practice resulting in contact with high consciousness; the transfer of the human consciousness into that of soul awareness. A science that helps us attain a direct experience of God, usually through periods of silence in which the work of concentration, contemplation and gestation brings about soul growth.[30]

Monad: The spark of Divinity that you are. It is the highest body in consciousness; pure Light. Each person begins as a Monad, the initial stage of personal development. The Monad drops down the vibratory scale of involution, building bodies of Consciousness. As one grows and advances in consciousness, one begins to travel back up the vibratory scale of evolution to the Godhead.[31]

Occult: That which is hidden and must be studied to be understood. In Latin, *to conceal*. The true study of occultism seeks to penetrate the causal mysteries of being.[32] Modern media has given the neutral term *occult* a negative connotation.

Oversoul: A blended group of souls working as one in consciousness, occurring as the same individuals participate regularly in an action, i.e., family, team, class.

Pages of Shustah: Shustah: literally, "Footsteps Back to Truth." This Wisdom of the Ancients is a compendium of the Laws of Evolution as they have been carried forward through civilizations of development. A wisdom school founded by Ann C. Manser, this course unfolds correct procedures of the Western Tradition for right thinking and right acting in time, place and order. It is a text of sixty-six lectures and exercises given to aspiring students as disciplines to be absorbed and practiced in the daily living.

Pages of Shustah Cards:
The "Pages of Shustah Card Book" with an accompanying deck of divination cards is a treatise and working method depicting the value of symbolism combined with Astrology and Meditation, inducing increased sensitivity and greater intuitive awareness in the daily living of a more comprehensive and constructive life.[33]

Perfect Pattern:
When pertaining to an individual, it is the pattern or blueprint for one to follow during an embodiment. It is based on what the soul needs to experience for self-development and what karmic conditions must be met. Violet is the color for accessing your Perfect Pattern, as in meditation.

Prana:
Sanskrit for *breath*. It is the cosmic life-force on all planes of being; the *breath of life*. Life-force energy from the Sun.[34]

Reincarnation:
Reincarnation is the rebirth of the soul into a new physical body following the death of the body presently in use. This necessitates the repeated dying of the physical body and the creation and rebirth of another until it has garnered all the knowledge and wisdom that is possible while living on Earth.

Rishis:
Sages of Vedic India who rose into prominence when Hinduism was in its earliest flowering, perhaps 1,000 to 4,000 years ago.[35]

Rolfing:
A scientific and organized system of manipulating the muscles into their correct alignment in the body. Developed by Ida P. Rolf, Ph. D., the system was originally termed *structural integration*.

Root Race:
Once our earth was established on the physical plane, its life was divided into seven great periods (seven days of Creation). During these periods,

life evolves upon seven great continents. Human beings progress through ensouling seven great successive root races. These are each sub-divided into seven minor races and so on into further sub-divisions, e.g., We are now living during the fifth great period, the fifth day of creation.[36] We are, as a whole, the fifth sub-race of the fifth root race. There is evidence of a developing sixth sub-race at this time.

Seed Atom: A reservoir of data encoded to preserve information to be used in the evolutionary pattern of an individual on a specific level of expression. These atoms, or small force centers, form the bodies of the personality— physical, emotional, mental and spiritual—each of which distributes a certain type of force and is able to respond to a particular vibration.[37]

Silver Cord: The silver cord is an invisible etheric thread fastened in the left ventricle of the heart by the seed atom. Its rupture stops the heart, resulting in death of the physical body. It is not broken in any case where resuscitation is accomplished.[38]

Solar Plexus: The third chakra, as we ascend the etheric spine, is usually identified with power, control, the degree of confidence and sense of self one embodies; the home of will and lower mind for the individual. The psychic sense associated with this center is *clairsentience*, resonant with "gut feelings" and "butterflies."

Soul: A vehicle of self-expression for the mind. It is comprised of the subconscious mind/soul, the conscious mind/soul and the Super-conscious Mind/Soul. It is the vehicle of experience that contains the entire history of the journey through incarnations.[39]

Spectrochrome System: Invented by Dinshah P. Ghadiali of Bombay, India, the original Spectrochrome system uses five matched glass slides or filters to produce twelve colors. An apparatus with high wattage bulbs, 500-1000 watts, is used to project the prescribed color onto an area of the body for the healing of that body part or organ. The theory states that the chosen color will return the vibratory frequency of the body part to its optimum vibratory frequency for healing. This works on the organs and all cells of the body, digestive and respiratory systems, as well as the biochemistry, such as circulatory and lymphatic systems. For example, for thyroid underactivity or hypothyroidism, treatment or tonations using orange, lemon and green at different times on different parts of the body will correct the condition, according to prescribed tonations in a book by Dinshah's son, Darius Dinshah.[40]

Spirit: The Life-force energy that is in everything within and without the Universe.

Spiritual Science: A term coined by Rudolf Steiner for wisdom teachings of an esoteric nature which he perceived as an extension of the science of a purely material nature. Making available and understanding other dimensions of matter. A methodology to evolve higher consciousness as it relates to the human being, to the universe and to all creation, as taught by the Ageless Wisdom studies and Theosophy.[41]

Subtle Bodies: Vehicles or sheaths of the Monad, higher in frequency than the physical body and corresponding to our multidimensional levels of consciousness.

Super-conscious Self: An eternal part of Divinity that contains the wisdom, spiritual awareness and memory of the Perfect Pattern of the individual soul.

Symbol: A divine language; a form designed to portray some abstract quality. A symbol must convey an impression; it must cause the mind to see something which, though not actually in the symbol itself, is suggested by the symbol.[42]

Theosophy: Literally *divine wisdom*. From the Greek *theos*, divine, and *sophia*, wisdom. A major esoteric school of thought. It includes Eastern philosophy and philosophy of metaphysics. The Theosophical Society was established November 17, 1875, co-founded by Madame Helena P. Blavatsky and Colonel Olcott. Alice Bailey, Annie Besant, Charles Leadbeater and Geoffrey Hodson were major contributors and authors in the development of Theosophy. Much of the information was given by ascended masters: Master Morya, Master Kuhumi, Master Djwal Khul and Master Comte de St. Germain (Master Rakcozy).[43]

The work: *The work* is referred to several times in this book. It connotes here a general reference to any spiritual body of work or writing or expression through teaching or service.

Trance: An altered state of consciousness. There are three levels of trance: light, semi, and full trance.

Transition: The passing of consciousness from the physical realm into the nonphysical. According to Webster, a passing from one condition or place to another.[44]

Transmission: Inspirational writing and mediumship. Some transmitters work entirely on the astral levels and their work is part of the great illusion. They are unconscious mediums and are unable to check the source of their information. Some work only on the mental levels bringing into consciousness, through telepathy, the higher teachings from the higher realms.

Transmigration: Belief that human souls can incarnate into the bodies of animals. Most Western wisdom teachings do not accept a backward movement of evolving egos into lesser kingdoms as do some Eastern teachings. It is the *life atoms* that transmigrate into the lower kingdoms of Nature—never the soul of humans into the bodies of animals.[45]

Universal Law: Immutable Laws of the Universe.

Universal Love: Unconditional love for all life.

Wisdom: Spiritual knowing. Knowledge is learned; Wisdom comes with experience.

RESOURCES

Blogs and Websites

Afterlife Research Centre: Cross-Cultural Ethnographic Research
www.afterliferesearch.co.uk

Along the Path: Ancient Wisdom Teachings
www.annfrazierwest.com

Center for Quantum Activism: Quantum Consciousness
www.amitgoswami.org

Death Café: "To increase awareness of death with a view to helping people make the most of their (finite) lives." www.deathcafe.com

Doreen Virtue, Ph. D., Author; Spiritual Doctor of Psychology, Metaphysician.
Angel Therapy: www.angeltherapy.com

Dr. Eben Alexander, Neurosurgeon, Author.
www.lifebeyonddeath.net

Dr. Gary Schwartz, Author; Professor of Psychology, Medicine, Neurology, Psychiatry and Surgery at University of Arizona and Director of the Laboratory for Advances in Consciousness and Health. www.drgaryschwartz.com

Karen Noe, Psychic Medium; Author. Angel Quest Center.
www.karennoe.com

Lysa Mateu, Psychic Medium, Author.
www.channelingspirits.com

Penney Peirce, Author; Intuitive; Counselor: Bringing Higher Awareness to Life
www.penneypeirce.com

Robert Moss, Dream Teacher; Author:
Dream Gates, http://blog.beliefnet.com/dreamgates/ and
The Robert Moss Blog, www.mossdreams.blogspot.com

The Newton Institute: For Life Between Lives Hypnotherapy
www.spiritualregression.org

The Windbridge Institute for Applied Research in Human Potential
Julie Beischel, Ph. D., Director
www.windbridge.org/mediums.htm

Media

Bob Olson, Psychic Medium Researcher and Afterlife Investigator.
www.bestpsychicdirectory.com

Eben Alexander, M. D., Neurosurgeon, Author.
www.lifebeyonddeath.net/radio-broadcasts
www.lifebeyonddeath.net/national-broadcasts
www.lifebeyonddeath.net/online-broadcasts

Gary Schwartz, Ph. D., Professor, Author.
Celebrating the Evolution of Science and Spirit
www.drgaryschwartz.com/INTERVIEWS-AND-MEDIA.html

Robert Moss, Dream Teacher, Author.
Way of the Dreamer Radio Show
www.healthylife.net

Karen Noe, Psychic Medium.
Angel Quest Radio Show
www.throughtheeyesofanother.com/angel-quest-show

Victor Zammit, Attorney, Afterlife Researcher, Author.
Afterlife Evidence
www.victorzammit.com/index.html

Neale Donald Walsch, Author: *Conversations with God*
www.nealedonaldwalsch.com

Animal Communicators

Animal Communicator Forum
http://animalcommunicatorforum.com

Danielle MacKinnon, Intuitive Life Coach, Soul Contract Consultant, Animal Communicator.
www.daniellemackinnon.com

Jacquelin Smith, Animal Communicator, Author.
www.jacquelinsmith.com

Marta Williams, Animal Communicator, Author.
http://martawilliams.com/WhatIsAnimCom.htm

Psychic and Intuitive Counseling/Consulting

Reverend LeRoy E. Zemke, Spiritual Teacher, Senior Minister, Intuitive Counselor, Author. Temple of the Living God of St. Petersburg, FL, Inc.: Non-denominational Metaphysical Church and Educational Center. 1950 Second Avenue North, St. Petersburg, FL 33713
727-822-8628
www.templeofthelivinggod.org

Steve A. Engel, Metaphysical Teacher, Psychic Counselor/Consultant, Author.
2907 NE Couch Street, Portland, Oregon 97232-3224
503-231-9122 after 11:00 AM Pacific Time

Robert Murray, Psychic Counselor/Consultant, Author.
James Murray, Artist.
www.TheStarsStillShine.com

Lysa Mateu, Psychic Medium, Author.
www.channelingspirits.com

Other Resources

Afterlife Knowledge Guidebook: A Manual for the Art of Retrieval and Afterlife Exploration with CD
Bruce Moen, Author of *The Exploring the Afterlife Series*.
www.Afterlife-Knowledge.com

Hemi-Sync: A scientifically based and clinically proven "audio-guidance" technology. Facilitates a whole brain state known as hemispheric synchronization.
www.monroeinstitute.org

Pages of Shustah, Inc. Study Course, Ann C. Manser, Author.
Pages of Shustah Divination and Meditation Cards and Book by Ann C. Manser and Cecil North.
www.templeofthelivinggod.org and 727-822-8628.

BIBLIOGRAPHY

Ahlquist, Diane. *The Complete Idiot's Guide to Life After Death*. New York: Alpha Books, 2007.

Alder, Vera Stanley. *From the Mundane to the Magnificent*. York Beach, ME: Samuel Weiser, Inc., 1980.

Alder, Vera Stanley. *The Fifth Dimension*. London: Rider & Company, 1983.

Alder, Vera Stanley. *The Finding of the Third Eye*. York, ME: Samuel Wieser, Inc., 1981.

Alder, Vera Stanley. *The Initiation of the World*. New York: Samuel Weiser, Inc., 1972.

Alder, Vera Stanley. *The Secret of the Atomic Age*. New York: Samuel Weiser, Inc., 1974.

Anderson, George and Andrew Barone. *Walking in the Garden of Souls*. New York: G. P. Putnam's Sons, 2001.

Andrews, Ted. *How to Meet and Work with Spirit Guides*. St. Paul: Llewellyn Publications, 2001.

Anonymous Author. *The Boy Who Saw True*. London: Rider, Random House, 2005.

Arcangel, Dianne. *Afterlife Encounters*. Charlottesville, VA: Hampton Roads Publishing Company, Inc., 2005.

Bailey, Alice A. *Discipleship in the New Age, Volume I*. New York: Lucis Publishing Company, 1972.

Bailey, Alice A. *Esoteric Healing*. New York: Lucis Publishing Company, 1977.

Bailey, Alice A. *Esoteric Psychology I*. New York: Lucis Publishing Company, 1979.

Bailey, Alice A. *Glamour: A World Problem*. New York: Lucis Publishing Company, 1971.

Bailey, Alice A. *Letters on Occult Meditation*. New York: Lucis Publishing Company, 1972.

Bailey, Alice A. *Ponder on This*. New York: Lucis Publishing Company, 1978.

Bailey, Alice A. *The Consciousness of the Atom*. New York: Lucis Publishing Company, 1973.

Bailey, Alice A. *The Externalisation of the Hierarchy*. NewYork: Lucis Publishing Company, 1957.

Bailey, Alice A. *The Rays and the Initiations*. New York: Lucis Publishing Company, 1971.

Bair, Deirdre. *Jung: A Biography*. Boston: Little, Brown and Company, 2003.

Baker, Douglas. *The Opening of the Third Eye*. New York: Samuel Weiser Inc., 1978.

Balcombe, Betty F. *The Psychic Handbook*. Boston: Weiser Books, 2000.

Barborka, Geoffrey A. *The Divine Plan*. Wheaton, IL: The Theosophical Publishing House, 1980.

Barker, A.T. Transcription, complilation: Christmas Humphries, Elsie Banjamin, Eds. *The Mahatma Letters*. Wheaton, IL: The Theosophical Publishing House, 1962.

Barker, Elsa. *Letters from the Afterlife*. Hillsboro, OR: Beyond Words Publishing, Inc., 1995.

Berkowitz, Rita S. and Deborah S. Romaine. *The Complete Idiot's Guide to Communicating With Spirits*. Indianapolis: Alpha Books, 2003.

Begg, Deike. *Rebirthing*. Berkeley: North Atlantic Books, 1999.

Besant, Annie. *Death-and-After*. Wheaton, Ill: The Theosophical Publishing House, 1999.

Besant, Annie. *Man and His Bodies*. Adyar, Madras, India: The Theosophical Publishing House, 1971.

Borgia, Anthony. *Life in the World Unseen*. http://anthony3741.tripod.com, 1951.

Borgia, Anthony. *More About Life in World Unseen*. www.rait.airclima.ru/books, 1951.

Boyer, Peter J. "Little Boy's Death Was Just a Walk into Another Galaxy," in *The St. Petersburg Times*, Jan. 19, 1978.

Bridges, Robbin Renee. *A Bridge of Love Between Heaven and Earth: Self-induced Contact in the Afterlife*. www.spirit-sanctuary.org, 2004.

Bro, Harmon H., Ph. D. and Hugh Lynn Cayce. *Edgar Cayce on Dreams*. New York: Paperback Library, Inc., 1968.

Browne, Sylvia. *All Pets Go to Heaven*. New York: Fireside, A Division of Simon & Shuster, Inc., 2009.

Browne, Sylvia. *Conversations with the Other Side*. Carlsbad, CA: Hay House, Inc., 2002.

Browne, Sylvia. *Life on the Other Side*. New York: Dutton, 2000.

Browne, Sylvia and Lindsay Harrison. *Visits from the Afterlife*. New York: Dutton, 2003.

Bruce, Robert. *Astral Dynamics: A New Approach to Out-of-Body Experience*. Charlottesville, VA: Hampton Roads Publishing Co., Inc., 1999.

Chopra, Deepak. *Life After Death*. New York: Harmony Books, 2006.

Choquette, Sonia, Ph.D. *The Psychic Pathway*. New York: Three Rivers Press, 1995.

Codd, Clara M. *The Ageless Wisdom of Life*. London: The Theosophical Publishing House, 1969.

Coleman, Graham, Ed., with Thupten Jimpa. *The Tibetan Book of the Dead (English title); The Great Liberation by Hearing in the Intermediate States (Tibetan title)*. New York: Viking Penguin Group, 2006.

Currie, Ian. *You Cannot Die*. New York: Methuen, 1978.

Dalai Lama. *The Art of Living*. New York: Gramercy Books, 1995.

Diamond, Harvey and Marilyn. *Fit for Life*. New York: Warner Books, Inc., 1985.

Dinshah, Darius. *Let There Be Light*. Malaga, NJ: Dinshah Health Society, 1990.

Dresser, Charlotte Elizabeth, Fred Rafferty, Ed. *Life Here and Hereafter*. San Francisco: Chase and Rae Publications, 1927.

Eadie, Betty. *Embraced By The Light*. Placerville, CA: Gold Leaf Press, 1992.

Engel, E. Charles (Steve A.). *Esoteric Definitions*. Portland, Oregon: Angel Estates Publishing, 1992.

Farnese, A. *Wanderer in the Spirit Lands*. Scottsdale: AIM Publishing Company, 1993.

Fortune, Dion. *The Cosmic Doctrine*. New York: Samuel Weiser, Inc., 1976.

Gallenberger, Joseph. *Brothers Forever: An Unexpected Journey Beyond Death*. Charlottesville, VA: Hampton Roads Publishing Co., Inc., 1996.

Greer, Jane. *The Afterlife Connection*. New York: St. Martin's Press, 2003.

Hall, Manly P. *Invisible Records of Thought and Action*. Los Angeles: The Philosophical Research Society, Inc. 1975.

Hall, Manly P. *Lectures on Ancient Philosophy*. Los Angeles: Philosophical Research Society, Inc., 1984.

Haich, Elisabeth. *Initiation*. Palo Alto, CA: Seed Center, 1974.

Heath, Pamela Rae and Jon Klimo. *Handbook to the Afterlife*. Berkeley: North Atlantic Books, 2010.

Heindel, Max. *The Rosicrucian Cosmo-Conception*. Oceanside, CA: The Rosicrucian Fellowship, 1969.

Heline, Corinne. *New Age Bible Interpretation: Mystery of the Christos, Volume VII.* Santa Monica, CA: New Age Press, Inc., 1985.

Hinz, Walter, Ph. D. *The Corner Stone*. Suffolk: Neville Spearman, 1977.

Hodson, Geoffrey. *Hidden Wisdom in the Holy Bible—Vol. I*. Wheaton, IL: Quest Books, 1993.

Hodson, Geoffrey. *Man's Supersensory and Spiritual Powers*. Adyar, Madras, India: The Theosophical Publishing House, 1969.

Hodson, Geoffrey. *The Kingdom of the Gods*. London: The Theosophical Publishing House, 1976.

Holland, John. *The Spirit Whisperer*. New York: Hay House, Inc., 2010.

Holmes, Ernest. *The Science of Mind.* New York: Dodd, Meade and Company,1938.

Ingerman, Sandra and Hank Wesselman. *Awakening to the Spirit World*. Boulder, CO: Sounds True, Inc., 2010.

Jung, Carl G. *Man and His Symbols*. New York: Doubleday & Company, 1964.

Kazantzakis, Nikos. *The Last Temptation of Christ*. New York: Simon & Shuster, Inc., 1960.

Kubler-Ross, Elisabeth. *The Wheel of Life*. New York: Touchstone, 1997.

Kubler-Ross, Elisabeth. *On Life After Death*. Berkeley: Celestial Arts, 1991.

Larsen, Stephen. *The Mythic Imagination*. Vermont: Inner Traditions International, 1996.

Larson, Patricia R. *Ageless Wisdom for Today's World*. Omaha: Study Course, 1989.

Lawson, Lee. *Visitations from the Afterlife*. New York: HarperSanFrancisco, 2000.

Leadbeater, C. W. *Invisible Helpers*. Adyar: The Theosophical Publishing House, 1973.

Leadbeater, C. W. *The Beginnings of the Sixth Root Race*. Adyar: Theosophical Publishing House, 1931, (out of print).

Leadbeater, C. W. *The Chakras*. Wheaton, Ill: The Theosophical Publishing House, 1972.

Ledwith, Miceal, D.D., LL.D. and Klaus Heinemann, Ph.D. *The Orb Project*. New York: Beyond Words Publishing, 2007.

Lee, Leonard. www.positivearticles.com, 2009.

Linn, Denise. *The Secret Language of Signs*. New York: Ballantine Books, 1996.

Lonegren, Sid. *The Pendulum Kit*. New York: Simon & Schuster, Inc., 1990.

Long, Max Freedom. *Growing Into Light*. Marina del Rey, CA: DeVorss Publications, 1955.

Long, Max Freedom. *Self-Suggestion*. Vista, CA: Huna Research Publications, 1956. Republished by Ancient Wisdom Publications, Sacramento, CA., 2009.

Long, Max Freedom. *The Secret Science at Work*. Vista, CA: Huna Research Publications, 1953.

Long, Max Freedom. *The Secret Science Behind Miracles*. Vista, CA: Huna Research Publications, 1954.

Lumari. *Akashic Records: Collective Keepers of Divine Expression*. Santa Fe, NM: Amethyst, 2003.

Macy, Mark. *Spirit Faces:Truth About the Afterlife*. San Francisco: Weiser Books, 2006.

Manser, Ann C. *Pages of Shustah, Inc.* Omaha: Study Course, 1974.

Martin, Joel and Patricia Romanowski. *Love Beyond Life*. New York: Dell Publishing, 1997.

Mateu, Lysa. *Psychic Diaries*. New York: HarperCollins Publishers, Inc., 2003.

Meek, George W. *After We Die, What Then?* Columbus: Ariel Press, 1987.

Moen, Bruce. *Afterlife Knowledge Guidebook*. Charlottesville, VA: Hampton Roads Publishing Company, 2004.

Moen, Bruce. *Afterlife Knowledge Guidebook CD Recordings*. Englewood, CO: Shaydan, Inc., 2004.

Moen, Bruce. *Voyages into the Afterlife*. Charlottesville, VA: Hampton Roads Publishing Company, 1999.

Moen, Bruce. *Voyage to Curiosity's Father*. Charlottesville, VA: Hampton Roads Publishing Company, 2001.

Moody, Raymond A., Jr., M. D. *Reflections on Life After Life*. St. Simons Island, GA: Bantam, 1978.

Moss, Robert. *Active Dreaming*. Novato, CA: New World Library, 2011

Moss, Robert. *Conscious Dreaming*. New York: Crown Trade Paperbacks, 1996.

Moss, Robert. *Dreamgates*. Novato, CA: New World Library, 1998.

Moss, Robert. *Dreaming the Soul Back Home*. Novato, CA: New World Library, 2012.

Moss, Robert. *Dreaming True*. New York: Pocket Books, 2000.

Moss, Robert. *The Dreamer's Book of the Dead*. Rochester, VT: Destiny Books, 2005.

Myss, Caroline, Ph.D. *Anatomy of the Spirit*. New York: Harmony Books, 1996.

Myss, Caroline. *Sacred Contracts*. New York: Harmony Books, 2001.

Newton, Michael. *Destiny of Souls*. Woodbury, MN: Llewellyn Publications, 2006.

Newton, Michael. *Journey of Souls*. Woodbury, MN: Llewellyn Publications, 2008.

Noe, Karen. *Through the Eyes of Another*. New York: Hay House Inc., 2012.

Parrish-Harra, Carol W. *A New Age Handbook on Death & Dying*. Marina del Rey, CA: Devorss & Company, 1982.

Parrish-Harra, Carol E. *The New Dictionary of Spiritual Thought*. Tahlequah, OK: Sparrow Hawk Press, 2002.

Peirce, Penney. *Frequency: the Power of Personal Vibration*. New York: Beyond Words Publishing, 2009.

Powell, A. E. *The Astral Body*. London: The Theosophical Publishing House, 1965.

Rafferty, Fred, ed. *Spirit World and Spirit Life*. Los Angeles: J. F. Rowny Press, 1922.

Rafferty, Fred, ed. *Life Here and Hereafter*. San Jose: Cosmos Publishing Co., 1927.

Ralenno, Franzie. *Amazing Realities from Life After Death*. Morges, Switzerland: Spiritual Perceptions Publishing, 2007.

Randall, Edward C. *The Dead Have Never Died*. New York: Alfred A. Knopf, 1917.

Ray, Sondra. *Celebration of Breath*. Berkeley: Celestial Arts, 1983.

Redfield, James. *The Celestine Prophecy*. New York: Warner Treasures, 1994.

Rinpoche, Tenzin Wangyal. *The Tibetan Yogas of Dream and Sleep*. Ithaca, NY: Snow Lion Publications, 1998.

Roberts, Jane. *Seth Speaks*. San Rafael, CA: 1972.

Saraydarian, H. *The Science of Meditation*. Sedona: Aquarian Educational Group, 1981.

Schwartz, Gary E. and William L. Simon. *The Afterlife Experiments*. New York: Pocket Books, 2002.

Schwartz, Gary E. with William L. Simon. *The Truth about Medium*. Charlottesville, VA: Hampton Roads Publishing Company, Inc., 2005.

Singer, June. *Boundaries of the Soul*. New York: Anchor Books, 1973.

Stead, W. T. and Estelle Stead. *The Blue Island*. Washington, D. C.: ESPress, Inc., 1979.

Steiner, Rudolf. *Life Between Death and Rebirth*. Hudson, NY: Anthroposophic Press, 1968.

Storr, Anthony. *The Essential Jung*. New York: MJF Books, 1983.

Student of Max Heindel. *Etheric Vision and What it Reveals*. Oceanside, CA: The Rosicrucian Fellowship, 1965.

Tart, Charles T. "What Death Tells Us About Life." *Shift: At the Frontiers of Consciousness*. No. 17, December 2007-February 2008.

Thompson, Edward K., ed. *The World's Great Religions, Vol. 2*. New York: Time Incorporated, 1957.

Three Initiates. *The Kybalion*. New York: Tarcher Cornerstone Editions, 2008.

Van Praagh, James. *Heaven and Earth*. New York: Pocket Books, 2002.

Virtue, Doreen, Ph. D. *Angel Visions*. Carlsbad, CA: Hay House, Inc., 2000.

Virtue, Doreen, Ph.D. *Chakra Clearing*. Carlsbad, CA: Hay House, Inc., 1998.

Virtue, Doreen, Ph. D. *Divine Guidance*. Los Angeles: Renaissance Books, 1998.

Virtue, Doreen, Ph.D. and Becky Prelitz., M.F.T., R.D. *Eating in the Light*. Carlsbad, CA: Hay House, Inc., 2001.

Virtue, Doreen, Ph.D. *The Lightworker's Way*. Carlsbad, CA: Hay House, Inc., 1997.

Walsch, Neale Donald. *Home With God in a Life that Never Ends*. New York: Atria Books, 2006.

Wambach, Helen. *Life Before Life*. New York: Bantam, 1979.

Wands, Jeffrey A. *Another Door Opens*. New York: Atria Books, 2006.

Weed, Joseph J. *Psychic Energy*. West Nyack, NY: Parker Publishing Co., 1970.

Weil, Andrew, M. D. *Spontaneous Healing*. New York: Fawcett Columbine of The Ballintine Publishing Group, 1995.

Williams, Bill, Muriel Williams and Ian Currie. *Life in the Spirit World*. Victoria, BC: Trafford Publishing, 2006.

Wilson, Ted, Jr. *O Master Let Me Walk With Thee (CD).* Music arranged and performed by Ted Wilson, Jr., 2003.

Woolger, Roger J. *Healing Your Past Lives.* Boulder: Sounds True, Inc., 2004.

Woolger, Roger J. *Other Lives, Other Selves (A Jungian Psychotherapist Discovers Past Lives).* New York: Bantam Books, 1988.

Wright, Machaelle Small. *MAP: The Co-creative White Brotherhood Medical Assistance Program.* Warrenton, VA: Perelandra, LTD., 1990.

Yogananda, Paramahansa. *Karma & Reincarnation.* Nevada City, CA: Crystal Clarity Publishers, 2007.

Yogananda, Paramahansa. *The Second Coming of Christ.* Los Angeles: Self-Realization Fellowship, 2004.

Zammit, Victor James. *A Lawyer Presents the Case for the Afterlife, Fourth Edition.* www.victorzammit.com, 2006.

ANN FRAZIER WEST IS AN Educational Therapist, Spiritual Teacher and Spiritual Counselor and holds a doctorate from Vanderbilt University in Human Development Counseling. She has a background in nursing, psychological counseling and as a teacher and workshop leader in spiritual science, color healing and related disciplines. Currently a teacher of Spiritual Science, she resides in Nashville, Tennessee. www.annfrazierwest.com

Index

scientist(s) ix, 8, 14, 19, 75, 97, 135, 136, 193, 194, 196, 198-201, 212

seed-atom 21, 22, 183, 219

Shustah *See also Pages of Shustah*

silver cord 21, 22, 24, 183, 219

sixth sense 155, 184, 199

Smith, Susy 198, 199

Society for Psychical Research 98, 194, 200

soul xi, xvi, xx, 10, 14, 15, 18-23, 30, 32, 34, 39, 53, 64, 77, 85-87, 95, 122, 133, 134, 150, 173, 175, 182, 185-191, 199, 211-213, 215-221, 225

sphere 6, 29-33, 76, 77, 96, 150, 171

spirit(s) xiii-xv, xviii, 8, 10, 11, 13, 14, 16-18, 20, 23-25, 28, 29, 31-37, 39, 60, 63, 75-78, 80, 98, 99, 101, 106, 113, 115-117, 120, 123-125, 129-131, 134, 135, 138, 139, 143, 144, 149-151, 155-157, 166, 167, 171-173, 175, 177-179, 182-184, 186, 189, 195, 201, 213-215, 220, 223, 224, 226

spiritual ix, xi, xiii-xvii, xx, 10, 14, 15, 20-22, 28, 33-38, 44, 49, 50, 54, 58, 62, 64, 71, 72, 76, 80, 86, 88, 89, 93, 95, 102, 104, 105, 107, 125, 126, 130, 133, 134, 149-151, 158, 163-165, 169, 170, 173, 175, 176, 182-184, 187-191, 196, 201, 211, 215, 216, 219-221, 223-225, 233

Spirit World xv, 23-25, 29, 31, 32, 35, 87, 98, 115, 150, 156-158, 182

Stead, W. T., Estelle ix, 77, 156, 157

Steiner, Rudolf ix, 150, 220

subconscious 22, 81, 82, 149, 151, 157, 159, 160, 212, 213, 216, 219

suicide 22, 23

Summerland 31, 76

super-conscious 149-151, 159, 220

symbol(s) 35, 36, 48, 49, 56, 59, 72, 75, 89, 99, 105, 106, 122, 123, 133, 151, 166, 174, 177, 184, 220

symbolic 75, 89, 99, 117, 122

symbolism 59, 175, 218

T

Tammy 126, 136-139, 145

Tao/Taoism/Taoist 189

Tart, Charles 196

Tassajara Zen Retreat 45, 48

teacher(s) ix-xi, xiv-xvii, xx, 13, 14, 16, 35, 45, 50, 56, 58, 60, 62, 63, 65, 67, 69, 71, 78-81, 85, 86, 102, 104, 105, 115, 121, 123, 130, 133, 153, 154, 160, 169, 173-175, 181, 183, 224, 225, 233

teachings ix, xiv, xv, 9, 16, 18, 34, 37, 39, 43, 54, 57, 60, 62, 65, 69, 73, 74, 77, 79-81, 83, 89, 90, 104, 115, 160, 162, 191, 214, 215, 220, 221, 223

telepathic xviii, 33, 107, 133, 136, 139, 156, 177, 184, 214

telepathy 4, 24, 36, 96, 99, 106, 136, 172, 201, 221

temple 56, 57, 125

Temple of the Living God xiv, 50, 55, 57, 71, 86, 125, 225, 226

Theosophy/Theosophical/Theosophist xiv, 18, 57, 67, 181, 220, 221

third eye 34, 74, 104, 165, 166

three remarkable women xiii, xvi, 7, 183

trance 50, 73, 133, 213, 221

transition ix, xi-xiv, xvi, xix, 10, 18-21, 23-25, 28, 36-39, 61, 71, 72, 74-76, 79, 80, 86, 94, 104, 107, 110, 115, 117, 118, 122, 124, 129, 130, 139-142, 151, 155, 167, 175, 176, 178, 181-185, 221

transmission(s) xii, 38, 53, 87, 96, 97, 99, 122, 156, 159, 167, 184, 221

tunnel 38, 95, 105

U

unconscious 31, 32, 163, 187, 221

Universal Law/law 57, 80, 221

V

Vaughn, Patrika/Pat xiii, xv, 168

vehicle(s) x, 18, 20-23, 29-31, 53, 67, 97, 125, 134, 153, 164, 169, 183, 186, 197, 212, 214, 217, 219, 220

vibration(s) 17, 28, 30, 31, 36, 49, 75, 76, 96-98, 101, 165, 167, 190, 211, 213, 219

vibratory/vibratory frequency xviii, 18, 27, 28, 30, 31, 34, 36, 37, 39, 57, 62, 73, 76, 81-83, 96, 98, 99, 105, 107, 117, 156, 158, 162, 163, 165, 166, 171, 174, 177, 181, 184, 190, 191, 213, 216, 217, 219, 220

violet flame 83, 159, 165, 168

vision(s) ix, xiii, xviii, xix, 6, 18, 21, 23, 33-36, 39, 51, 56, 69, 72, 74, 83, 95, 117, 130, 135, 150, 155, 157, 165, 166, 173, 174, 176, 181, 187, 200, 212

visualize xx, 31, 81, 83, 85, 101, 129-131, 136, 139, 157, 159, 160, 164-169, 171, 173, 174

vital body 21, 22, 134

W

Wallace, Alfred Russell 194

West, Ann ix, 19, 90, 91, 97, 102, 103, 118, 119, 121, 130, 223, 233

    Jim xv, 60

    J. Thomas/Tom xvi, 9, 16, 43, 45-50, 64, 65, 126, 175-179

    Julia/Julie xvi, 46, 47, 60, 72, 137

    Mark 46, 47, 60, 67

    Wendi xv, 10, 11, 50, 60, 62, 63, 71, 73, 114, 126, 136

Williams, Marta 139, 140, 142, 143, 225

Williams, Muriel xviii, 167

Windbridge Institute for Applied Research in Human Potential 199, 224

wisdom teachings xi, 39, 57, 65, 220, 221, 223 *See also ancient wisdom teachings*

Y

Yogananda, Paramahansa 29, 30, 165, 173, 189, 190

Z

Zammit, Victor James 193, 194, 200, 225

Zemke, LeRoy E. x, xv, xvi, 50, 57, 64, 71, 86, 90, 102, 103, 105, 120, 123, 225

Zemke, Bertha 123